THE COMPLETE IDIOT'S GUIDE® TO

ACT!™ 2000

by Douglas Wolf

QUE®

A Division of Macmillan USA
201 W. 103rd Street, Indianapolis, IN 46290

Trademarks

All terms mentioned in this book that are known to be trademarks or service marks have been appropriately capitalized. Que cannot attest to the accuracy of this information. Use of a term in this book should not be regarded as affecting the validity of any trademark or service mark. ACT! is a registered trademark of Symantec.

Warning and Disclaimer

Every effort has been made to make this book as complete and as accurate as possible, but no warranty or fitness is implied. The information provided is on an "as is" basis. The author and the publisher shall have neither liability nor responsibility to any person or entity with respect to any loss or damages arising from the information contained in this book.

Associate Publisher
Greg Wiegand

Acquisitions Editor
Stephanie J. McComb

Development Editor
Gregory Harris

Managing Editor
Thomas F. Hayes

Project Editor
Tom Stevens

Copy Editor
Sossity Smith

Proofreader
Jeanne Clark

Technical Editor
Deb Newell

Illustrator
Judd Winick

Team Coordinator
Sharry Gregory

Interior Designer
Nathan Clement

Cover Designer
Michael Freeland

Copy Writer
Eric Borgert

Production
Dan Harris
Lisa England

Contents at a Glance

Table of Contents

vii

viii

Part 4: Hey, Why Didn't They Tell Me You Could Do That with ACT!?   221

15 Working with Groups   223

16 Customizing Your Layout   237

About the Author

Douglas Wolf has written over 30 computer books (which have not made him rich or famous), including three others on ACT!. In 1986, he wrote his first book, *1-2-3 Made Easy*. He is a Minnesota native and graduated to California in 1984—mainly to play tennis year around. He has worked as an aide to a member of Congress, was State Director for the Concord Coalition, and has been a radio talk show host. A true Renaissance man, he lives in San Diego with his lovely and talented wife, Gloria, his above-average children, Ilsa and Alexander, and their poodle, Nietzsche.

Dedication

I hereby dedicate this book to my tennis buddies who really are more fun than a barrel of monkeys: Michael "PQ" Kelley, Harlan "The Forehand" Reese, Jerry "The Gentleman" Von Teuber, and Robert "Overhead" Howe. I am privileged to know and play with them.

Acknowledgments

A lot of very smart folks went into the process of making this book a reality (besides me): my wife, Gloria, for one and my talented agent, Matt Wagner, who negotiated this book deal when his world was temporarily in chaos.

The folks at Macmillan are Stephanie McComb, who risked her career by selecting me as the author; Gregory Harris, for his virtuous text editing; Debra Newell, for the technical editing; Mandie Rowell, for formatting; Amy Neidlinger from marketing, who made a tough advertising call; and Tom Stevens, for the overall management of this enterprise.

Several ACT! Certified Consultants gave me their informed opinions on this work and will gladly charge you for ACT! advice:

Chris Lagarde, Computer Information Associates, New Orleans at 800-331-9615

Michael Moldofsky, Los Angeles at 818-344-1909

Geoffrey Blood, New Hampton Group, Mountain View, CA at 650-967-3543

Steve Chipman, Lexnet Consulting Group, San Rafael at 415-256-1155

Bud Rice, Global Technology Partners, Pleasanton at 510-727-6366

Tell Us What You Think!

As the reader of this book, *you* are our most important critic and commentator. We value your opinion and want to know what we're doing right, what we could do better, what areas you'd like to see us publish in, and any other words of wisdom you're willing to pass our way.

As an Associate Publisher for Que, I welcome your comments. You can fax, email, or write me directly to let me know what you did or didn't like about this book—as well as what we can do to make our books stronger.

Please note that I cannot help you with technical problems related to the topic of this book, and that due to the high volume of mail I receive, I might not be able to reply to every message.

When you write, please be sure to include this book's title and author as well as your name and phone or fax number. I will carefully review your comments and share them with the author and editors who worked on the book.

Fax: 317-581-4666

Email: consumer@mcp.com

Mail: Greg Wiegand, Associate Publisher
          Que
          201 West 103rd Street
          Indianapolis, IN 46290 USA

Introduction

"To understand is hard. Once one understands, action is easy."

Sun Yat-Sen

When I was writing my first book on ACT! in late 1991 and early 1992, Windows 3.0 had just become a bestseller and Contact Software was working furiously on the Windows version of ACT!. In the summer of 1992, the product shipped and became the best selling contact management software in the world. Why? Because the preponderance of users of ACT! are salespeople who hate paperwork, cannot type, and always manage to lose that crucial phone number when most needed. ACT! made it easy for them to get their schedule under control, make the phone calls they were supposed to, and reminded them of their anniversary!

How to Use This Book

The purpose of this book is to take you through the various components of ACT! in the same way I teach my clients. In the beginning chapters, I focus on the aspects that get you productive immediately. Then, as you become more comfortable with ACT!, you can read the chapters on more advanced ACT! tools; reporting, for example. So, if you are brand new to ACT!, read the first several chapters in order, up to Chapter 9, "Checking Your Calendar." Then look to the chapters you need to fill in your knowledge. If you are an experienced ACT! user, you should go ahead and take a look at the new sales forecasting tools and the Internet links. Both of these new features have benefits to anyone using ACT! to manage their time.

Extras

To help you understand the online jungle, this book also gives you extra secrets, inside tips, and bits of information that will help you get the most out of your money. You'll find them in these boxes:

Check This Out!

The "Check This Out" sections throughout the book point out things that are noteworthy, stuff to be leery of, great tips—basically, they are full of information that adds to your understanding of security or gives insightful background.

Techno Talk

"Techno Talk" boxes highlight terms, methods, or brainy stuff that you don't necessarily need to know, but that definitely help you make more sense out of security and privacy.

Notes

The "Note" boxes are used as a catchall to pass along cross-references pointing you to other sections of the book, to provide interesting facts, to alert you to actions or procedures that you must avoid in order to maintain the integrity of your ACT! database, or for anything else you should take a look at.

A Short History of ACT!

Contact Software was founded in 1986 by Pat Sullivan and Mike Muhney. They are both dynamic salespeople who were continually frustrated by the lack of a good software tool for sales-related tasks. For example, there are many database programs that are very good at retrieving reams of data, but the average user doesn't have the time or sophistication to learn how to use such a tool. Besides, the other features that Pat and Mike felt were necessary—alarms for important events, word processing, and so on—weren't available in database programs. So they sat down and drew up their ideas for a software program. (At that time, the term contact management had not yet entered the computing vocabulary.) With the help of a couple of programmers, version 1.0 of ACT! was written. It took time, but by boot-strapping and a little luck, ACT! became recognized as the contact management software tool of choice. Then in June of 1993, Contact Software and all its products were purchased by Symantec Corporation. They have produced versions 3.0, 4.0, and now 2000.

My Story

I was introduced to ACT! version 1.0 by a friend in 1989. He was insistent that ACT! was the best software on the market for managing all the names, phone numbers, meetings, and tasks that any busy person must keep track of. At that time, I was a mortgage broker and writing books, generally going crazy trying to juggle all I was supposed to do, so I started using it. I too had searched for a program such as ACT! to aid me in my business endeavors. I had just written a book on Agenda, the Lotus product, and had decided that, though it was very powerful, it was difficult to master the conceptual nature of the product. I also had used Sidekick, but it wasn't a very robust product and it too required a little too much thinking on the part of the user. So ACT! was a pleasant surprise. It was obviously designed by real salespeople. I've used it continuously since.

When version 2.0 of ACT! for DOS was ready to ship, Contact Software asked me to assist them in preparing the documentation. On a very tight schedule, we managed to get the product out. I have written three other books on ACT! and since 1995 I have been busy installing, customizing, and troubleshooting ACT! for my clients, as part of the Symantec ACT! Certified Consultants program. I also was the founding editor of *Easy ACT!*, the monthly newsletter for ACT! users.

Training Tools

In addition to this book, I've created training videos and a CD-ROM that cover Windows 98 and ACT!. To order, contact me directly at (800) 449-9653, or visit my Web site, www.howtosoftware.com. All of my customers can call me directly for help.

Time Management, Goals, and ACT!

Goal-setting is crucial to success in any endeavor, yet it's amazing how many people set out upon their lives each day with little thought as to the result. The best book on the market for goal-setting and life management is Steven Covey's *The Seven Habits of Highly Effective People*. In it, he extols the absolute necessity of defining your life principles so your goals and priorities are in harmony with your overall life mission. I highly recommend this book as part of your effort to become more organized and efficient.

Time management means that you've planned what you're going to do and when you're going to do it. The earliest proponents of time management taught that people should sit down at the end of the business day and list the important things they had to do the next day, by using the previous day's list of tasks as a guide. Those tasks that weren't accomplished would be carried over to tomorrow's agenda. The next evolution in time management was the idea of prioritizing those tasks, so the most important items received immediate attention.

ACT! facilitates the execution of the tasks you've decided to undertake, implementing the best ideas in time management. By recording calls to make, meetings to go to, and things to do, you've created your task list. After a business day, you can sit down with ACT! and review your task list, erase those tasks that have been accomplished, and add new tasks for tomorrow, prioritizing or reprioritizing as you go. ACT! automatically reminds you of activities you didn't complete the day before and asks you if they should be rescheduled for the current day. Computers are supposed to simplify your life and ACT! is one of the tools that can do that for you.

Terminology

Each person or company you enter in ACT! is a contact record. So, the two terms, *record* and *contact*, are used interchangeably. A set of contact records constitutes an ACT! database. The designers of ACT! took the view that people do business with other people, not with companies. Ergo, ACT! is a person-centered database. Also, ACT! has you schedule activities with those other people, but then those activities are placed on, among other places, the Task List. They could have called it the Activity List, but that would make it to easy.

Moving from 4.0 to 2000

The most dramatic change is the set of icons on the left side of the record layout. Instead of searching for the tiny icons that opened your calendars, task list, and email, the icons are now prominent on the screen. The second aspect is the addition of sales forecasting tools. Long requested, these tools enable you to easily keep track of your sales pipeline without having to modify ACT! fields and reports on your own. ACT! 2000 is more closely tied to the Internet with links directly to the most useful sites and the ability to save the information directly into ACT!.

Contacting Symantec for Help

If you really get stuck on a problem and can't find the answer in my book or the ACT! manuals, here are the numbers to contact for help:

- ➤ Customer service (U.S. and Canada only)   (800) 441-7234
- ➤ Technical support, standard care   (541) 465-8645
- ➤ Technical support, premium care (or 25 cents a call)   (800) 927-3989
- ➤ Technical support, premium care (or $2.00 a minute)   (900) 646-0001
- ➤ Fax-back retrieval system   (800) 554-4403
- ➤ Web Site   www.service.symantec.com

Live Update

Symantec now provides a way for you to get the no-fee upgrade releases of ACT!. In other words, when they go from release 2000 to 2000.01 you can get it free by doing the following:

1. In ACT!, click the **Help** menu.
2. Click the **LiveUpdate** option.

ACT!'s Live Update Wizard will walk you through the process. Of course, you have to have a modem installed. You can get the same update files via the Web site, but you have to apply the install yourself.

Certified Consultants Program

If you, or your company, need specialized help for customization, synchronization, or custom programming, you can call upon a Certified Consultant for help. They do charge for their time, but you will likely save money and frustration if you call upon their expertise.

Part 1

Where in the Heck Is the Address for...?

First things first, and in the case of using ACT!, you have to put information in, in ACT!'s case, companies or contacts, and then find them. So, Chapters 1–5 are focused on getting your contacts into ACT!, finding them, and then using it to manage your time. After you get the sense of how ACT! stores contact information, you can leverage that knowledge to make ACT! your essential time-management tool.

Installing and Creating a New Database

"Nothing in the world is so powerful as an idea whose time has come."

Victor Hugo

Hugo had it right, and I have an idea that you purchased ACT! to bring order out of chaos. It can do that for you if you make the commitment to use it the way it is supposed to be used. If you work at a desktop most of the day, it should be running in one of your windows. If you are mobile, a laptop, PalmPilot, or Windows CE device should be your constant companion. If you are accustomed to a paper system, such as a Franklin Planner or Day Timer, you should begin to wean yourself away, gradually and inevitably. Why? Because no matter how good your memory is, ACT! is better.

Where to Start?

If you are an experienced ACT! user and have an existing ACT! database, skip to the section on converting from 2.0, 3.0, or 4.0. If you're starting from a brand-new installation and you have never used ACT!, start reading the next section.

Adding Your Installation Preferences

The installation program of ACT! includes a series of dialog boxes that ask questions, called the QuickStart Wizard. This wizard is not at all like the man from OZ, in that these questions guide you into correctly setting up ACT!. You will not be asked to kill a witch.

After you install ACT!, you may be asked to restart your computer. After you've rebooted, click the **ACT!** icon to start ACT! or click the **Start** button, select **Programs**, choose the **ACT! 2000** group, and then click the **ACT! 2000** icon. The next thing you see is the QuickStart Welcome dialog box. Click the **Next** button. The second dialog box asks if you want to connect to Symantec's Live Update server. This option is a way for you to get the most recent version of ACT! directly from Symantec to your desktop. If you choose this option, your computer's modem dials a number that connects to a Symantec computer. The Symantec computer checks the version of ACT! that you have, and if it is out-of-date, sends and installs the update automatically. I suggest that you take a few minutes and click the **Connect** button to make certain you are working with the latest release.

Word Processor, Faxing

Move on by clicking the **Next** button. ACT! now gives you the opportunity to select the word processor you want to use and, if installed, the fax software, as shown here. Most computers have a word processor, most likely Microsoft Word, WordPerfect, or AmiPro. Select the word processor you prefer. For faxing, I recommend that you purchase WinFax, also made by Symantec, because it is tightly integrated with ACT!. In fact, you can edit an ACT! contact record directly from WinFax! If WinFax is installed on your computer, ACT! finds it automatically. Move to the next dialog box by clicking **Next**.

The QuickStart Wizard lets you select your word processor and fax software.

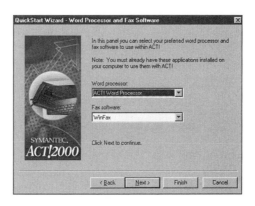

Email

Again, ACT! searches for installed versions of Lotus Notes, Eudora, or Outlook 98 programs that ACT! can use for email. ACT! lists any email software found on your system. If you have none of these programs, I suggest that you select Internet Mail. ACT! has built-in email software that can work with virtually any Internet service provider (ISP), except America Online. Click the box preceding the name of the email software you have and then click the option button to begin setting up email now. (If you don't intend to use email, skip the next paragraph.) Click **Next**.

At this point, the dialog box for your email settings should look like this.

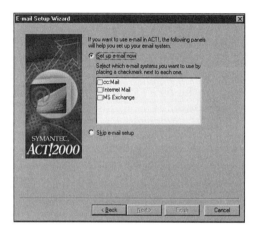

The ACT! E-mail Setup Wizard enables you to configure your email account.

In the resulting wizard, click the **New Account** button. You can now supply your account information as provided by your ISP. Table 1.1 shows how to make the entries.

Table 1.1   Account Information to Supply

Field	Description
Default Account (User Name)	Enter the first part of your email address only. My email address is DWOLF@HOWTOSOFTWARE.COM, so my entry is simply DWOLF.
Outgoing SMTP server	This is provided by your ISP. Type it in exactly as given to you.
Incoming POP3 server	This is provided by your ISP. Type it in exactly as given to you.
Real Name	Enter your proper name, such as Douglas J. Wolf.
Organization	If appropriate, make an entry—not required.
Reply to address	Enter your own email address.

The next check box involves passwords. You can choose to have ACT! remember your password so that you are not required to type it every time you send or receive email. Or, you can elect to enter your email password every time you use email. In an office, you may want to require the password, so that you are the only person who can read your email.

Stop Snoopers

Entering your password each time you use email may be a little inconvenient. However, it ensures that only you can read or send email from ACT!. If ACT! enters the password for you, anyone who can access your computer can read your mail.

The next option, Leave Retrieved Messages on Server, requires a bit of thinking. Usually the ISP deletes your email from its server when you download it. However, you can select this check box so that the email remains on its computer. You may want to do this if you access your email from two locations—say, from office and home—and you want to leave messages on the ISP computer so that you can read the messages from either location, regardless of whether it has been downloaded already at the other location. My suggestion is that you turn this option off so that your email doesn't get deleted.

If you connect to the Internet by modem, you may want to disconnect automatically from the phone line when all your messages have been sent and received. This option is particularly useful if you use ACT! in a home office and have a single phone line for email and faxing.

You can also select the way you connect to the Internet, with the Connect to the Internet Using option. The default setting is via a direct network connection, which shows the bias of the programmers, who are of course connected to a network themselves. But most ACT! users are still dialing via a modem. Chances are, you already have your ISP's dialup information configured. In that case, it appears on the pulldown list, so you can just select your ISP from this list.

The Advanced button is used to test your email connection. Click it and you see a dialog box that allows you to indicate the authentication style used by your ISP, (usually Passwords) and provides a button you can click to run a test. I suggest that you test the connection at this point. If it works, you can begin sending and receiving all those email jokes you have heard so much about but could never get.

Click **OK** after the test. You'll return to the wizard. Now, click **Next** to get to the big enchilada: setting up your database.

Setting Up Your Database

This next section applies only to those users who do not have an existing ACT! database from any version. The QuickStart Wizard asks you to create a name for the database. ACT! recommends *contacts*, but I suggest that you use your company name or your own name. For example, Wolf's Byte or Doug's Contacts. Click **Next** after entering a name.

The QuickStart Wizard is ready to complete the process. The dialog box shows you the choices you have made. Click **Finish** and ACT! starts creating the database.

The My Record

After ACT! finishes creating the database, it presents the My Record dialog box, and you'll see My Record whenever you start ACT! My Record is a key point in ACT!. The information you enter is used in many places in ACT!, as you can see in the dialog box. When you start ACT! on a single-user database, the first record you will always see is the My Record. If you are working on an ACT! database that is to be used on a network with multiple people accessing the database, each person will have their own My Record and they will see it every time they start ACT!. With the My Record dialog box, ACT! knows which activities belong to which user. For example, if I have scheduled four phone calls, two meetings, and six things to do for today, ACT! displays those activities. Other users get their own activities.

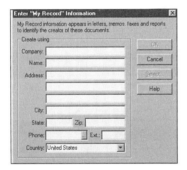

ACT! presents this dialog box for entering My Record information.

My Record Myopia

Another important concept about the My Record, which I will repeat ad nauseam, is that whenever you think of scheduling a call, meeting, or to-do, always do so for the contact with whom the activity will be scheduled. Many times, I have been asked to come to a company and fix ACT!. ACT! was working fine—the problem was the way it was being used. The customer had been putting all his activities on his My Record. So, I erased all the activities one by one and as I did, I located the contact record with which he was planning the activity, and scheduled the activity there.

Enter your information carefully. The most important field is the Name field. All the other fields can be changed later, but the Name field can cause problems if not completed properly.

After you enter the information, click **OK**. ACT! asks if the information is correct. Click **Yes**.

Congratulations! You now have a brand-new ACT! 2000 database.

Converting Existing 2.0, 3.0, or 4.0 Databases

ACT! is such a popular program that it is likely that many of you already have an ACT! database that was created in a former version. It is easy to convert the old database, but before you do, you need to know from which version you are converting.

ACT! 2.0

Converting a 2.0 version database requires that you first open the database in 2.0 and perform maintenance. First, make sure there are no email messages in your outbox. Second, perform a reindex. Next, open ACT! 2000 and follow these steps:

1. Choose **File**, **Open**. The Open dialog box appears, as shown here.

The Open dialog box is your first step in converting an existing ACT! database.

2. Select the **ACT! 1.0–2.0 Database (*.dbf)** option from the **Files of Type** drop-down list.

3. You must know where the old database is stored, because it probably is not in the folder that you see in the Open dialog box. To browse to the correct folder, click the **Up One Level** button (arrow pointing up on top of a folder) at the top middle of this dialog box. Doing so moves you up a level and you can continue to move up until you locate the folder in which the old database resides.

4. Click the old filename.

5. Click the **Open** button.

ACT! alerts you with a dialog box that the file you are about to open is from a previous version of ACT!, and asks if you want to back up the file before it is converted. Click **Yes**. Depending on the number of records, and the speed of your machine, this process will take some time. Now might be a good time to check out the sports section.

ACT! 3.0, 4.0

Importing an ACT! 3.0 or 4.0 database is also fairly simple. Just follow these steps:

1. Choose **File**, **Open** and the Open dialog box appears.
2. Select the database type you have from the **Files of Type** drop-down list.
3. You must know where the old database is stored, because it probably is not in the folder that you see in the Open dialog box. To browse to the correct folder, click the **Up One Level** button (arrow pointing up on top of a folder) at the top middle of this dialog box. This moves you up a level and you can continue to move up until you locate the folder in which the old database resides.
4. Click the name of the database.
5. Click **Open**.

ACT! alerts you that the database you are trying to open was created in an older version of ACT!, and asks if you want to create a backup and if you want to move the converted database to the default folder. Click the check box for creating a backup—unless you have already backed up the database yourself. In addition, you should click the check box for moving the database to the default folder.

If all went well, your old database should appear in a new idiom.

Starting ACT!

You might think this section should be first. As you can see, it isn't. It isn't because not everyone goes through the install process, and as you've seen, installing ACT! involves a number of configuration issues.

But now all that is behind you, and you're ready to go. The following steps show you how to start ACT!:

1. Click the **Start** button.
2. From the menu, select **Programs**.
3. From the submenu, select **ACT! 2000**.

    A second submenu appears, with ACT! 2000 listed again, as shown here.

Choose the ACT! 2000 icon from the ACT! program group under the Start menu.

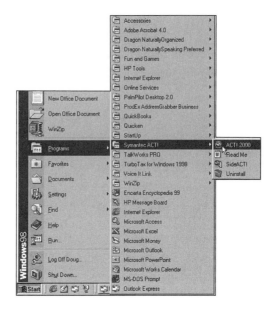

4. Click **ACT! 2000**. You'll see the ACT! startup screen.

You'll see this ACT! opening screen when you launch ACT!.

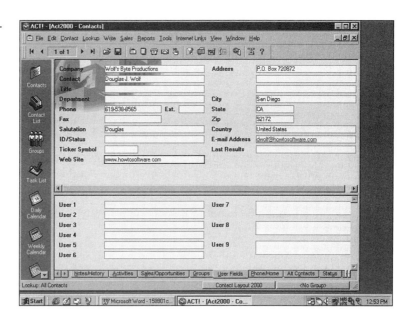

ACT! opens the same database you had open when you last exited the program. So, if you have been working in an existing database, that database appears. If you haven't created a database or converted one as described in the preceding section, you will see the Database Wizard. Follow the prompts to create a new database.

16

The ACT! install program also puts a pair of shortcut icons on the desktop: one to start ACT! and another for its cousin, SideACT!. You can click the ACT! icon to start ACT!, too.

SideACT!, Briefly

Before the arrival of ACT! 4.0, one of the criticisms of ACT! was that it did not include an easy way to create a simple list of to-dos. The ACT! thinking has always been that everything you do should be attached to a contact record. But customers disagreed, and they have the gold. So following the golden rule (those that have the gold make the rules), ACT! now includes SideACT!. This application is simply an easy way for you to enter your grocery list, a series of stops you have to make after work, or your personal goals. The list can be easily printed and thrown on the dashboard. To find out more about what you can do with SideACT!, read Chapter 20, "Using SideACT!."

Opening the ACT! Demo Database

To learn ACT!, you need to have some contact records with which to work. Anticipating this, Symantec includes a database that has a number of records you can use to follow the examples in this book. Open the demo database as follows:

1. Open the **File** menu and choose **Open**, as shown here. The Open dialog box appears.

You can open the ACT! File menu by clicking the menu bar or by pressing Alt+F.

2. Click the **ACT5demo** filename.
3. Click the **Open** button.

If all goes according to plan, the first record you see is Chris Huffman. Chris is the My Record for this demonstration database. That is why it is the initial record on the ACT! screen.

Network or Standalone Database Creation?

The ACT5demo database allows you to consider the difference between a standalone and a network database. If you are working with ACT! on your desktop or laptop computer and are not connected directly to a network, then you are a standalone user and do not need to create a place for the database that other users can access. Also, a single

My Record will be in the database, because only you will be entering records, scheduling activities, and so on. It is possible to allow multiple people to use ACT! as a standalone. For example, you might have an administrative assistant who enters names for you. If you plan to have that sort of arrangement, read the next section on networks.

Network Databases

The only differences between ACT! on a standalone system and a network is where the database is located and who can use it. The first consideration is who is going to be using ACT!. This process is called defining the users of the database. Unless a person is defined as a user, none of the information he or she enters will be identified as coming from that person. Let's take a look at defining a user of a shared database.

1. If you have not done so, open the ACT5demo database.

2. Open the **File** menu and select **Administration**. The submenu appears, as shown here.

You access the Administration option from the File menu.

3. Select **Define Users**. The Define Users dialog box appears.

You'll define your network users in the Define Users dialog box.

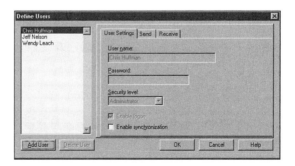

18

This demonstration database has three predefined users. Chris Huffman is automatically defined as the Administrator because he created the database. The other two users have standard security, which means that they can open the ACT! database and add new records, edit existing records, and delete records. Yikes! You might be thinking that you don't want all the users of your ACT! database to be able to delete records, but there's no other choice. It is your responsibility to make backup copies and train the users not to delete contact records except under specific circumstances. You also can assign a user the Browse level of security—that way, all that person can do is look at contact records. Any changes they make are not saved.

Defining Users on a Shared Database

Adding a new user of a database is easy—just follow this procedure:

1. Click the **Add User** button. ACT! inserts the placeholder, User1, into the User Name field.

2. Type a new name.

3. Add a password if desired.

4. Set the security level.

5. Click the **Enable Logon** check box.

6. Click **OK**. ACT! responds with a dialog box asking you to create the My Record for the new user.

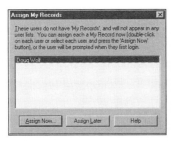

The ACT! dialog box asks for the My Record for a new login user of the database.

You have two options at this point:

➤ If the user is already a record in the database, click **Assign Now**, use the **Select** button to locate that person's record, and click it to use the information.

➤ If that person is not in the database, click **Assign Later**. When the new user tries to access the database, ACT! asks him to complete his My Record.

In Search of Login History

Login The term login has nothing to do with forestry. In computer parlance, it is a term that originated in computer systems many years ago to keep a track record, a log, of when, for how long, and where they went on the system. ACT! uses the login on a multi-user database to connect the activities, notes, and other items to the person logging in.

A Simple Login Test

To test the way ACT! tracks the login, click the name **Jeff Nelson** and click the **Enable Logon** check box. Then, click **OK** to close the dialog box and follow these steps:

1. Close the ACT5demo database by opening the **File** menu and selecting **Close**.

2. Open the ACT5demo database by opening the **File** menu and selecting **Open**.

3. From the Open dialog box, double-click the **ACT5demo** filename. The Login to ACT5demo dialog box appears, as shown in the following figure. As you can see, ACT! thinks you are Chris Huffman, because he is the last person to open this database from your computer.

ACT! launches and prompts Chris Huffman to log in.

4. Change the username by deleting Chris Huffman, and typing Jeff Nelson.

5. No password was assigned to Jeff, so click **OK**.

6. Because this is the first time that Jeff Nelson has logged into the database, ACT! asks you to add the My Record information. Jeff already has a record in this database, so click the **Select** button.

7. The Select My Record dialog box appears. Scroll the list of names until Jeff Nelson appears. Click the name.

8. Click **OK**.

Voilà! You are now logged in to the ACT5demo database as Jeff Nelson and his My Record appears on the screen.

Locating the Network Database

Now that you know how to set up a new database and add users, you must think about where you want the database stored. When you installed ACT!, it created a series of folders. One of those folders is named Database and is located on your C drive. You can see this arrangement in the Open dialog box, which you can access from the **File** menu.

The Open dialog box shows your folder hierarchy.

You probably don't want the other members of your team accessing your C drive to use ACT!. After all, that is the purpose of a network server—having the data on a fast computer that can be easily accessed by everyone. Talk to your Network Administrator about setting up a folder on the network drive for the shared ACT! database. In Chapter 23, "Network Tricks and Traps," I provide more information on using ACT! on a network.

You need to know a few key ideas about putting an ACT! database on a network drive. Chapter 25, "Synchronizing with Remote Users," covers the needs of each user and the information for the Network Administrator.

The Least You Need to Know

➤ On a standalone system, your database is located on your C drive, and after creating a new database, you are ready to go.

➤ On a multi-user system, the database is located on a network drive and each user has to be defined by the ACT! Administrator before using ACT!.

"As life is action and passion, it is required of a man that he should share the passion and action of his time, at peril of being judged not to have lived."

Oliver Wendell Holmes

Chapter 2

Getting Around in ACT!

In This Chapter

➤ Moving from record to record

➤ Looking at different layouts

➤ Checking the menus and toolbars

➤ The tabbed information

"I have learned that success is to be measured not so much by the position one has reached in life as by the obstacles he has overcome while trying to succeed."

Booker T. Washington

Now that you've successfully installed and configured ACT!, it's time to take a look at the various components of the program window. Fortunately, the ACT! window provides a plethora of tools for navigating records and manipulating your data. ACT! 2000 also features a new toolbar that groups a number of commonly performed functions in a convenient location.

It's time to take a look at the components of the ACT! window. Before you do, you'll need to make sure you're viewing a database.

Moving from Record to Record

At this point, your database, might have many records. ACT! has a demonstration database with lots of records that you can use for learning purposes. If you do have a database with more than five records, you can use it for the examples in this chapter. If not, open the ACT5demo database as follows:

1. Start ACT!.
2. Open the **File** menu and select **Open**. The Open dialog box appears.
3. Click the **ACT5demo** database name.
4. Click the **Open** button.

If you changed the login to Jeff Nelson following the directions in Chapter 1, "Installing and Creating a New Database," you will see the Login dialog box, with Jeff Nelson's name.

1. Type **Chris Huffman** as the login name.
2. Click **OK**.

The Chris Huffman My Record appears, as shown here.

When you log in as Chris Huffman, the appropriate My Record appears.

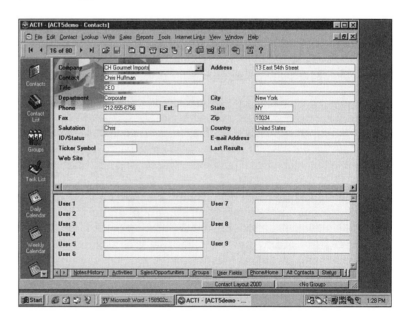

Take a tour of the ACT! interface. Begin at the upper-left corner of the screen. Across the top is the name ACT! and the name of the database. Directly below them is a series of menus, beginning with File and ending with Help. Beneath the menus is the toolbar, which has a series of icons that perform ACT! functions. The illustration shows each of the icons with a short description of what they do.

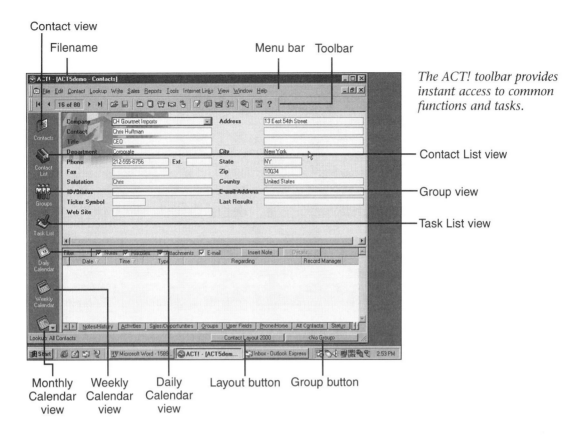

Contact view

Filename

Menu bar   Toolbar

The ACT! toolbar provides instant access to common functions and tasks.

Contact List view

Group view

Task List view

Monthly Calendar view   Weekly Calendar view   Daily Calendar view   Layout button   Group button

In the left side of the screen, running from top to bottom, is a series of graphics labeled Contacts, Contact List, and so on. (If you are an ACT! 3.0 or 4.0 user, you'll note that these icons used to be in the lower-right corner of the screen.)

At the bottom right are two buttons: No Group and Contact Layout 2000.

Navigating Records

The first buttons to consider are the four buttons on the far left of the toolbar. Between the four buttons is the record counter; in the preceding figure, it reads 16 of 80. Because the demo database has just been opened, the record counter indicates that there are a total of 80 records in the database. It does not mean that the Chris Huffman record has been assigned record number 16. To see a different record, click the first button (the one with the triangle pointing left to a solid line) at the far left of the toolbar.

When you click this button, you'll see the first record in the database. ACT! sorts the contact records by company and then by last name. All the records lacking a company name, such as the one shown here, appear at the beginning of the sort order.

Your initial contact record looks like this.

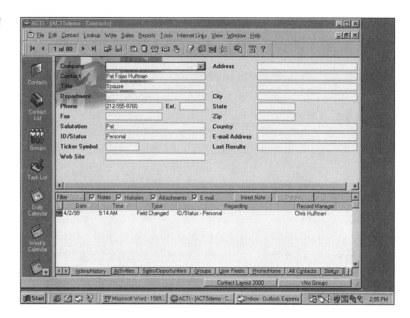

Next, click the button that is pointing to the right and has the vertical line. This button takes you to the final record in the database. The buttons with only a triangle, on either side of the record counter, move you from record to record, one at a time. Try clicking either one to see how it works.

If you want to use the keyboard to move through the records, the PgUp key takes you to the previous record and the PgDn key takes you to the next record. Holding down the Ctrl key and then pressing the Home key moves you to the first record in the database, and Ctrl+End moves you to the final record.

The movement buttons are useful after you have performed a lookup. For example, if your database had 1,000 records and you wanted to find all contact records in the city of San Diego, ACT! might find 12 records. The movement buttons enable you to flip from one record to another easily. This notion will be clearer when you perform a lookup, which I'll cover in Chapter 4, "Locating Records."

Using the Toolbar

Each of the buttons on the toolbar is discussed briefly in the following table. When you move your cursor on top of a toolbar button, a pop-up window appears revealing the name of the button. At the bottom left of the screen, ACT! displays a short message telling you what the button does. Table 2.1 covers some prominent toolbar buttons.

Table 2.1   Useful Toolbar Buttons

Button	Name	Description
	File Open	Use this button to open a different ACT! database.
	Save	The beauty of ACT! is that it saves information automatically when you move to a different record or close the database. So, you never have to worry about reminding yourself to save a newly entered record or edited information. Use this button to actively save information entered into a record. One common use of this button is when you are editing a record on a network database. If someone else is looking at the same record on a different computer, they will not see any new information you have entered unless you move to a different record or close ACT!. Clicking this button saves any changes, and other users can see them immediately.
	New Contact	This button is used to enter a new contact. When clicked, the ACT! fields are blanked out, ready for new information.
	Insert Note	Use this button to add notes easily to a contact record. Clicking this button starts the process.
	Schedule Call, Meeting, and To-do	These three buttons do almost the same thing. They open the Schedule Activity dialog box. The only difference is you can set up defaults for each activity—for example, maybe you like to block five minutes on your calendar for calls and reserve two hours for meetings.
	Letter	This button fires up your designated word processor and sends the information from the current contact record to a letter as the inside address and salutation. This feature is every lazy typist's dream. No excuses now not to write mom!
	Quick Fax	If you have faxing software installed and the current contact record has a fax number, you can send a fax. This method does not provide a cover sheet. More on faxing in Chapter 11, "Creating Documents."
	Email	If instant communication is desired, click this button to begin an email message.

continues

Table 2.1 continued

Button	Name	Description
	Dial Phone	The Dial Phone button not only dials the number you want, but also automatically starts the process of logging the call. That is, a dialog box appears and asks you what happened—was the call completed, or did you leave a message? The dialog box also includes a button for starting the call timer.
	SideACT!	This button opens the SideACT! window. Use it to jot down those items you need to pick up at the store after work. More on SideACT! in Chapter 20, "Using SideACT!."
	Live Update	This is your most valuable tool against software problems. The Live Update button connects your computer to Symantec and downloads and installs any new free updates of ACT!. This feature is particularly useful when Symantec finds a problem with ACT! and fixes it. You don't have to wait for a disk from them to fix the problem—you can use Live Update.
	Help	This button opens the Help Topics dialog box. With the dialog box open, you can enter a topic and ACT! searches for help text.

The View Bar

On the left side of the ACT! screen is a list of icons that are accessed more frequently than others, which is why they have an elevated status. ACT! calls this series of icons the View bar. Table 2.2 discusses their functions in detail.

Table 2.2 View Bar Buttons

Button	Function
Contacts	The top icon opens the view at which you are looking.
Contact List	The Contact List button changes the view of your ACT! records from one record at a time to many, as shown in the following figure.
	The list view is another way to work with your contact records. See Chapter 6, "Working in the List View," for more information.

Button	Function
Groups	This button opens the Groups window where you can create, edit, or delete groups. A group is a way to identify contact records by an affiliation you have determined. For example, you might create groups identifying your golfing foursome or purchasers of your new cure for male pattern baldness. See Chapter 15, "Working with Groups," for more information.
Task List	This button opens the Task List window that displays all your activities that you have scheduled. See Chapter 8, "Tackling Activities," for more information.
Daily, Weekly, Monthly Calendars	See your calendars quickly by clicking the appropriate button. See Chapter 9, "Checking Your Calendar," for the calendar insights.
Email	Email is so important that it gets buttons on more than one toolbar. Click the icon to start creating an email message to the current contact. More about email is found in Chapter 14, "Internet and Email."

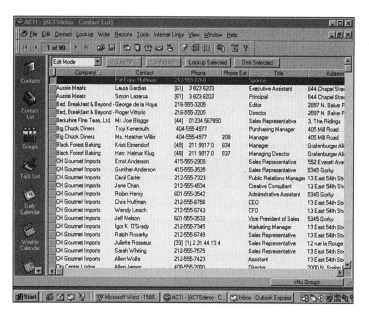

The Contact List view displays many database records at once.

Menus

The menus in ACT! can be opened by mouse clicking the name, or by pressing the Alt key and then typing the underlined letter in the menu name. For example, Alt+F opens the File menu.

You can open the File menu by clicking the menu name or by typing its keyboard shortcut, Alt+F.

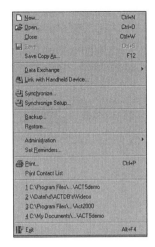

With any menu open, you can press the right or left arrow keys to open the adjoining menus. Note that many menu items can be activated by a combination of keystrokes. For instance, you can print the current document by pressing Ctrl+P. These keystrokes are listed next to the corresponding menu item.

I'll describe many of the menu commands as you need them throughout the book. For now, you can cruise through and try a few by opening a menu and clicking an item or two.

The Tabbed Information

One of the major changes to ACT! occurred with the release of version 3.0. This change was the addition of tabs to access more information on a particular contact record. Click each tab to see the kind of information each holds, as shown in the following figure. Table 2.3 describes what the various tabs do.

Table 2.3　Information Tabs

Tab	Function
Notes/History	This tab contains four pieces of information. Notes are text entries that you add. History entries are added automatically by ACT!. As an example, when you schedule an activity, ACT! records the disposition; the result is written to the tab as a history entry. Suppose you changed the Id/Status field from *prospect* to *customer*—ACT! automatically records this event in the History tab. When you send a letter to a contact, you can save it as a word processor file and then attach it to the contact record. Later, when you want to see exactly what you sent to the contact, clicking the attachment icon opens the letter for you.

Tab	Function
	Email works the same way. When you send an email, the action is recorded automatically by ACT!. You can also attach the entire email message if desired.
Activities	The Activities tab lists your scheduled activities with a contact. Each activity appears on its own line. You have a variety of options for filtering the information displayed, such as Today's Activities Only or Today and Future. The filtering process is discussed in detail in Chapter 8.
Sales/Opportunities	This tab is new to version 2000. ACT! now makes it easy to keep track of your sales pipeline. All good sales people and sales managers need this information, but if you aren't in sales, you also can use it. For example, if you use ACT! to track the progress of grant proposals, you can create a report that shows where each application stands. Chapter 19, "Working with Reports," goes over using the Sales/Opportunities tab.
Groups	When you click this tab, you see to which groups the contact record belongs. ACT! allows for an unlimited number of groups, and a particular contact record can be in any number of groups. Groups are covered in detail in Chapter 15.
User Fields	You can customize this tab for your own use. A series of fields is already available that you can modify. Chapter 17, "Creating New Fields," discusses various customization techniques.
Phone/Home	This tab includes several more fields for the seemingly unending stream of phone numbers we all now have. There also are fields for the home address of the contact.
Alt Contacts	In many cases, a contact will have an assistant or perhaps a financial advisor—someone who does not need to have a complete contact record, but does need some information. This tab provides fields for that situation.
Status	The Status tab has a number of system fields—that is, fields in which the information is generated for you by ACT! and you can't edit this information. An important field on the Status tab, if you are on a network, is the Public/Private field. Because ACT! is the tool for your time management, include your personal activities. So, if you put your proctologist's record in the database, be certain to make it a Private record! If you subsequently schedule an appointment, it will show up on the network calendar as "private activity," not "Harry is getting his hemorrhoids removed." You can modify additional user fields that I'll discuss in later chapters.

The information tabs in ACT! provide access to additional contact information.

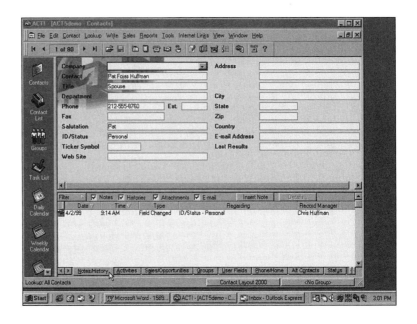

Scrollbars

Scrollbars are located on the bottom and on the right side of the ACT! record screen. Your use of them depends on the screen resolution setting of your monitor. If the resolution is set to 800 × 600, you will have to use the scrollbars to see all the contact record. At 1024 × 768, all the information is visible. In Windows 98, you can change the screen resolution by clicking the Adjust Display Properties button in the lower-right corner of the screen. Remember, in Windows you can maximize an individual window to see more. If you cannot see the Notes/History tab and so on, maximize the ACT! program window and the contact record window.

The Least You Need to Know

➤ Moving from one contact record to another is easy—click the movement buttons to go to the previous or next contact record.

➤ ACT! provides access to useful functions via the menu bar, the toolbar, and the new View bar.

➤ You can click tabs at the bottom of a contact's window to access additional information fields.

"There is nothing more demoralizing than a small but adequate income."

Edmund Wilson

Chapter 3

Entering Records

In This Chapter

➤ Entering a new record

➤ Editing drop-down menus

➤ Adding notes

➤ ID/Status field

"The great end of life is not knowledge, but action."

Thomas Huxley

Entering a New Contact Record

Whether you start ACT! in a new database or one with many records, the first record you will always see is the My Record. In a new database, with only the My Record entered, the record counter will read "1 of 1." In a database with many records, the record counter will read "YY of XX." The YY number tells you the current position in the database of the My Record. The XX number tells you the total number of records in the database. Here you can see the record counter in a new database and the My Record.

This new database shows the record counter as "1 of 1" and displays the My Record.

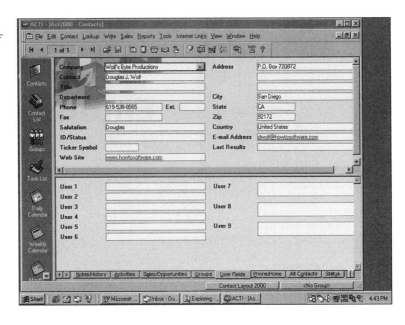

The My Record in the illustration is mine—Douglas Wolf. I'll use this new database to show you how to enter a new record. Open your own database and follow along.

The first step to entering a new record is to click the **New Record** icon, or open the **Contact** menu and select **New Contact**. Take a look at the opened Contact menu.

Open the Contact menu and select the New Contact option.

When you do, ACT! presents a blank contact record.

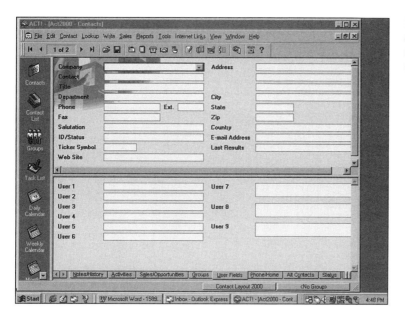

When you create a blank contact record, the insertion point begins in the Company field.

At this point you are ready to begin typing. If the person works for a company, go ahead and enter that information. For example:

1. In the **Company** field, type ABC Company.

2. Press **Tab** to move the insertion point to the next field, which is **Contact**.

3. Type Sam Wells.

4. Press **Tab** to go to the **Title** field.

   Because ACT! was designed by nontypists for nontypists, many fields have drop-down lists that contain the most likely entries for the field.

5. At the right end of the Title field is a gray box with a down arrow. Click it. The drop-down list appears with a set of common options, as shown in the following figure.

   As you can see, you can select a title from the list, eliminating a typing chore. The list is sorted alphabetically, so scroll to get to the President entry.

6. Select the title **President**. ACT! inserts it into the Title field for you.

7. Press **Tab**. The insertion point is now in the **Department** field.

   You might not need this field. If not, you can skip it. If you find that you never use this field, or any other, it easily can be deleted from the layout. Chapter 16, "Customizing Your Layout," covers modifying the layout.

   For this example, enter a department, using the drop-down list. But, instead of opening it and looking for the entry you want, assume that you want the word "Corporate" in the field.

The drop-down list in the Title field supplies some common choices.

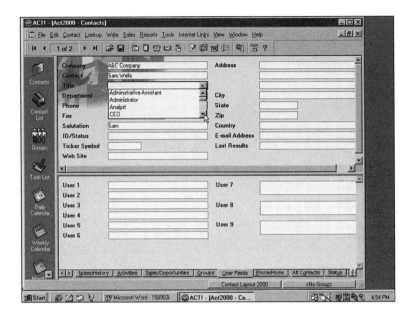

8. Type c.

   When you type c, ACT! searches the drop-down list for the first entry that has the letter C as its first letter. It finds Corporate, and enters it into the field. If there was a Cost Accountant entry in the drop-down list, and that is what you want, typing cos will cause ACT! to insert that title into the field.

9. Press **Tab** to move the insertion point to the Phone field. This field has special formatting capabilities. At the right end of the field is a gray box. Click it to reveal the Country Codes dialog box, shown here.

The Country Codes dialog box with the phone number formatting shown.

If you are entering phone numbers for the United States, and do not intend to make phone calls out of the country, the default settings for phone numbers are fine. However, if you are not in the United States, you can select the name of your country and the phone format will match. The pound sign (#) determines where a number must be entered, and ACT! automatically inserts the appropriate parentheses or dashes for you. After selecting the country, click the radio button in front of Apply This Format for Country Code.

If you are going to enter numbers from all over the world, your best choice is Free Form.

For our purposes, select the **United States** format.

10. Enter a phone number by typing 619-555-1212.

11. Press **Tab** and the insertion point goes to the **Ext** field. Use this field if the contact has an extension.

12. Press **Tab**. The active field is **Fax**. The same rules apply to this field as to the Phone field.

13. Press **Tab**. The **Salutation** field is filled for you. The default in ACT! is to enter the first name of the contact. This default can be modified, as explained in Chapter 10, "Setting Your Preferences."

14. Press **Tab**. The insertion point is now in the **ID/Status** field. For this example, type PR and ACT! enters Prospect into the field.

ID/Status Considerations

This field is important because it is one of the choices on the Lookup menu and works with several of the reports in ACT!. Let me offer a few suggestions on how to use this field. ACT!'s pull-down list suggests that you identify your contacts by category—as a vendor, shareholder, competitor, and so on. This arrangement may work for you. Other companies, particularly those in sales, use this field to distinguish the position of the contact record in the sales funnel. So, when the record is created, the ID/Status would begin as Suspect; when the contact shows some interest, the ID/Status is changed to Prospect; and when the contact buys, the ID/Status is changed again to Customer. The benefits of this method are several, the most salient of which is the capability to see how many of each type of entry your company has. Secondly, one aspect of sales is trying to determine the conversion time of a customer—that is, how long it takes for a suspect to buy. The key idea is to think through how you want to use this field before entering many records. Chapter 15, "Working with Groups," focuses on groups, another means of identifying contact records. The ID/Status field can be used in concert with groups, making the identities of your contacts clear.

15. Press **Tab** to move to the Ticker Symbol field. This field is used to enter the symbol for this contact record's stock, assuming he or she works for a publicly traded company. This entry comes in handy when using the Internet links, covered in Chapter 14, "Internet and Email."

16. Press **Tab** to enter the Web Site field. For this example, enter a useful Web address: `www.symantec.com`.

    Note that the entry displays in a color, and is underlined, alerting you that this is an *active* field. Assuming that you can connect to the Internet from your computer, clicking the entry in this field starts your browser and opens the Internet site you have entered. This is handy, because companies often post their latest product announcements, financial reports, and other important news on their Web sites. So, when you look at the contact record, you can click the Web Site field and go directly to that Web site and be on top of what is happening with your customer's business.

Selecting and Editing Web Addresses Can Be Tricky

If the Web address changes, a special trick is required to edit the field. Instead of clicking and dragging the field, right-click it. A menu appears; choose the **Select All** option. The entire Web address is highlighted and your browser does not fire up. Now, select **Delete** to erase the old address and enter the new.

17. Press **Tab** to go to the Address field. ACT! provides three fields for the address. No need to make any entries at this point. Press **Tab** twice to go to the City field.

Editing the City Drop-Down

The City field is a good place to learn how to add or delete an entry in a drop-down list. The steps you'll perform here are consistent for any drop-down you find in ACT!:

1. Open the drop-down list by clicking it.

2. Scroll down the list and click **Edit List**. The Edit List dialog box appears, as shown in the following figure.

3. If your city is already in the list, you can just read along. If not, click the **Add** button. This opens the Add dialog box.

4. For this example, type `Poway`.

    There's no need for a description (despite Poway's reputation!). If you were entering codes for salary levels, you could add that as the description. On a network, you, as Administrator, can prevent other users from editing the drop-down list, thereby stopping them from seeing the description field.

5. Click **OK**. Poway is added to the list.

6. Click **OK** again. Poway appears in the City field.

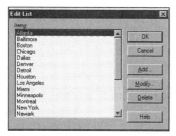

The Edit List dialog box lets you add a city to ACT!'s defaults.

I suggest that you add the names of most of the cities that you anticipate having to enter.

Finishing the New Record Entry

The State and Zip fields are straightforward. By the way, there is an add-on program that fills in the City and State fields for you when you enter the zip code. (See Chapter 26, "ACT! Add-on Products," for the information on that product and others.)

The Country field may be superfluous in your business. Use it if needed.

The E-mail Address field is also special—similar to, but not the same as, the Web Site field. You can enter an email address by typing. Once entered, the field becomes active, and when you click it, ACT! opens the E-mail window, assuming that you want to create an email message. Web site addresses do not change much, but email addresses do, and many people have multiple email addresses. Fortunately, ACT! enables you to edit the address and to save several email addresses for the contact.

To see how this process works, enter an email address:

1. Type Swells@pacbell.net.
2. Press **Tab**. The email address displays in color and is underlined, alerting you that it is an active field.
3. Press **Shift+Tab**, which moves the insertion point back to the E-mail Address field. You can't click to do this, because you will open an email window.
4. Add a second email address. Click the down arrow at the right edge of the E-mail Address field, and select **Edit E-mail Addresses**.

The E-mail Addresses dialog box lets you add a second email listing for a contact.

5. Click the **New** button and the New Address dialog box appears.
6. Type swells@bugfoot.com.

7. You have the opportunity to make the new address the Primary Address—that is, the address that shows in the field and is used by default when you create an email to this contact. Click **OK** twice to leave it as is. In Chapter 14, I'll show you the way to use the secondary address.

The final field on the top half of the contact record screen is labeled Last Results. In a way, it is a holdover from the DOS version of ACT!—before it was easy to enter a note in a contact record. Consider it a shorthand way of entering an update to the record. The field has a drop-down box containing a series of selections that are general enough for every business. The Last Results field also has the History attribute. That is, when you make an entry into the field, a copy of the entry is also entered automatically on the Notes/History tab.

Does This Person Need a Record?

In deciding whether to enter a person as a contact record, the important idea is whether you will need to

➤ Look up the person

➤ Schedule activities

➤ Keep a running history of what has occurred with that person

If not, then perhaps the person can be added as an alternative contact on another contact record. Or, you could go to the My Record and enter the person's name and phone number as a note.

Entering a Duplicate Record

You do not want to save duplicate records in your database! Why, then, this section title? Because many of your contact records maybe similar—that is, you may be doing business with a number of people from the same company. So, many of the fields are identical, like the address fields. The main difference is probably the name and phone number. As a result, you can create a duplicate record, change just a few pieces of information, and save yourself a lot of time.

To hasten the entry of new contact records that are virtually identical, do the following:

1. Look up the contact record that is close to the new one you plan to enter. For more information on locating the record you want, see Chapter 4, "Locating Records."

2. Click the **Contact** menu.

The Contact menu lets you duplicate a contact, saving time when adding people who work for the same company.

3. Select **Duplicate Contact**. The Duplicate Contact dialog box appears, as shown.

The Duplicate Contact dialog box lets you copy some or all of a contact's data.

There are two options. One is to grab the information from all the fields and the other is to get the information from only the Primary fields. The Primary fields are the Company field and all the address fields.

4. Click the radio button in front of the option that works best for your purposes.

5. Enter the contact name and phone number to complete the new record.

A Special Note on Entering Names

ACT! is a bit unusual in that both the first and last names of contacts are entered into a single field. The Lookup menu in ACT! enables you to find contacts by either name. So, it is important to understand how ACT! reads the entry in the Contact field.

If you enter a name such as Sam Wells, as in the example, ACT! easily identifies the first name as Sam and the last name as Wells. ACT! also identifies honorifics such as Dr., Mr., and Ms., and suffixes such as Ph.D., M.D., and Sr., not as names but as what they are—additions to the name. It also correctly identifies last-name prefixes such as Von, de, da, and St. But there are names that can cause trouble, such as hyphenated names—the vogue of the 80s—like Gloria Wheeler-Wolf. ACT! tries to guess which of the parts of the entry are the last name that you would use to lookup the contact. Sometimes it may be right and other times wrong. Plus, you may prefer to lookup a contact by the last name with which you are most comfortable—"I never call her Gloria Wheeler-Wolf, just Gloria Wheeler. Why she married that idiot, I'll never understand." In such an unhappy case, you would want to lookup Gloria by the last name Wheeler, not Wolf. Anyway, follow the steps here to see how ACT! identifies the name parts:

1. In any contact record, click on the **Contact** field.
2. Press the **F2** key. The Contact Name dialog box appears.

The Contact Name dialog box highlights what ACT! assumes are the first and last names.

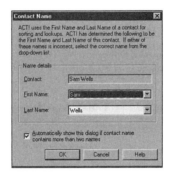

If you can look up a contact record by company or phone number, but ACT! refuses to find the same record when you use the Lookup menu's Last Name option, click the **Contact** field and press **F2** to check out what ACT! thinks is the correct part of the name. If it is wrong, use the pull-down list and select the correct part. Note that you can have this dialog box open automatically for those trendy names.

One last rule: If you imported your records—see more on this in Chapter 21, "Importing/Exporting Data"—and the names came in formatted as Wolf, Douglas, ACT! assumes that the last name is Wolf and the first name is Douglas, saving you the trouble of editing all the records. The comma between the names does the trick. However, if the names came in Wolf Douglas, with no comma, you have work to do—unless you use an add-on tool to fix this problem, as detailed in Chapter 26.

Inserting a Note

In early incarnations of ACT!, it was a bit of a chore to add a note to a contact record. With the arrival of 3.0, the task was made very easy, and this ease continues in ACT! 2000.

To add a note to a contact record:

1. Click the **Notes/History** tab. (Make sure there is a check mark in front of the word Notes to the right of the Filter.)
2. Click the **Insert Note** button.
3. For this example, type This is an example note.
4. Click anywhere in the contact record, and the note appears, as you can see here.

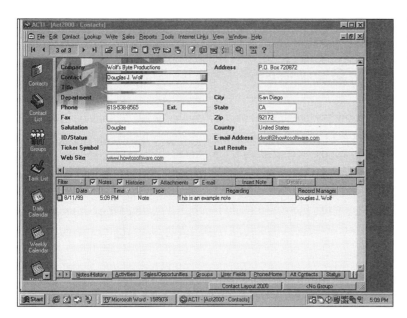

Your example note appears in the Notes/History tab.

As you can see, the date and time are inserted for you, plus the type of entry. To the right of the note, there is a column named Record Manager. On a standalone system, your name appears. On a network, the Record Manager entry is taken from the My Record of the person entering the note. Usually, this is your name. But, suppose you are out of the office, playing golf. If your best client calls to leave important information, and one of your co-workers goes to the client's contact record and inserts the important information as a note, the co-worker's name is inserted as the Record Manager for that note. When you toddle in from the 19th hole, you can see who talked to your client and thank them for entering the note.

You can enter a note of any length that you need. At the right margin, ACT! wraps the text. You can modify the display of the note in several ways. You can make the note field longer, for example, by positioning the mouse pointer on the right border, holding down the mouse button, and then dragging the border to the right. You also can change the font of a note, the current size being eight teeny-tiny points, to whatever size your failing eyesight enables you to read. Check Chapter 10 to see how to edit this setting.

The Least You Need to Know

➤ Adding a new record to ACT! is as simple as clicking the New Contact icon and typing away.

➤ Determine beforehand how you are going to use the ID/Status field.

➤ The Web Site and E-mail Address fields are active fields and start your browser or email program automatically.

"However brilliant an action, it should not be esteemed unless the result of a great motive."

Francois De La Rochefoucald

NOTHIN' NET!

Locating Records

"Fishing is a delusion entirely surrounded by liars in old clothes."

Don Marquis

Easy Lookups

In this chapter, you will learn how to locate your "fish," finding the contact records that you have entered. The Lookup menu includes easy ways to lookup contact records and several ways that require detailed explanation. So, this chapter covers the easy methods, and Chapter 5, "Advanced Record Lookups," covers the esoteric.

The Lookup Menu

After entering hundreds and possibly thousands of records into ACT!, the next logical step is that you will want to find a particular record. You could use the movement buttons to flip from record to record, as described in Chapter 2, "Getting Around in

ACT!," but that becomes impractical when hundreds of contacts are in your database. The movement buttons work best when used *after* you create a lookup that narrows the number of contacts.

You find a record by using the Lookup menu.

The Lookup menu is where you go to find records in your database.

Now, I'll discuss this menu's components in some detail.

My Record

When you open the Lookup menu and click the My Record menu option, ACT! finds and displays the My Record contact screen. Now, try the following steps:

1. Click the **My Record** option. The contact record appears. Notice that the entry in the status bar under Lookup reads My Record. This is to remind you how the contact was found.

2. Click the **Next Contact** button. ACT! beeps at you!

This short example serves to illustrate an important concept in ACT!. That is, when you execute a lookup, ACT! creates a subset of contacts in the database based on the lookup criteria you specify. In this example, there is only one contact record that can be put into the My Record subset, so you can't move to the Next or to a Previous record. Expanding this idea a little further, suppose that you want to work with just the contacts that are in a specific city. Using the Lookup menu and the City option, ACT! creates a subset of contacts of the database containing just those contacts living in the city you specified. This is a subset of the entire set of contacts in your database.

All Contacts

As you might suspect, the All Contacts option accesses the contacts in their entirety. In other words, if you click the Next/Previous buttons, you can walk through every contact in the entire database, one at a time.

Keyword Search

The keyword search method has been changed dramatically in ACT! 2000. Because ACT! includes many user-definable fields, has a note-taking facility for each contact, stores email addresses, and records sales opportunities, information can be stored in many places. The Keyword Lookup is the catchall for information that you need, but have forgotten where it's hiding in your database. For example, in a conversation two years ago a contact mentioned a hot stock pick and you entered the ticker symbol and type of business into the Notes tab for that contact. This morning you saw a news story on a technology that promises to be a big winner for

The Rest of the Database Remains Accessible

Even though a lookup creates a subset of the records in the database, you do not have to execute an All Contacts lookup to access the rest of the database.

companies in that field. You remember that your contact said the same thing about this hot stock pick, but, you have long forgotten the name of the contact or anything to do with it except that it is somewhere in Notes. Relax! ACT! will find the stock information for you. Here's how:

1. Open the **Lookup** menu and select **Keyword**. The Keyword Search dialog box opens.

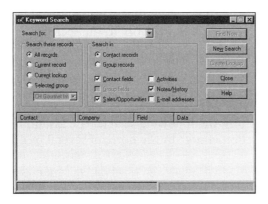

The Keyword Search dialog box is your first step to find records based on the information they contain.

2. In the **Search For** text box, enter the word or phrase you want to find.

3. Click **Find Now**.

While taking a moment to look at your search options, consider that a keyword search is a brute-force method for locating the contact record or records. ACT! looks at every piece of information in each record to match the entry you make. So, if you have 20,000 records with five years of Notes/History, this search could take some time. That's why ACT! has a number of switches, set by the radio buttons, that you can use to reduce the mass of data to be searched. For example, you could have ACT! search the Current Lookup in Notes/History only, by clicking the appropriate radio buttons.

These are the options in the Search These Records section of the Keyword Search dialog box:

➤ All Records	Searches every record for a match
➤ Current Record	Searches only the record that was onscreen when the dialog box was opened
➤ Current Lookup	Searches the records you have selected from a previous use of the Lookup capability
➤ Selected Group	Searches in the specific group you select

In addition to choosing what records to search, you can select which fields, tabs, or even groups you want to search. Here are your options as presented in the Search In section of the Keyword Search dialog box:

➤ Contact Records	Searches the contact records, not groups
➤ Groups Records	Searches the groups, not the contact records
➤ Contact Fields	Searches the contact fields
➤ Groups Fields	Searches the group fields
➤ Sales/Opportunities	Searches the information in the Sales/Opportunities tab
➤ Activities	Includes activities in the search
➤ Notes/History	Includes Notes/History in the search
➤ E-mail Addresses	Includes email addresses in the search

Performing a Keyword Search

Use the ACT5demo database to perform the following search. The assumption is that you have entered the word "product brochure" in the notes of several records, but you cannot remember which ones.

1. Open the ACT5demo database.
2. Click the **Lookup** menu and select **Keyword**.
3. Click the **All Records** radio button.
4. Click the **Contact Records** radio button.
5. Click the **Contact Fields** check box.
6. Click the **Activities** check box, so that it's deselected.
7. Click the **Notes/History** check box, so that a check mark appears.
8. In the Search For text box, type product brochure.
9. Click the **Find Now** button. ACT! responds with a list of the records something like this one.

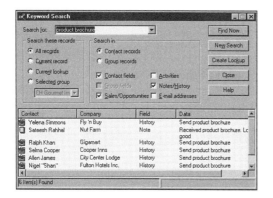

When you perform a keyword search, ACT! displays a list of matching records.

The result of the lookup shows the Company, Contact, and Field in which ACT! found the matching data. The search also shows the search text with some surrounding text.

After performing this lookup, you have several choices. Click the **Create Lookup** button to see the records in Contact view. You can select a single record by clicking part of it. To select multiple adjacent records, click the first record, hold down the **Shift** key, and click the last record. To select records that aren't adjacent, click the first record, hold down the **Ctrl** key, and then click on the other records you want. After selecting a record or records, right-click one of your selections. A menu appears listing these options:

➤ Click **Go to Record** to see that single record.

➤ Click **Lookup Selected Records** when you have selected multiple records.

➤ Clicking **Lookup All in List** is the same as clicking the Create Lookup button.

After you create a keyword lookup, ACT! saves the lookup's settings. The keyword you entered to match is stored on a drop-down list so you can access it later. Because the settings are saved, you can run another search after changing a single setting like this:

1. Click the **Lookup** menu and select **Keyword Search**.

2. In the Keyword Search dialog box, click the check box in front of **Activities**. Leave all other settings the same.

3. Click the **Find Now** button.

There should be one additional record located. Remember, the earlier exercise assumed that all the matches could be found in the Notes/History. But, this example should teach you not to trust your assumptions and to try several settings before being satisfied with the result.

Searching by Company

Use this option to find a contact or contacts that are identified with a certain company or with companies that have specific letters in their names. ACT! assumes that you are entering the name of the company in the Company field of the contact record.

1. Click the **Lookup** menu.
2. Click **Company**. The Lookup dialog box appears with the Company criterion selected.

The Lookup dialog box lets you search for information by company name.

ACT! prompts you to enter the company name in the Search For field. What ACT! doesn't tell you is that you don't have to know the exact spelling of the name. For example, if you know that the company name in a hypothetical database begins with the letters "MULT," you can type those letters into the field and click OK. ACT! finds all contacts with company names beginning with MULT:

Multiplexing Systems

Multiple Sources

Multimation

Multiplying Inc.

Multisource

The idea here is to see that the first four letters are matched in the Company field. In the MULT example, five contacts were found. In the Record Counter, ACT! indicates 1 of 5. If you enter only the letter "M" as the match, ACT! returns all companies that have a name beginning with "M," which would probably result in a much longer list.

This ACT! concept sometimes confounds new users. Despite the fact that the previous lookup assembled matching contacts into a subset of the contacts, you don't have to use the Lookup, Everyone, option to "unselect" the contacts before you can execute another lookup. So, after finding the MULT subset, you can immediately execute a lookup for contacts Last Name is Smith, and ACT! will dutifully find that group of contacts from among your entire contact list.

The reason for the subset creation is to enable you to easily locate specific contacts for form letters, mailing labels, or a list of calls that you want to direct to a smaller portion of the entire database. You can perform these actions on your subset without affecting the larger contact list.

Lookup Options

The Lookup dialog box has switches to refine the lookup. After you create a lookup, you can add more records or reduce the number of records by using the switches described in Table 4.1.

Table 4.1 Lookup Refinement Switched

Switch	Function
Replace Lookup	This is the default setting in ACT!. That is, if you run a lookup and then decide to run a second lookup, ACT! assumes that you want to select an entirely different set of contact records from the entire database. So, all you have to do is type a new lookup entry in the field to execute a new lookup.
Add to Lookup	After executing a lookup, you may find that you want to keep the set of contact records you have found and then add another set of records.
Narrow Lookup	After executing a lookup, you may find that you want to narrow the scope of the lookup. When you do this, ACT! uses only the first set of contacts to look for the next batch.

How to Add Records to Your Lookup

One useful and timesaving feature of ACT! 2000 is the capability to combine lookups to create lists matching multiple criteria. Here's how you do it.

Suppose that in your database, you have entered the customer's product interest, in the ID/Status field, and you look up all contacts that are interested in Product A. Then, you decide you want to see the customers who are interested in product D, but you want *both* sets of records to be included in the same lookup. All you have to do is execute a second lookup to add the contacts interested in Product D, like this:

1. Click the **Lookup** menu.
2. From the menu, select the field on which you want to perform the lookup, as described previously.

51

3. After executing the lookup, open the **Lookup** menu and select the field you want to use for the second lookup.

4. Before clicking **OK**, click the **Add to Lookup** radio button.

The lookup now contains both sets of contacts. There's no limit to the number of subsequent lookups you can perform to get the set of contacts that you want.

This is a great way to create groups of contacts that you will need to use in the future. After the lookup is complete, create a permanent group so that you do not have to repeat the steps. See Chapter 15, "Working with Groups," for more on groups.

Narrow Your Lookup

Sometimes you may run a lookup that returns more records that you need, possibly because there's something extra the records you really want have in common. For example, suppose that you used the lookup to find all your contacts in the city of San Diego. But you really want to find only those contacts interested in a specific product, which is listed in the ID/Status field. You can narrow your lookup results like this:

1. Click the **Lookup** menu and pick the field you want to search.

2. Enter the search criteria and click **OK**.

3. ACT! responds with a set of contacts that meet the criteria. In this example, you looked up all contacts in San Diego.

4. Click the **Lookup** menu again and select the second field on which to search. For this example, choose the **ID/Status** field, which contains the name of a product in which your contact is interested.

5. Enter Product A as the next criteria for the search.

6. Click the **Narrow Lookup** radio button.

7. Click **OK**.

ACT! executes the second search in only those contacts that were identified by the first search criteria. So, it will find all the contacts in San Diego with an ID/Status indicating interest in Product A.

First Name, Last Name

I'm going to discuss these two lookup methods in the same section because they work together. When you enter a name into the Contact field, you may enter it as JOHN SMITH or as SMITH, JOHN. The operative distinction is the comma. When ACT! sees a comma between two entries in the Contact field, it assumes that the first entry is the last name of the contact. So, it doesn't matter how you enter the first and last names—as long as you have the comma between them when you use the second method, ACT! recognizes the first and last names. If you enter SMITH JOHN, though, ACT! assumes that the last name of the Contact is JOHN. The key is to be consistent in the way in which you enter the names. Choose one method or the other.

Combine Names from Imported Databases

If you import data from another database, and the first name is in one field and last name is in another, you can map both the names into the Contact field. ACT! provides the field names First and Last as target fields, even though the contact records do not have separate fields. See Chapter 21, "Importing/Exporting Data," for exact steps.

Selecting either the First Name or Last Name option from the Lookup menu opens the Lookup dialog box. The match entry is identical to the Company lookup: You do not have to enter the entire name to find the contact. If you know the exact spelling, all the better, but it isn't critical.

Mr. Courtesy Title

Besides the order in which you enter the names, you may include a courtesy title such as Mr., Ms., or Professor, because ACT! recognizes those entries for what they are: prefixes and not a first or last name. You can add your own prefixes for recognition as described in Chapter 15.

Phone

It's happened to you; it's happened to everyone—you get a message on voice mail or from a temporary secretary, and the name is so mangled that you cannot make out who it is. Never fear, ACT! saves the day by enabling you to look up the entire phone number or just the first digit and returns the matching contact record you have in the database.

City

The City lookup finds contacts on the same match criteria as the other lookup options. If you enter the first three letters, such as "SAN," then ACT! finds all city names that begin with "SAN," such as San Francisco, San Antonio, Santa Fe, or Santiago.

The Add Lookup feature works great in conjunction with this lookup. You can add cities or whatever you need on-the-fly.

Using a Drop-Down List

Instead of typing the data into the field, you can use the drop-down list to select a city. Click the drop-down arrow in the Lookup dialog box and the same drop-down list that appears when you are entering a new contact is displayed. Click a city in the list, and click **OK**. The city is inserted into the Lookup dialog box. Click **OK** to execute the lookup.

Lookup by State

Again, entering the state as either an abbreviation or as a full name works for lookup purposes, but be consistent. Don't enter Texas as both TX and Texas and expect that ACT! can easily find all the contacts from Texas. Using the drop-down list to enter the state when creating the contact record means that you can easily use it again in the Lookup dialog box to find the contact.

Try this lookup example. To do so, you need to open the ACT5demo database that is shipped with ACT!. If you are not already in that database, then:

1. Click the **File** menu and select **Open**.
2. Click the filename **ACT5DEMO.DBF**.
3. Click **OK**. The My Record of the ACT5demo database appears.

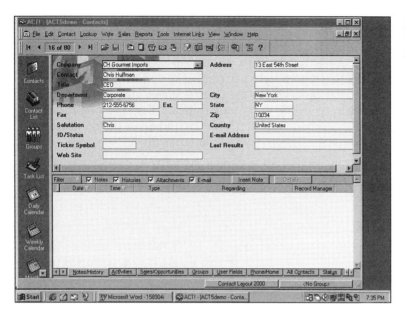

In the ACT5demo database, Chris Huffman's My Record is visible.

4. Click the **Lookup** menu.

5. Click the **State** option.

6. The Lookup dialog box appears. Click the drop-down arrow. The list of state names appears.

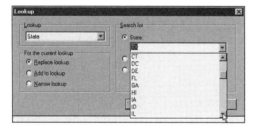

You can choose a state's abbreviation from the Lookup dialog box.

7. Click **TX**.

8. Click **OK**. ACT! inserts the abbreviation TX into the Lookup dialog box.

9. Click **OK**.

ACT! locates the contacts that meet the lookup criteria. In the demo database, four contacts hail from the Lone Star state.

Remember, the Add to Lookup feature enables you to add another state if needed to comprise the set of records you need. The Narrow Lookup feature works great in conjunction with the State lookup in that you can then specify a city within the state as a further search. Or, as I pointed out previously, you can use the ID/Status field as the next level of the search.

Lookup by Zip Code

The zip code lookup is powerful for a number of reasons. Imagine being able to group all of the contacts in your database that live in a certain zip code. The capability to target market, or to plan trips based on a tight geographic region, is yours with this lookup. Even though this entry is numeric (in the United States, anyway) you enter the matching data the same way as in the other lookup fields. For example, for all the contacts in zip 92XXX, enter 92 only. But, if you want to find all of the contacts in Rancho Penasquitos (a suburb of San Diego) you would enter the full zip code, 92129.

Here again, the Add to Lookup or Narrow Lookup features make selecting exactly the records you want quite easy.

Lookup by ID/Status

This option works the same way as the other lookups. Enter the first couple of letters or the entire entry. A drop-down list is available in this dialog box, too. This is probably the most important field in each record because you can use this field with the Group feature to locate contacts in specific ways. For example, you can enter the level of interest the contact has in a purchase by ranking him with numbers 1, 2, 3,... or with words such as *suspect*, *prospect*, and *likely customer*. Combine this ranking with Grouping and you can have a Group of contacts interested in a specific product, ranked by interest level. Or, you can reverse the process and use the ID/Status field to indicate the product and then create groups by interest level.

Lookup by Email Address

Use this lookup to locate records by the entry in the email address field. It works the same as the other lookup fields—enter a partial or full entry and ACT! tries to make a match.

Lookup by Other Fields

When software developers started creating database programs, one of the first problems they ran into was being able to locate a particular record quickly. Imagine trying to locate a record in a database consisting of thousands of records, where each record contains hundreds of pieces of data. It would be similar to having to read every word of an encyclopedia to find the topic you needed! Even a fast computer would get bogged down. The solution was to create an *index* of selected fields in the record.

When you open the Lookup menu, the fields such as Company, City, ID/Status, Phone, State, and Zip Code are *indexed* fields. In addition, ACT! creates an index for the Contact's first and last names. So, when you ask ACT! to locate records with a zip code of 92129, it skips all the other data in the records, goes to the zip code field index, reads the index until it finds the number 9, and then finishes the lookup.

The Other Fields lookup gives you easy access to the fields *not* on the Lookup menu. Because the other fields are not indexed, this is a slower search, especially if you are working in a large database—10,000 records or more. But, if you want to look up a record by, say, the Referred By field, this is the fastest way:

1. Open the **Lookup** menu.
2. Select the **Other Fields** option. The Lookup dialog box opens.
3. Pull down the list in the Lookup field.

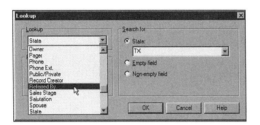

The Lookup dialog box with the drop-down list opened.

4. Select the **Referred By** field (or any field you want to use) from the drop-down list.
5. Finish the lookup by entering the text you want to find and set any switches, such as **Add to Lookup** or **Narrow Lookup**.
6. Click **OK**.

Notice that all the fields appear in this drop-down list. This list is available every time you open the Lookup dialog box. If you start the lookup by using the Company option and then decide that you really need the State field, you can easily change the field you want to use in the search by pulling down this list and selecting the field.

If you have customized a field and need to look up information in that field on a regular basis, you can create an index for a user field. This process is covered in Chapter 17, "Creating New Fields."

Previous Lookup

Often, you will want to toggle between lookups, and ACT! provides the Previous item to do that. You can create a lookup and get the records you want. Then, you execute another lookup. At that point, you want to see the other set of records from the previous lookup. Click the Previous item to do so. This tool is useful when used with the Narrow Lookup and Add to Lookup options in the Lookup dialog box. If you ran a lookup and then executed a second lookup by selecting the Add to Lookup option, you might find that you did not want to add the second set of contacts after all. Fortunately, you can use the Previous lookup to return to the original set of records.

Lookup for Empty Fields and Filled Fields

New to version 2000 is the capability to locate records that have any entry in a particular field, or records in which a particular field has no entry—in other words, records in which a certain field is blank or not. This type of lookup used to require a high level of query expertise in ACT!. No longer. The best example of the use of this type of lookup is for email addresses or fax numbers. When you want to send an email or fax to many recipients, similar to a mail-merged letter, the job is easier if you eliminate records that lack an entry in the field. This will become more apparent as you create mass email or faxes.

To search for records that have an empty field:

1. Open the **Lookup** menu.
2. If the field is one of the ones listed, select it. If not, use the **Other Fields** option.
3. In the Lookup dialog box, check the **Replace Lookup** radio button.
4. Click the **Empty Field** radio button.
5. Click **OK**.

ACT! responds with the records with no entry in the field. The record counter indicates the total number, in the format "1 of x," where x is the total number of matching records.

Non-Empty Lookup

Another way to use this type of lookup is to eliminate the records that do not have an entry. Suppose you created a lookup by ID/Status and then wanted to send an email to those contact records. To eliminate the records lacking an email address:

1. Open the **Lookup** menu.
2. Select the field you want to locate with an entry. If the field is not on the menu, select **Other Fields** and use the drop-down list to select the field. In this example, you would select the **E-mail Address** Lookup option.
3. In the Lookup dialog box, click the **Narrow Lookup** radio button.
4. Click the **Non-Empty Field** radio button.
5. Click **OK**.

The records that have an entry in the field chosen are displayed. ACT!'s record counter indicates the total number found, in the format "1 of x," where x is the total number of matching records.

The Least You Need to Know

➤ When you have an ACT! database with hundreds of records, you can find the one you want using the Lookup menu.

➤ You can search for the information that you remember about the contact, the company, his or her name, the phone number, or a keyword.

➤ You can combine lookups to create new groups of contacts with common criteria.

➤ The entry does not have to exactly match the record for which you are searching.

"All politics are based on the indifference of the majority."

James Reston

Chapter 5

Advanced Record Lookups

In This Chapter

➤ Finding records by example

➤ Finding records by Sales Stage

➤ Using the Internet Directory

➤ Modifying the Lookup menu

"When it is a question of money, everyone is of the same religion."

Voltaire

Looking Up Contact Records By Example

In Chapter 4, "Locating Records," you looked up records by a single criterion at a time, narrowing the list by repeated lookups. Fortunately, ACT! enables you to streamline this process by allowing you to ask for records matching multiple criteria at once.

You'll use the By Example option when you need to make a complex *query* of your database. A query asks a question of the database. The previous lookup options, discussed in Chapter 4, were simple queries, because they examined only a single field at a time. The By Example option enables you to create complex queries with multiple variables. For example, you may want to find all the contacts identified as prospects who are in the 92000 zip code area and have purchased more than $1,000 worth of goods in the past.

The By Example option also allows for the use of Boolean logic. That is, you can include arithmetic operators in the queries and specific words such as AND, OR, NOT, and CONTAINS that can combine or exclude criteria. Suppose that you want to find all your contacts identified as prospects whose zip code is 92000 or greater. In Boolean terms, the operators would be >=92000 (greater than or equal to 92000). So, ACT! would find 92000, 92001, 93000, and so on.

Let's create a sample query using the By Example option. In this exercise, I'll use the ACT5demo database to illustrate the query. It contains 14 records in the state of New York. The query example locates the records in New York that have a zip code greater than 10100:

1. Open the **File** menu.
2. Click the **Open** option.
3. From the Open File dialog box, click the **ACT5DEMO.DBF** filename.
4. Click **Open**.
5. Open the **Lookup** menu.
6. Click the **By Example** option. The Query screen appears.

The blank Query screen lets you specify criteria for one or more fields.

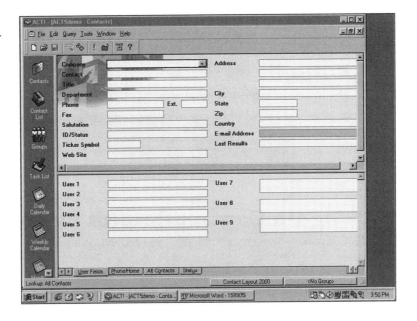

7. Click the **State** field.
8. Press **F2**. From the resulting list, click **New York**. NY is entered as the first search criterion in the Query screen.
9. Click the **Zip** field.
10. Type >10100.

    The completed query looks like this.

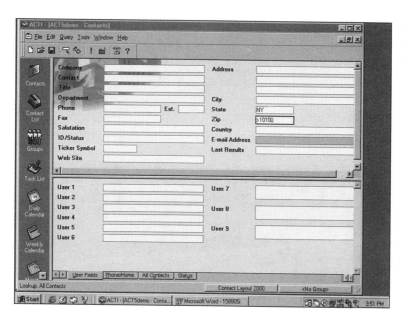

You've entered a query into the State and Zip fields.

This query translates into plain English as: Find all the contacts whose City entry equals New York and whose zip code *is greater than* the number 10100.

11. Click the **Query** menu.
12. Click the **Run Query** option.
13. The pop-up dialog box asks if you want to Replace, Add, or Narrow the lookup. Select **Replace**.

ACT! finds the three contacts that matched the query. By combining the city with the zip, you would be assured that the contacts located are physically contiguous. (Because of the paucity of contact records, you could have simply entered a single search criterion, either the State or Zip code, because you knew both. But the example shows how to combine two search elements to find contacts. Similarly, you could enter search criteria in other fields as necessary to locate the contact.)

Let's take this query idea a step further by adding another logical operator (another term for a Boolean operator) to the search expression:

1. Open the **Lookup** menu and select the **By Example** option.
2. Click the **Edit** menu.
3. Click **Clear**. This option removes any previous query data. It's a good practice to do this, because you might have entered data into a field that is not visible. If so, you might get strange results when you run the query.
4. In the State field, type NY.
5. In the Zip field, type >10030.
6. Click the **Query** menu.

The Query menu lets you generate an advanced lookup request.

7. Click the **Convert to Advanced Query** option.

The Advanced Query window appears, featuring the Query Helper dialog box.

The Advanced Query window includes a dialog box that helps you build queries.

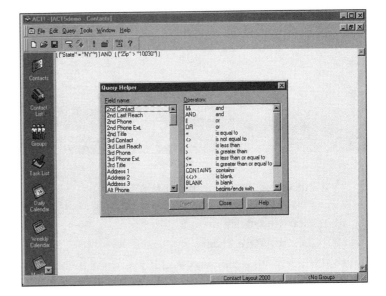

As you can see in the window, ACT! has converted the entries in the query screen into the logical expression (("State"="NY"*)) AND(("Zip">:"10030")).

No, you haven't opened a window into ACT!'s program code. This obscure-looking formula is simply how ACT! represents the criteria you entered into the nice, friendly dialog box. As such, it just means that the State field must contain NY and the Zip field must be larger than 10030. Not too difficult, is it?

Now, let's edit this arcane formula to produce a more accurate lookup.

Adding Another Level of Complexity

Now that you've examined the Boolean expression ACT! creates from your query, it's time to add a third variable. Suppose that you want to find the contacts in New York in the >10030 zip code area that are co-workers. The ID/Status field can be used for, among other things, identifying interest level. In this demonstration database, Coworker has been entered for contacts in the ID/Status field.

There are two ways to enter a new variable. You can go back to the Lookup dialog box and enter the variables in the respective fields. But, if you want to use a Boolean operator, you must do it in the Advanced Query window, as in the following example:

1. If you aren't looking at the Advanced Query window, follow the steps in the previous section to access it.

2. Click to the right of the expression.

3. To the right of the expression, click the **AND** operator from the Query Helper dialog and then click **Insert** to enter it.

4. Type two opening parentheses: ((.

5. Next you need the field name for ACT! to look in. From the Query Helper dialog box, double-click the **ID/Status** field. ACT! inserts the name of the field for you. You must add a pair of quotation marks around the phrase ID/Status.

6. Double-click the **equal sign** (=) to insert it into the expression.

7. Type "Coworker"0 (including the quotation marks). You might have to press the spacebar to see the quotation marks. If they do not appear, add them.

8. Close the variable with a pair of closing parentheses:)). The completed query should look something like this.

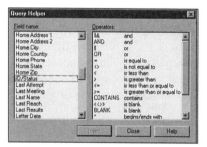

You've completed a three-criteria query.

Now the search expression reads, "Find the contacts that have a State entry of New York *and* a zip code that's *greater than* 10030 *and* the entry Coworker in the ID/Status field."

9. Click the **Query** menu.

10. Click **Check Query Syntax**. If you have followed the directions, you will get the message "Query Correctly Formatted". If not, it will indicate at what character position it thinks you have made a mistake. Be advised, ACT! is *very* picky, and everything has to be exact in order for queries of this sort to work.

11. When your query syntax checks out, click the **Run Query** button (the one with the exclamation point).

12. ACT! asks you if you want to save the query. Click **Yes**. The Save As dialog box appears.

Save your query so you can run it again later.

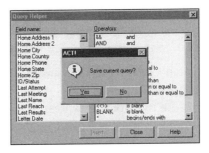

13. Type a name for the query, and click **Save**.

14. The Run Query Options dialog box appears. Click the radio button for **Replace Lookup**.

15. Click **OK**.

ACT! finds seven contacts in the ACT5demo database that meet all three criteria.

Complex Queries Take Longer

This type of lookup takes longer than the previous lookups (particularly in a large database) because of the complexity of the query. Each contact must be searched for the matching data, whereas the other lookup options are indexed fields and therefore are much faster to use.

More on Smart Query

This next example cannot be duplicated using the ACT5demo database unless you modify a record. If you decide not to, follow the steps outlined and look carefully at the figures, so that you can re-create this type of query in your database. (If you want, you can use the Save As command to save a duplicate of your demo database before making any changes.)

The Advanced Query window included a way to insert not only logical operators, but also field names and Boolean operators. One of those Boolean operators is CONTAINSC. An example of using the CONTAINS operator is when you are in the executive search business (okay, a headhunter), and you specialize in computer programmers. Rather than enter the languages that the prospects are trained to use in several different fields, you enter all their abilities in the User 1 field. The entries in that field could be: C+, BASIC, Visual Basic, COBOL, and SQL. Plus, you need to enter a range of zip codes so you can determine if the job seeker is within a reasonable driving distance of the potential new job.

Now, you need to find someone who can program SQL in the New York City area. In English, the search is: Find me the contacts who can program in SQL and live in the 10000-to-10034 zip area.

To duplicate this example, you need to add an entry to a record in the ACT5demo database (or the copy you just made):

1. Open the **Lookup** menu and select the **Last Name** item.
2. In the Lookup dialog box, type Newsom.
3. Click **OK**. The record with the name Joshua Newsom should appear.
4. Click the **User 1** field.
5. Type SQL.
6. Open the **Lookup** menu again and select **My Record**.

Obviously, you know which record has the information you are trying to find, but follow the steps to see if you can make the lookup work:

1. Open the **Lookup** menu and select **By Example**.
2. In the blank record, go to the zip code field and enter the lower zip number by typing "10000" (with quotation marks).
3. Click the **Convert Query** button.
4. In the Query Helper dialog box, click the operator >= (is greater than or equal to).
5. Double-click to highlight the = sign in the expression, and click **Insert**.
6. After the first expression, insert the AND operator. You may have to click to the right of the expression to activate the insertion point.
7. Type ((to start a new expression.
8. In the Query Helper dialog box, click **Zip** from the **Field Name** list.
9. Click **Insert**. Be sure to add quotes.
10. In the Query Helper dialog box, click the operator <= (is less than or equal to).
11. Click **Insert**.
12. Type the higher zip code value: "10030" (don't forget the quotation marks).
13. Close the expression by typing)).

    Entered correctly, the expression looks like the following figure. If an asterisk (*) appears in the expression, be sure to delete it.
14. After the first expression, insert the AND operator by clicking it from the Query Helper dialog box.
15. Type ((.
16. Remember, the field in which you entered the programming skills is User 1. Click the **User 1** field and click **Insert**. The field name is added to the expression.
17. In the Query Helper dialog box, select the **CONTAINS** operator.
18. Make sure your insertion point is after the field name User 1 and click **Insert**.
19. Type the text or numbers you want to find in the User 1 field; in this example, "SQL".

20. Close the second expression with)).

Check your screen to see that it matches the following figure.

You've entered your query expression.

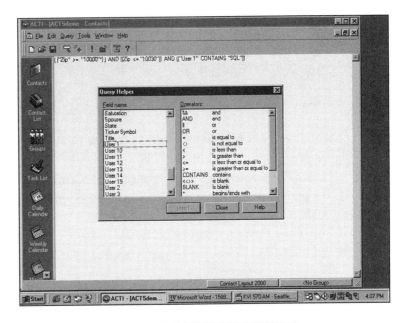

You've now completed a three-expression query.

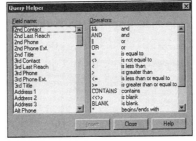

21. Click the **Run Query** button.

Joshua Newsom should be the single record returned by the query.

Note the position of parentheses and quotation marks. Without those, ACT! gives you an error message when you try to execute the query. The foregoing sample query would find the contact, assuming it had been entered into ACT!. This example should give you an idea on how the Smart Query feature can be effectively used.

What Those Operators Mean

They might look complicated, but the logical operators and the Boolean operators really aren't. Read through this list and you will discover how easy and useful they can be.

Table 5.1 Boolean Operators

Sign	Meaning and Use
=	Equals. An exact match: 2=2.
>	Greater than. 3 is greater than 2 (3>2), or B is greater than A (B>A).
<	Less than. 2 is less than 3, or A is less than B.
<>	Less than or greater than. 3 is less than 4 but greater than 2.
>=	Greater than or equal to. 3 is greater than 2, and equal to 3.
<=	Less than or equal to. 2 is less than 3, and equal to 2.
CONTAINS	The field contains a sequence of characters: Software contains WAR.
*	Begins/ends with: Carpet ends with PET (not pet stains, we hope).

Symbol	Definition
&&	Same as the AND operator.
AND	The contact must have both matching words or values. The contact is a Dealer and Requested more information.
II	Same as the OR operator.
OR	The contact must have at least one matching value. The contact is a Dealer OR Requested Information.
NOT	Contact does not have a matching value. Contact is NOT from Omaha.
Blank	Field has no entry; is blank.
<< >>	Same as Blank.
..	Field has a range of values. 5..9 means the contact has 5, 6, 7, 8, or 9.
!	Same as NOT.

Checking a Query for Precision

As I've mentioned, ACT! is notoriously picky about how you create queries. Even though you think you have correctly created a complex query, you may have missed a nuance. ACT! can give you a hand by checking the query for you before you run it and receive an error message.

After creating a query:

1. Click the **Query** menu.
2. Click the **Check Query Syntax** option.

ACT! processes the query, stopping if there is incorrect syntax. The most common error is "Value Expected." Check to see if quotation marks enclose each of the matching values. This feature can save you plenty of headaches when you're creating complex queries!

69

Sorting on a Query

ACT! sorts the contacts that match your query by the entry in the Company field, and if there is no entry in the Company field, the sort is done on the Last Name in the Contact field. Changing the sort order is a snap, but you need to do so before clicking the Run option in the Query menu.

To change the sort order, open the **Query** menu and select **Specify Query Sort**. The Sort Contacts dialog box opens.

The Sort Contacts dialog box lets you change the default order of the results.

As you can see, you can specify up to a three-level sort, and specify the order within each sort level. This does not affect the sort order of the entire database, only the lookup. I describe how you can change the sort order for the database in Chapters 6, "Working in the List View," and 12, "Mail Merge, a.k.a. Form Letters." One practical use of the sorting is by zip code when you anticipate doing a bulk mailing to the contacts found by the lookup.

Executing a Saved Query

You'll probably find yourself executing certain queries repeatedly. For example, you might want to create an email list by finding contacts' email addresses or by finding all contacts that were edited last week. Fortunately, you don't have to create these queries from scratch; you can save a working query and use it any number of times. That's why you saved the query in this chapter's first example.

To access and execute a saved query, use the following steps:

1. Click the **Lookup** menu and select the **By Example** option.
2. Click the **File** menu and choose **Open**. The Open dialog box appears.
3. Double-click the name of the saved query. The search criteria are inserted into the query screen.
4. Click the **Run** button (it looks like an exclamation point) to execute the query.

That's all there is to it! Now you can update your lists as your database grows by performing the same query at different times.

Modify Menu

In a previous example, you used the Lookup By Example option to create a highly specialized query and then saved it as a file. The designers of ACT! anticipated that you might want to have a faster way to access a saved query. So, the program lets you add a saved query to the Custom menu. Here's how to do it:

1. Save a query as a file.
2. Click the **Lookup** menu and choose the **Modify Menu** option.
3. The Modify dialog box appears.

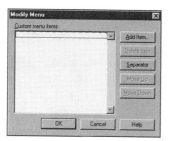

The Modify Menu dialog box lets you add a useful query to ACT!'s Lookup menu.

4. Click the **Add Item** button. The Add Custom Menu Item dialog box appears.

Use this dialog box to add a query to your menu.

5. If you know the exact name of the query file, type it into the **Filename and Location** field. If you don't know the name of the file, click the **Browse** button (it is mysterious gray box with three tiny dots to the right of the field), which invokes the Open dialog box listing the saved query files. Double-click the filename, and ACT! inserts it into the Filename and Location field of the Add Custom Menu Item dialog box.
6. Type a description of the query in the **Description** box. You must add the description for the process to work, as it appears on the menu.
7. Click **OK**.
8. Click the **Lookup** menu to see your new query in place.

Gotta Keep 'Em Separated

If you add several items to this menu, using the Add Line button to separate them on the menu makes each query easier to read. You can also click on an item and move it to a different position on the menu by using the Item Up and Item Down commands.

I've added the "example.QRY" query to the Lookup menu.

Sales Stage

Because the Sales Stage is a new feature of ACT!, I've devoted Chapter 18, "Forecasting Sales," to describing it. Essentially, it lets you determine the point at which your sales contacts are in your sales process. Imagine the power of combining this lookup with ID/Status! You could lookup the prospects in ID/Status and then use the Sales Stage lookup to check the sales pipeline. To use this Lookup to its fullest, please take the time to learn how to enter the information needed as described in Chapter 18.

At its most basic, you can look up contact records as you have defined them using Sales Stage.

1. Open the **Lookup** menu.
2. Click **Sales Stage**.

3. Click the radio buttons that determine which records are to be included in the lookup.

4. Enter the sales stage you want to match.

5. Click **OK**.

Internet Directory

ACT! 2000 provides an exciting new feature that can bring you contacts from around the world. No longer do you have to enter your contacts and search only the records you've entered. Now you can go online to find people via the Internet!

In other words, this Lookup option connects your computer to one of three popular Internet search engines: Bigfoot, WhoWhere, or Yahoo!. When you want to find a person's phone number, physical address, or email address by searching the Internet, you can do so—provided you have an account with an Internet service provider (ISP) or your company has a direct Internet connection.

This lookup is most useful when the contact is not already in your database. If you want to look up information on a contact in your database, you can use an option on the Internet Links menu called Yahoo! Person Search. If you access the Internet that way, the name of the contact is transferred automatically to the search engine fields.

To get information on a person not in your database:

1. Open the **Lookup** menu.

2. Select the **Internet Directory** option. The Internet Directory Lookup dialog box appears.

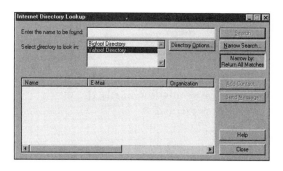

The Internet Directory Lookup dialog box lets you search online for contact information.

3. Enter the name of the person you want to find.

4. Click the directory where you want to search. You may have to try both search engines to locate the target—and remember, not *everyone* is in a directory.

5. Click **Search**.

73

If you are on a dial-up connection (via a modem), your browser starts, the dialer starts, and the search begins. Here are the results using a certain famous author's name searching Yahoo!.

This is the result of a Yahoo! directory search using your curmudgeonly author's name.

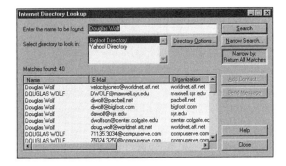

As you can see, there are many names that match the search criteria. If you recognize the correct name when you run the search, click the name to select it. Then, create the new contact record by clicking the **Add** button.

Click the Add button to open the Add Contact dialog box.

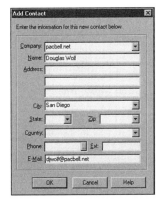

Whatever information was included with the name from the directory automatically appears in this dialog box. Most of the time you will get only the city, state, country, and email address. Click **OK** to add the new record.

Narrow the Search

Depending on the name you're looking for, it's possible that the search returns so many names that it's impractical to look at them all. You can narrow the search, provided you have some data on the contact. To narrow the search, click the—you guessed it—**Narrow Search** button. The Narrow Search dialog box appears.

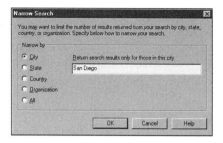

The Narrow Search dialog box lets you restrict your Internet name search.

To restrict the search to a specific state, click the **State** radio button and enter the full name of the state. Click **OK** to close the Narrow Search dialog box and then click the **Search** button again.

Sending Email

You may also immediately send an email message to someone your Internet search found by clicking the name and then the **Send Message** button to begin creating an email message. The email message window you see depends on which email system you have set up. Chapter 14, "Internet and Email," covers the different email systems compatible with ACT!.

Adding Other Search Directories

Although ACT! provides two directories, you can add as many as you like to the list, provided you have the technical information from the directory service. To add a new directory:

1. Click the **Directory Options** button. The Directory Options dialog box appears.
2. Click the **Add** button. The Directory Options dialog box appears.
3. Click the **Add** button again. The Add Directory Service dialog box appears.

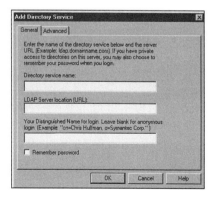

The Add Directory Service dialog box lets you send your Internet search to other search engines.

To add a directory, you need the name of the service, the LDAP, and perhaps a login name if it is a private directory. You might also have to select the **Advanced** tab to limit the search scope and port. These settings will likely require the assistance of your network administrator. Click **OK** twice after entering the information to save the new directory service.

Lookup by Synchronized Records

This lookup is designed to be used in the situation where there is a master database and remote databases that have shared contact records. Synchronization is the process whereby each contact record is checked to ascertain which version—the one on the master database or the one at the remote location—has the most current information. Then, the record is updated. This topic is covered in detail in Chapter 25, "Synchronizing with Remote Users."

The Least you Need to Know

➤ Advanced lookups are not that complicated as long as you think through the process when you begin entering the lookup criteria.

➤ To create an advanced lookup, open the **Lookup** menu and select **By Example**. Enter the characters you want to match in as many fields as you want, and then click the **Run Query** button.

➤ Although the query editor is not in demand as much as previously because of the Add Lookup and Narrow Lookup options in the Lookup dialog box, there are still times when you may need to tweak a lookup very tightly.

➤ New features of ACT! let you, among other things, search the Internet for contact information.

"The chief value of money lies in the fact that one lives in a world in which it is overestimated."

H.L. Mencken

Part 2

I Was Sure That Meeting Was Scheduled for Today

What would civilization be without a schedule? A mess, because everything would be happening at once! In this part, you begin scheduling your activities with contacts, seeing how they are handled by ACT!. The calendars in ACT! can be adjusted to show your activities and the activities for everyone on your ACT! network. Chapters 6–9 focus on making your hectic workday more pastoral.

Chapter 6

Working in the List View

In This Chapter

➤ Opening the List view

➤ Arranging the columns

➤ Edit versus Tag mode

➤ Printing the List view

"Life is too serious a thing to ever talk seriously about."

Oscar Wilde

Opening the List View of Contact Records

If you started reading this book from the beginning, you have been working in what ACT! calls the Contact view. You may have heard this presentation style referred to as the single-record-at-a-time view or as the *form* view, because data is laid out in a pre-designed form. Underlying all databases are *tables*—columns of information with headers that tell you what the data is in the particular column. If you have worked with database programs such as Microsoft Access or FoxBASE, or a spreadsheet such as Excel, you are familiar with columns of information. ACT! uses tables of data, too, and you can look at your contact records using the List view.

To see how to work in the List view in ACT!, open the demonstration database. If you have a database with more than five or six contacts, that will work just fine.

To open the demonstration database:

1. Open the **File** menu and choose **Open**.

2. From the Open dialog box, click the **ACT5demo** database.

3. Click **Open**.

The demonstration database should open with Chris Huffman as the My Record.

To see the contact records in List view, click the **Contact List** icon at the left of the record form. When you switch to List view, the contact record you were viewing when you switched is highlighted on the screen.

You can look at contact records in List view.

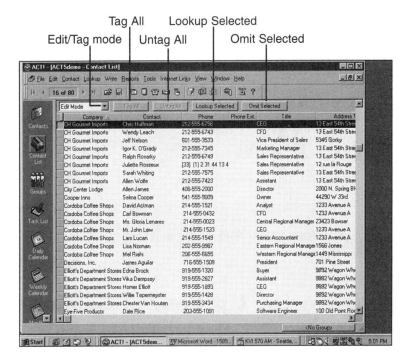

Scrolling the List

You should see two scrollbars in the List view: the vertical and horizontal. The vertical scrollbar moves the list so that you can view the previous or next records. The horizontal scrollbar shifts the view so that you can see the columns to the right or left.

Scroll the list so that the first record in the database, Pat Huffman, is visible. That is the first record, because by default, ACT! sorts records in ascending (ABC...) order by company. If no company name is in the record, ACT! displays those records at the top of the list, using the Last Name field to sort them. Because the Pat Huffman record is the *only* record without a company, it appears in the first position.

The columns that are in the list by default start with Company and end with ID/Status to the far right. Depending on your screen resolution, you may have to scroll the list to the left with the horizontal scrollbar to see the columns to the right. You can insert more columns in the whitespace at the far right.

Sorting Records

Scroll back to the far left so that the Company field is visible. Note that on the column name, there appears a small gray triangle pointing up. This triangle is the sort indicator. Remember, by default, ACT! sorts records in ascending (ABC...) order by company. If no company name is in the record, ACT! sorts by the Last Name.

To sort the list, click any column header. For example, the list is currently sorted by the Company name. Click the **Contact** header, and ACT! sorts the list by name.

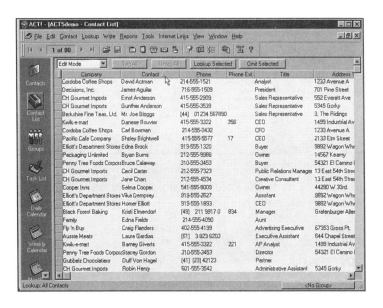

You can sort the List view by contact last name.

Now, click the **Contact** header again. Doing so sorts by contact in *reverse* fashion, in descending alphabetical order (ZYX...).

You can sort the list on any field in the view. This is particularly handy for sorting by zip code for bulk mail or form letters. The sorting in the List view does not affect the Form view, so you can sort your list as often as necessary.

Resizing the Columns

Each of the columns can be resized—made wider or narrower. To change the width of a column, move the mouse pointer to the line that separates the names of the columns. The pointer changes from a pointer to a line with an arrow pointing left and right. Click and hold the left mouse button, and then drag the mouse to the left to narrow the column, or to the right to lengthen the column. Here, I've narrowed the Phone field so that only the area codes are visible.

The phone column has been narrowed to show only the area codes.

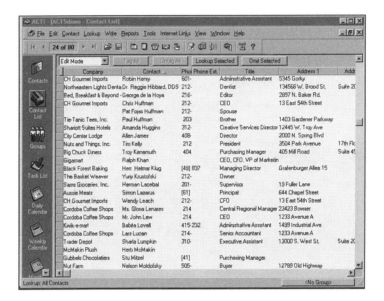

The process can be repeated to designate the column widths as you want them to appear. When you close the List view and then reopen it, the list appears as you have customized it.

Rearranging the Columns

Not only can you resize columns, you can drag the columns around to create the order you want. Supposing you want the Title column next to the Company column, just follow these steps:

1. Click and hold the left mouse pointer on the **Title** column header.

2. Drag the column header to the right of the Company column header and on top of the Contact column header. As you drag the column header, the mouse pointer appears as a small hand.

3. Release the mouse button. The columns are rearranged as shown in the following figure.

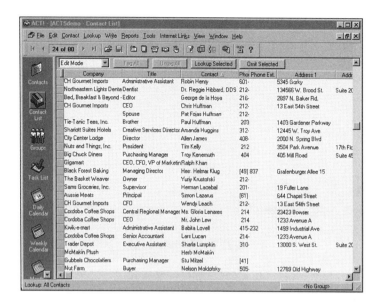

You can rearrange the column order in List view.

Caution! Slow Sorting

One caution at this point. If you have a large database—over 5,000 records—and you click the column header and do not begin moving the column immediately, ACT! might think you want to resort the database and it might appear that ACT! is not responding.

Adding New Columns

The columns that you see in List view might not include the field or fields you want to see. Suppose you wanted to see the date that each of the records in your database was created. The field that has that date is not included in the default List view. To add a column or columns to the view:

1. Scroll the List view window to the left until you have plenty of whitespace.
2. With the mouse pointer in the whitespace of the window, right-click the mouse. When you do, a pop-up menu appears.

In the List view, a pop-up menu enables you to add columns.

3. From the menu, select **Add Columns**. The Add Columns dialog box appears.

The Add Columns dialog box is your key to displaying more fields in List view.

From this dialog box, you can scroll the list to find the field or fields you want to add to the List view. The fields are listed in ascending alphabetical order.

4. Click the name of the field you want add, and click **Add**. To add a second column, select it and click **Add** again. In this example the field you want as a column is the Create Date field. The result of adding the new field as a column is shown here.

A new field always appears at the far right. Because you already know how to move columns, you can position the column at any place in the List view. Just click the column header and drag the field to the desired location.

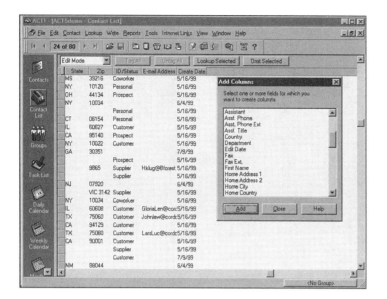

Presto! You've added a new field to the List view.

Deleting a Column

Deleting a column from the List view might seem a little disconcerting, but rest assured that doing so does not affect the database in any way. It is simply not visible. To delete a column, click the column header and hold the mouse button down. Drag the column head toward the top of the screen. When the mouse pointer appears as a small trash can, release the button and the column is deleted. It's that simple!

If you accidentally delete a field you want displayed, follow the procedure in the previous section to replace it.

Leave That Record Alone

Any changes you make to the List view appearance have no effect on the contact record data or on the fields.

Edit Versus Tag Mode

When you initially open the List view, the window is in Edit mode. That is, you can click a particular record and make changes. For example, if you click the Title field on a record, a drop-down list appears.

You can easily edit some fields via a drop-down list.

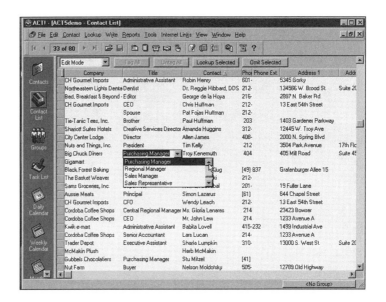

A benefit of being able to see the records in this fashion is the speed of editing. If the area code ever changes for a series of records (that *never* happens!), you can create a lookup by phone number using only the area code as the match, and then go to the List view and change each record. (In Chapter 26, "ACT! Add-On Products," I'll discuss a software product that keeps the area codes in your database up-to-date.)

You can also use the Edit mode when there are duplicate records in your database. Creating a lookup of the duplicates and then viewing the records in a list side by side makes it easier to decide if the records are truly duplicates (or merely similar), and if so, which one to keep.

The Lookup Selected, Omit Selected Buttons

List view also lets you create a lookup of records. To select a record, click the gray box at the far left of the record. When you do, the entire record is highlighted. To select several contiguous records, click the first record, hold the **Shift** key, and then click the last record. All the records between the first and last records are highlighted. To select a set of records, click the first record's gray box, hold the **Ctrl** key, and click the next record.

With a record or records selected, you can create a lookup by one of two methods. If you want to keep the records you have selected as the lookup, click the **Lookup Selected** button. Conversely, to get rid of the records selected and keep the others, click the **Omit Selected** button.

If you select a record by accident, click the mouse in whitespace and select again. Or, press the **Control** key and click the record.

Incidentally, all the Lookup menu methods discussed in Chapters 4, "Locating Records," and 5, "Advanced Record Lookups," work identically in the List view.

Changing to Tag Mode

The Tag mode is an easy way to mark records. Usually, the reason for marking the records is to generate form letters, create groups, or delete specific records from the database. Tagging is the best way to create ad-hoc lists of contact records because it's easy to select the records randomly.

To switch from Edit mode to Tag mode, move your mouse pointer to the drop-down list in the upper-left corner of the List view window. You should see the words `Edit Mode`. Click the drop-down arrow and select **Tag Mode**. The List view changes to resemble what you see in the following figure.

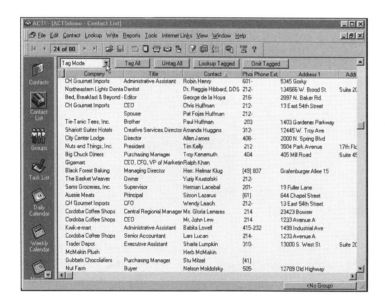

You can convert your List view into Tag mode for selecting records.

One record will likely be tagged by default—the record you were looking at before you switched to the List view. The tag is the big **+** to the left of the record. The buttons on the top of the List view change, too. The Tag All and Untag All buttons, for example, do what the labels say.

To tag a record, click anywhere on the record's information. ACT! adds the **+** symbol and draws a frame around the record. The purpose of the frame is to let you know which record was the last selected. To tag a series of contiguous records, click the first record, hold down the **Shift** key, and click the last record. To untag a record, click it again.

With a record or records selected, you can create the lookup by one of two methods. If you want to keep the records you have selected as the lookup, click the **Lookup Tagged** button. Conversely, to get rid of the records selected and keep the others, click the **Omit Tagged** button. Pretty easy, as is everything in ACT!.

Other Actions in List View

You can undertake several other actions in List view, in either Edit mode or Tag mode. One way to access several options is to right-click a record. The menu that appears in the next figure depends on whether you have selected records and whether you are in Edit mode or Tag mode. You can see the pop-up menu for a selected record in Tag mode. For example, you cannot enter a new contact or duplicate an existing contact in Tag mode. You can schedule activities with the contact (covered in Chapter 7, "Scheduling Activities"), as well as have ACT! dial the selected record's phone number; write a letter, fax, or email; and print the list per your design.

Right-clicking a record in List view produces a menu with handy options.

Printing the List

ACT! includes many ways to print your contact records: address book form, Filofax, Day Runner, and so on. Several reports are also available, such as the phone directory, which prints the company, contact, and phone number. The List view also gives you the ability to print an ad-hoc list with the exact columns and names that you want included. For example, one handy list is a phone and fax list. You can create a lookup, delete the columns you don't want, keep the phone column, add the fax column, and print the resulting list.

To print the list:

1. Right-click the mouse in any blank space. A pop-menu appears.
2. Click the **Print Column List** item. The Windows Print dialog box appears. Click the **Print** button. If the columns fit on a single page, the file is sent to the printer. If they don't fit, the Print List Window dialog box appears, as shown here.

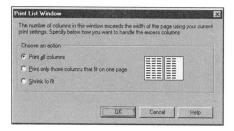

The Print List Window dialog box offers options for oversize printing.

Your can choose to print all columns, which means that the list will print across more than one page. Or, you can print only the columns that fit on a single page. The last choice, Shrink to Fit, may work best if you don't have many columns. Shrink to Fit allows ACT! to shrink the type font so that all the text fits. Too many columns, however, and the resulting list will be too small to read.

Move It on Over

Here's a tip if you're facing a spacing crisis: You can also try to get the columns on a single sheet of paper by changing the printer properties from portrait to landscape.

The Least You Need to Know

➤ Changing from the single contact record view to the List view is as easy as clicking the **Contact List** icon at the left of the ACT! program window.

➤ You can sort, resize, add, and delete columns in List view without affecting your database.

➤ You can use the List view to make ad hoc sets of records for mail merging, creating groups, editing fields, or deleting records.

"Life is an unbroken succession of false situations."

Thornton Wilder

Chapter 7

Scheduling Activities

In This Chapter

➤ Scheduling calls, meetings, and to-dos

➤ Dealing with alarms

➤ Checking your tasklist

"Never put off until tomorrow what you can do the day after tomorrow."

Mark Twain

Mark Twain might have had the luxury of procrastination but most of the rest of us don't. The next aspect of working with contacts I'll tackle is the scheduling of activities. ACT! categorizes activities into three areas: calls, as in telephone calls, meetings, and to-dos, which is short for a task to be undertaken.

The My Record contact that was created when you installed ACT! is for scheduling those activities that do not warrant entering a contact, such as stopping at the dry cleaners. This is a key concept in ACT!—always schedule your activities by going to the contact record of the person with whom you want to interact. One of the most common mistakes new ACT! users make is to schedule everything in My Record. Don't make that mistake—only use My Record to schedule tasks that you need to do apart from any contact in your database.

The steps to schedule activities are identical whether for calls, meetings, or to-dos. As I describe each, I'll highlight the differences.

Scheduling an Activity

As is true with most actions in ACT!, there is more than one way to schedule an activity. In fact, there are three ways to schedule an activity: with the menu system or the toolbar or by a combination of keys. The toolbar is the fastest, so I'll concentrate on that method in the following sections.

1. Use the Lookup menu to find the contact with which you want to schedule a call, meeting, or thing to do.

2. With the contact onscreen, click the **Schedule Call** button in the toolbar. ACT! opens the Schedule Activity dialog box.

You can schedule an activity with any contact in your database.

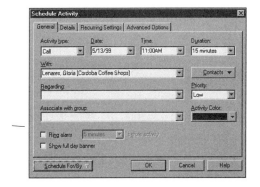

ACT! assumes that you want to schedule the call for the current day at the current time, but you can use the dialog box to change these assumptions. Let's look at the various settings in this dialog box:

➤ **Activity Type**   ACT! inserts the type of activity you have selected from the toolbar. If you decide that a call is not appropriate, click the drop-down arrow and select the activity you want.

➤ **Date**   By default, ACT! inserts the current date. Click the drop-down arrow to see a calendar.

You can use this calendar to pick a date for your activity.

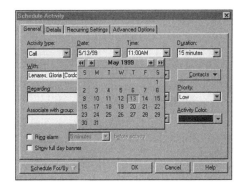

➤ **Time**   By default, ACT! inserts the current time as the time for the call. Click the drop-down arrow to select a time from the list of times presented. Or, you can select the **Timeless** option at the bottom of the list. The Timeless option means that the activity is scheduled for a specific date, but not a specific time.

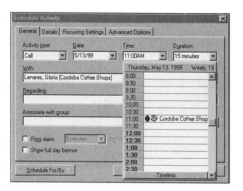

You can specify a time for your activity, too.

➤ **Duration**   In this window, you can click a single time period (15 minutes by default), or you can click the start time, hold the mouse button, and drag down through the time periods until the correct amount of time is blocked. Notice that the Duration window reflects the time period that you have blocked. ACT! has default settings for each activity—15 minutes for a call, 1 hour for a meeting, and 0 minutes for a to-do.

➤ **Priority**   With each activity, you can determine its priority. The chief importance of priority is that you can then locate activities by that designation. You can designate a certain call as a high-priority item, and then narrow your Task List so it only displays these items. The default for all activities is low priority.

➤ **With**   ACT! inserts the name of the contact you were on when you selected the activity button. If you decide that you want to schedule the activity with a different contact in the database, you can do it through this setting without having to close the dialog. Here's how:

1. Click the drop-down box at the right end of the **With** field. ACT! opens the list of other options to select contacts in the database. In this example, the **Select Contacts** option is clicked.

2. The Select Contacts dialog box opens.

3. From the list, click the contact name or names you want.

➤ **Regarding**   Enter a note to yourself as to why you have scheduled this activity. For example, you might designate some calls as first contacts and others as follow-ups. A drop-down list is available with a series of standard entries, and you can add your own by editing the list. Simply scroll the list to the bottom, and select **Edit List**. In the Edit List dialog box, click the **Add** button and type your entry. Click **OK** to close the editing process.

This list of contacts in the Schedule activity dialog box lets you plan the event with someone else.

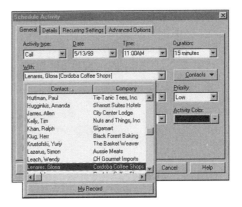

➤ **Associate with Group**   Creating and working with groups is covered in detail in Chapter 15, "Working with Groups." At this juncture, if you want an activity to be attached to a group, you can select a group from this drop-down list.

➤ **Ring Alarm**   One of the outstanding features of ACT! is the way it nags you until an activity you have scheduled is completed, deferred, or erased. A prime component of this nagging process is the alarm. Adding an alarm to a scheduled activity causes ACT! to open a dialog box on top of your ACT! screen at the appropriate time. When you click **Ring Alarm**, the Before Activity option is active. You then decide how long before the activity you want to be alerted to the activity. Later in this chapter, I'll discuss the options for handling alarms. If you scheduled an activity and added the Timeless attribute, the alarm appears as soon as you start your computer, or at 8 a.m., whichever is later.

➤ **Show Full Day Banner**   If you have a full-day activity, this option makes it very apparent by placing a banner across the day on the calendar. Some activities might not consume an entire day, but you want the activity to stand out on your calendar. Suppose you schedule a partial lobotomy for early morning—you might need the rest of the day to recover, so clicking this option places a banner on the day in your calendar.

➤ **Schedule For/By**   Clicking the Schedule For/By button expands the bottom of the Schedule Activity dialog box.

This expanded area is for scheduling activities for other users on a network. You might decide that one of your co-workers needs to have a meeting, make a call, or tackle a to-do with a contact in the database. So, you look up the contact, open the Schedule Activity dialog box, and enter the requisite information. Finally, you can click **Schedule For/By**, and then select the co-worker's name from the Scheduled For field. Your name automatically appears in the Scheduled By field and cannot be edited. The meeting then appears on the co-worker's calendar.

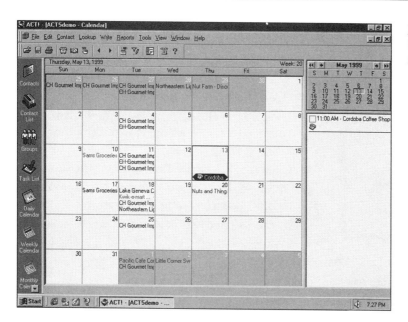

In this calendar, the 13th has a full-day event scheduled.

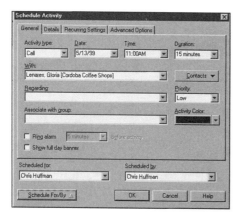

Clicking the Schedule For/By button expands the dialog box to show other users on the network.

The foregoing are the basic steps for creating any of the three kinds of activities with a single contact. Remember, you determine whether the activity is a call, meeting, or to-do by clicking the Activity Type drop-down arrow. Clicking OK adds the activity to the Activity tab of the contact and to your Task List and calendars. If you included an alarm as part of the scheduling process, the alarm will appear at the appropriate time on your desktop.

Scheduling a Phone Call

Try scheduling an activity for yourself in the default database:

1. Open the **ACT5demo** database.

2. Look up the Gloria Lenares contact record (if you need a reminder on how to do so, see Chapter 4).

3. Click the **Schedule Call** icon on the toolbar.

4. In the Schedule Activity dialog box, accept the default date, time, and the duration.

5. In the **Regarding** field, type Example Activity with an Alarm.

> ### ACT Can't Warn You if It Isn't Running!
>
> ACT! must be running for your alarms to be triggered. If you exit the program, you might miss a reminder.

6. Accept the Priority and Activity Color settings.

7. Click the **Ring Alarm** check box.

8. The Before Activity option is activated. Accept the 5 minutes default.

9. Click **OK**.

In a few moments, the Alarms dialog box appears. (If it doesn't, make certain that the clock in your computer is set to the correct date and time. To do so, double-click the time indicator on the right side of your Windows taskbar and make any necessary adjustments in the resulting dialog box.) Read on to the next section, where I discuss how to handle alarms.

Handling Alarms

At the time you specified, ACT! pops up a dialog box alerting you that you have a scheduled activity impending! Plus, ACT! plays the default sound when the Windows menu pops up, in case you aren't looking at the screen at the moment (ACT! can't help you if you stepped out of your office entirely, though). Now, I'll describe the options you can select when the alarm appears.

ACT! presents this alarm dialog box when you have a scheduled activity coming up.

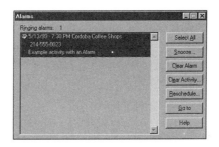

Select All

If more than one alarm appears, click the **Select All** button to select all alarms. After selected, you can use any of the other options to affect all the alarms at once.

Snooze

If you want to handle the alarm at a later time, click the **Snooze** button, and the Snooze Alarm dialog box appears. It works kind of like the snooze alarm you might have on your alarm clock, but it gives you more choices.

ACT!'s Snooze Alarm dialog box lets you defer action on a scheduled event.

Click the radio button that best handles the alarm, and then click **OK** to close the Snooze Alarm dialog box.

Clear Alarm

If you want the alarm to go away, click the **Clear Alarm** button. ACT! shuts off the alarm, but the activity remains on your calendar and Task List.

Clear Activity

To remove the activity from your calendar and Task List, click the **Clear Activity** button. ACT! opens another dialog box, prompting you to enter a disposition for the activity.

The Clear Activity dialog box asks you how you want to dispose of the event.

In clearing the activity, you can click the **Results** button to enter a message that is recorded with the History of that activity, or you can click the **Follow-up** button, which takes you back to the Schedule Activity dialog box, in which you can schedule a further activity.

If you select the Results option that indicates the activity is erased, no History record is kept.

Reschedule

Selecting the **Reschedule** option opens the Schedule Activity dialog box, allowing you to re-enter the parameters of the activity.

GoTo

Select the **GoTo** button to move from the current contact to the one with which the activity is scheduled.

Advanced Scheduling

Scheduling an activity with a single contact is straightforward. As you might expect, ACT! adds a plethora of options for scheduling. Taking advantage of these options can not only streamline your business day, but also make you a power user of ACT!.

Adding a New Contact from the Schedule Activity Dialog Box

The Contacts button comes in handy when you need to add a new contact record while in the Schedule Activity dialog box. Suppose that you're on the phone discussing a possible meeting date with someone who isn't already in your database. This button allows you to add the basic contact record information without closing the Schedule Activity dialog box, making a quick step to then scheduling the meeting. The next two figures illustrate this process.

Select the Contacts button in the Schedule Activity dialog box, and pick New Contact,...

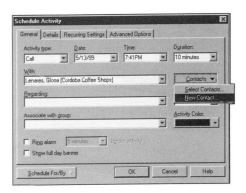

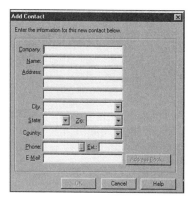

...and then enter the contact's information in the familiar Add Contact dialog box.

Enter the new contact record information. If you suspect that you already have the email address of the new contact—this often happens—you can add it to the record immediately. Click **OK** to save the information.

Selecting Multiple Contacts from the Schedule Activity Dialog Box

You might suppose that the only way to schedule the same activity with multiple contacts is to look them up one at a time and go through the scheduling process. Not so! After selecting a contact with which you want to schedule an activity, click the **Contacts** button, and then the **Select Contacts** option. The Select Contacts dialog box opens.

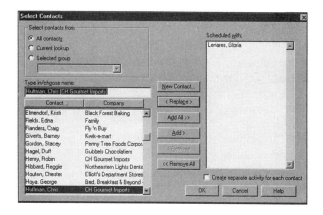

You can open the Select Contacts dialog box from the Schedule Activity dialog box.

Select Contacts From

Your first choice is to decide if the universe of contacts from which you can select is All Contacts, those in the Current Lookup, or from a Selected Group. The All Contacts choice means that you can scroll your entire database and select several contacts to be included in the activity. To add a contact to the activity, click the contact's name and then the **Add** button. ACT! inserts the name into the Scheduled With list box.

If you click the Current Lookup as your source for names, only those contacts that were in the lookup before you opened the Schedule Activity dialog box are available for inclusion.

If you click the Selected Group, ACT! lists the names of the groups that you have already created. By selecting a group, you have scheduled the activity with all members of that group. (Creating groups is covered in Chapter 15.)

The Contact and Company fields are listed in the dialog box. The default sort order is alphabetical ascending, as indicated by the gray triangle at the end of the word Contact. Change the sort order of the Contact field by clicking on the word **Contact**. Or, click the word **Company** and the list is sorted by company name.

To move to a specific name, you can scroll the list (or lists) or type the first letter of the contact's name—for Wolf you type w. When you type a W, the first contact with a last name beginning with W is highlighted. This search method is progressive—typing a second letter moves the highlight to next match. Typing wo highlights the first record that has a last name that matches both letters, such as *Womack* or *Woolworth*.

Random Selections

If you want to select several names at the same time, click the first name, press and hold the **Shift** key, and then click the names to select names that are juxtaposed. If you click a name and press and hold the **Control** key, you can jump around the list selecting names.

The New Contact, Replace, Add All, Add, Remove, and Remove All Buttons

In the Select Contacts dialog box, you have buttons to assist you in adding or subtracting names from the list box on the right. They're pretty much self-explanatory by their names, so take a quick look at them:

➤ **New Contact**   Click this button to begin a new contact in the database.

➤ **Replace**   Click this button to replace the contact or contacts in the list on the right with the selected contacts on the left.

➤ **Add All**   If you have selected multiple contacts on the left, click this button to add them to the list on the right.

➤ **Add**   Select a name on the left, and then click this button to add it to the list on the right.

➤ **Remove**   Click a name on the right, and then click this button to remove it from the list.

➤ **Remove All**   If you have selected several names on the right, click this button to remove them from the list.

Create Separate Activity for Each Contact?

This check box requires some thought. If you schedule with several contacts or a group, clicking this option creates an activity on each of the contacts. With it off, an activity is scheduled on the first contact record *only*. The benefit of adding the activity to every contact is that you can see all the names associated with the activity in the Task List or in a calendar. The negative is that the Task List and calendars become bustling with many names with activities scheduled for the same time—and, if you schedule a reminder, more alarms.

Adding Details

Although the Regarding field provides a short reminder of the activity, the Details tab opens a large field into which you can type an extended treatise of why you have to have this meeting at, oh, Las Vegas instead of at the office. This field can be printed and put in the "rationalizations" file for later inspection. On a practical note, the Details could hold your notes on negotiating session, price lists, or product specifications. If the information is in another application—say, a word-processed file—you could open that file and copy the text and paste it into the details field.

Scheduling Recurring Activities

ACT! has a specific tab in the Schedule Activity dialog box to handle activities that occur on a regular or not so regular basis. Clicking the tab reveals the following settings:

➤ **Once** This is the default setting for an activity.

➤ **Daily** Clicking this option lets you set the activity to recur every day, every two days, and so on, until the ending date you specify.

➤ **Weekly** Click this option to make the activity occur once a week, every two weeks, and so on, until the specified end date. ACT! also will make sure that the date is the correct day of the week, as specified by you.

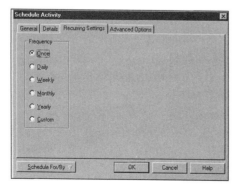

The Recurring Settings tab lets you handle repeating events.

➤ **Monthly**   This setting allows for the scheduling of an activity that might be regular in terms of the time, that is, the 3rd Thursday of every month, but not on a specific date. To use it, first select the **Every** option, which indicates every month, every two months, and so on. Enter the ending date, and then select the time value, 1st, 2nd, 3rd, and so on. Last, select the weekday on which the event falls.

You can establish settings for an activity recurring on a monthly basis.

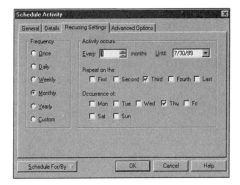

➤ **Yearly**   The marriage saver! Yes friends, never again forget your spouse's birthday, anniversary, or other significant date. You also can use this setting to remind yourself of important dates for your contacts, a yearly company event, or whatever else you want to be reminded of.

➤ **Custom**   This setting is used for those activities that do occur on a specific date. That is, if your club meeting is always the 15th of the month, you can enter 1 as the value for Every and the ending date, and then click the date itself.

Advanced Options

The Advanced Options tab adds the ability to send an email to the person or persons with whom you have scheduled the activity and to make the activity private.

The private activity works this way: If you have a job interview planned, and you are on a network system, the bet is that you do not want the entire office to be privy to your plans. By making the activity a private meeting, the other users of the network can look at your calendar and only see that you have a meeting marked private. Be careful not to add too much information to the Regarding field—it appears along with the activity and may reveal your plans.

The email options are to send, in ACT! format, the activity itself to another ACT! user, who can then apply it to his calendar. You also can email an event in Outlook 98 format, and the Outlook user can apply the meeting to her calendar. You also can email an event in both formats.

Setting Activity Defaults

One of the virtues of ACT! is its flexibility. Each of the three activities in ACT! can have its unique default settings. For example, you might want the Duration for all meetings to be set to three hours. Or you might want all your calls to be Timeless. Of course, when you actually schedule the activity, you can override these defaults.

To set the defaults for activities, open the Edit menu and select **Preferences**. From the Preferences dialog box, click the **Scheduling** tab. Select the activity type, and then select the defaults. These settings are user specific—that is, they can be unique for every user of the database, and ACT! recognizes your settings based on the name entered when you log in to the database. Chapter 10, "Setting Your Preferences," covers how to set all ACT!'s preferences.

Scheduling a Meeting, or Never Miss a Meeting Again

The steps to scheduling a meeting are identical to those for a call, except for the starting point. Click the **Meeting** icon to begin. Doing so automatically adds the default settings you have created as preferences for your meetings. You also can use the Contact menu to schedule the meeting. Those of you using a laptop on an airplane or otherwise preferring the keyboard, press and hold the **Ctrl** key and press **M** to open the Schedule Activity dialog box with Meeting as the default.

Scheduling a To-Do, or So Much To-Do and So Little Time

The steps to schedule a to-do are identical to scheduling a call or meeting, except for the starting point. To-dos are the tasks that you need to perform for your contacts, such as send a fax, send a letter, send apologies, and so on. Start scheduling a to-do by clicking the **To-do** icon—a finger with a string tied around it—and make your entries. You also can schedule a to-do from the Contact menu, or by pressing **Ctrl+T**. The Schedule Activity dialog box appears.

Creating a Series of Activities

New to ACT! 2000 is a feature that has been requested for many years and has finally arrived: the capability to schedule activities in a series.

Suppose that your company has a booth at a trade show. At the end of the show, you have collected many business cards and each requires a series of follow-up activities. The hard way to add the activities is to create the lookup and then add the activities, one at a time. ACT!'s new series scheduling feature saves you this trouble. As another example, if your business has a project with a due date, you can schedule a series of activities using the due date as the beginning point. In this case, each activity is scheduled moving backwards.

Take a look at how to create a scheduled series of activities:

1. Open the **Edit** menu and select **Create Activity Series**. The resulting dialog box presents two choices: You can create a new series of activities or edit an existing series.

The Create Activity Series dialog box begins the process of creating a new series, or editing an existing series.

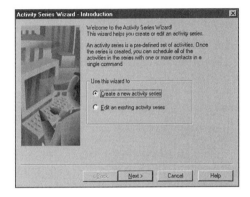

2. For this example, click the radio button to **Create a New Activity Series**.

3. Click **Next**. The Series Date dialog box asks if the new series has a Start date, or a Due date. Entering a start date schedules activities from that date into the future. Providing a due date schedules the activities working backward from that date. Select the **Start Date** option and click **Next**. The First Activity dialog box appears.

The First Activity dialog box is used to enter the initial activity in the series.

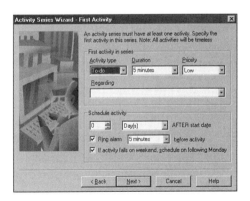

4. Select from the drop-down lists or enter the **Activity Type**, **Duration**, **Priority**, and **Regarding** attributes for the initial activity.

5. Determine the number of days, weeks, or months *after* the start date for the initial activity to occur. Set an alarm and determine whether a weekend date is appropriate for the activity.

6. Click **Next** and the Series Activity dialog box appears.

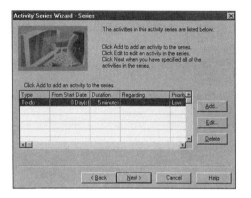

The Series Activity dialog box shows the initial activity that you have scheduled and the options to add, edit, or delete subsequent activities.

7. At this point, add the subsequent activities to the series. To begin, click the **Add** button. The Add Activity dialog box appears, in which you can add a second activity. Enter the attributes for this activity. You can drag the dialog box so that you can see the previous activities scheduled and determine the date spacing.

8. Add all the activities you want, and then click **Next**.

9. In the Finish dialog box, enter a name for the series and a description so that you can recall the purpose of the series. Click **Finish** to close the dialog box.

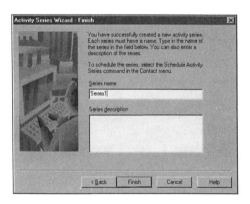

You add a name and a description for the series in the Finish dialog box.

Applying a Series of Activities to Contacts

With a series of activities created and saved, the next step is to apply the series to a contact or to multiple contacts. Here's how:

1. Lookup a contact record or create a lookup if you want to apply a series to multiple contacts.

2. Open the **Contact** menu and select **Schedule Activity Series**.

Here's the Schedule Activity dialog box, from which you can apply an existing series to a single contact or multiple contacts.

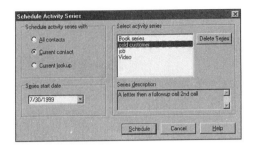

3. Lookup the contacts to which you want the series applied. Enter a start date, and then select the series to apply.

4. Click the **Schedule** button, and ACT! begins adding the activities to the contact records you have chosen.

ACT!'s new series scheduling ability is an extremely powerful tool and should save you many hours.

Clockwatching

If you select many contact records and the series has many activities, the process of ACT! adding the activites to the contact record could take considerable time. Have a tea break while this occurs.

Editing an Activity from the Contact Record Activity Tab

After creating an activity, you might need to make adjustments to it. The activity record is stored in several places. It is on the Activity for the contact. It is on the Task List. It is on the Day, Week, and Month calendars. Changes to the activity can be made from any of these locations. Let's start with the most direct method: the Contact.

1. Open the **Lookup** menu to locate the contact record that has an activity you want to modify.

2. Click the **Activity** tab. If the activity is listed, you can make the edit. If it isn't, then you must check the filter settings. The filter is used to customize the view of the activities on the list.

3. Click the **Filter** button in the upper left of the Activity tab. Select one:

   ➤ **Types to Show**   Be sure that all the types of activities are selected.

   ➤ **Priorities to Show**   Be sure that all priorities are chosen.

   ➤ **Dates to Show**   Be sure the setting is **All Dates**.

   ➤ **Select Users**   If you are on a network, be sure your name is selected.

4. Move the mouse pointer to the far-left activity onto the gray box that precedes the activity you want to modify.

5. Right-click the mouse. A pop-up menu appears.

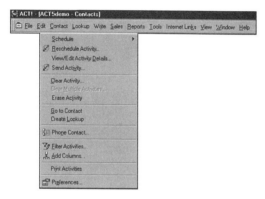

Right-click an activity to display this menu.

6. There is a plethora of choices. For this example, click **Reschedule Activity**. The Schedule Activity dialog box appears.

7. Make the change you want to the activity.

8. Click **OK**.

The dialog box closes and the activity is changed.

Editing an Activity from the Calendar

Chapter 9, "Checking Your Calendar," focuses on the ACT! calendars. However, take a moment to look at the Daily calendar to see how you can modify an activity.

1. Click the **Daily Calendar** icon to the left of the contact record form.

2. The Daily calendar appears.

You can modify activities in the Daily calendar.

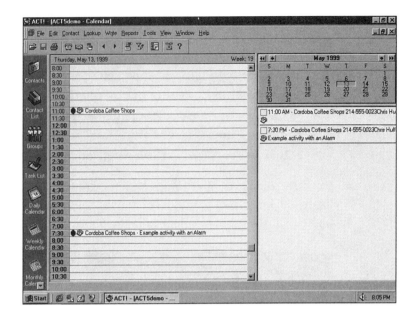

3. Right-click the activity you want to modify. The pop-up menu appears, identical to the one you saw in the previous section.

4. Click the **Reschedule Activity** item. The Schedule Activity dialog box appears.

5. Make the changes you want to the activity.

6. Click **OK**. The activity is modified in the calendar and on the Activity tab.

Modifying an Activity from the Task List

The Task List has so many attributes that I've devoted all of Chapter 8, "Tackling Activities," to it. But, because you can modify an activity by using the Task List, take a look at this quick example:

1. Open the Task List by clicking the **Task List** icon at the far left of the contact window.

2. All the activities, for all contact records, appear in the Task List. Click the gray box that precedes an activity.

3. Right-click your mouse to open the pop-up menu.

4. Click **Reschedule Activity**. The Schedule Activity dialog box appears.

5. Make the changes you want to the activity.

6. Click **OK** to save the changes.

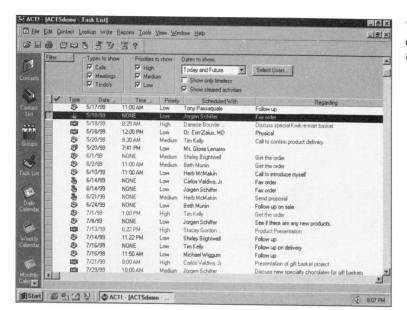

The ACT! Task List appears when you click its icon.

The Least You Need to Know

➤ The process for scheduling activities is identical for either a call, meeting, or to-do, except for the starting point.

➤ You can establish alarms at various intervals to remind you of appointments, and dismiss or defer them when they sound.

➤ Checking your tasklist ensures you stay on top of your activities.

"Everything in the world may be endured except continual prosperity."

Goethe

Chapter 8

Tackling Activities

In This Chapter

➤ Working with the Task List

➤ Clearing tasks

➤ Checking History

"I never did anything worth doing by accident; nor did any of my inventions come by accident; they came by work."

Thomas Edison

Your contacts are entered, the activities are scheduled, and now the time has come to tackle the activities. ACT! is intuitive, which makes it easy to understand how to access the activities you've scheduled and execute them.

Starting Your Day in the Task List

ACT! offers a condensed format, called the Task List, for viewing your scheduled activities. In addition, ACT! allows you to customize and modify the Task List to best fit your working style. So, to best use ACT!, start your business day by checking your Task List.

Accessing Your Task List

The Task List can be accessed in three ways: from the **View** menu, by pressing the **F7** key, or by clicking the **Task List** icon located to the left of the contact record screen, second from the right.

The Task List window looks like this.

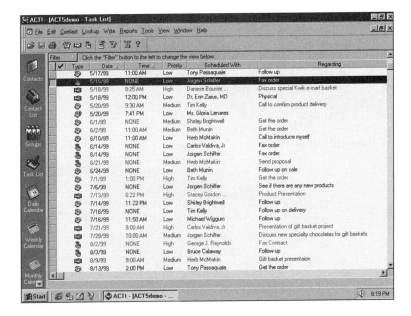

In this example, a multitude of tasks appears. The default filter for the Task List is to have ACT! show you only those activities that are scheduled for today, as determined by your computer's system clock. So, if the computer says that today is January 16th, the activities for that date are going to appear. Of course, you can change this filter setting. Before you do, though, take a look at the components of the Task List window.

Across the top of the window are some of the same menus that appear in the contact record window. Beneath the menu names are a set of icons relating to scheduling. You can click the call, meeting, or to-do icons to schedule an activity. ACT! automatically assumes that, if you click one of these buttons, the activity is to be scheduled with the contact you were on before opening the Task List. But, as I described in Chapter 7, "Scheduling Activities," you can select anyone in your database from the Schedule Activity dialog box.

Double-clicking any name in the contact column of an activity opens the Select Contacts dialog box, allowing you to change the name of the person with whom you have the activity scheduled, add a person to the activity, or add a group name.

Arranging Task List Columns

In Chapter 6, "Working in the List View," I covered the array of possibilities presented by the column list format that is used to list contact records. ACT!'s Task List offers the same options. You can

➤ Right-click and select **Add Columns** from the pop-up menu.

➤ Click a column heading and drag it to a different position in the list.

➤ Click a column heading and drag it up, and in so doing, delete it from the Task List view. Doing so only deletes the column from the view; no data is deleted.

➤ Click column headings to sort the list of activities. For example, if you want the list sorted by Priority, clicking that column heading re-sorts the list into Low, Medium, and High priorities. There is a visual cue in the column header: a small gray triangle that points either up or down, depending on the sort order. The only column that will not sort this way is the Scheduled With column.

➤ Clicking a column heading again reorders the list. For example, if the list has been sorted by Priority in Low, Medium, and High order, the column will sort in High, Medium, and Low order.

➤ Resize the columns by moving the mouse pointer to the line that divides two columns and, when the pointer changes to a right and left pointing arrow, clicking and dragging the line to a smaller or larger size.

To see the step-by-step instructions on the foregoing tasks, see Chapter 6.

Setting Filters

To understand the Task List, you have to grasp the concept of filtering. Assuming that you have scheduled a series of activities with different contacts, ACT! opens the Task List to the current date, and any activities you have scheduled appear, including Timeless activities. If you make changes to the filter, it will be in effect the next time you open the Task List. In this illustration, I selected the Filter button and the Filter settings appeared.

Let's examine the options that appear in this dialog box.

Types to Show

Need to see only your calls that are high priority? The Types to Show settings work with the other settings so that you can get to exactly what you want. Click the check box or boxes to select the activities you want to see.

With the Filter button clicked, its settings become visible.

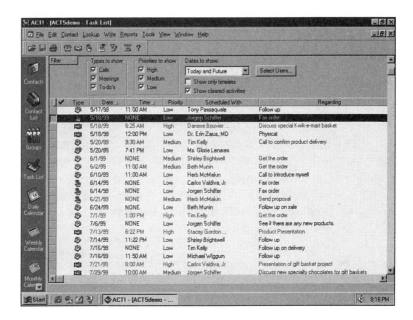

Select Users

This option applies to those of you on a network. You can select the public activities of a single user, of selected users, or of all users on the network. By clicking Select Users, you can click the names that appear in the list and see the public activities of those users. The default setting is for only your activities to be listed.

Dates to Show

The default setting of the Task List is the current date. However, you can see activities in a variety of ways. The All selection shows all activities scheduled and those cleared, unless you have checked the other option to not show cleared activities. Today shows the activities for the current date based on your computer's system date. Date Range allows you to select a range of dates for viewing. Past shows activities cleared and uncleared. Finally, you can choose to view Today and Future activities.

When you select any of the options, that is what will appear the next time you access the Task List. To see the effect of the change, click the **Apply** button. ACT! keeps the Filter dialog box open, so that you can make further changes if necessary.

Priorities to Show

Click the appropriate button to see the level associated with each activity. This ability reinforces a key point: When you schedule any type of activity, it is important to always indicate a priority level. One of the greatest mistakes to make in time management is to assign every task the same weight. Not every call is equally important, so make the assignment and your Task List will be more useful.

Show Only Timeless

This setting is particularly good when you have lots of activities that have been rolled over from previous days. It gives you an idea of what you have been missing and how to better schedule. On a network, it also might tell you who has been playing golf too much.

Show Cleared Activities

Time management experts suggest that you clear your activities by drawing a line through them, which is the default setting in ACT!. No one has a good enough memory to keep track of what they have done, so combining this option with the Date Range gives you a tool to see what exactly happened on a specific date or dates.

You also can change the filter settings from the toolbar by clicking the **Filter** button.

Creating a Task List Lookup

After setting the Filter options, the next step is to create a lookup based on the settings. Doing so gives you the list of records that have the activities you want to take on. It's easy:

1. Set the filter options.
2. Click the **Create Lookup** button.

ACT! returns the contact records based on the filter settings. So, if your record counter reads "1 of XX," the XX is the total number of records that meet the filter criteria.

Making a Call

Now that you have seen the ways in which you can look at the activities in the Task List and how to make changes, let's select a scheduled call and see how to execute that task. In the ACT5demo database Task List, a call is scheduled to Tony Passaquale. So, the first thing to do is to click the activity, and ACT! takes us to his record. To do this:

1. Click the gray box to the far left of the Task List. The entire line is highlighted.
2. Right-click the mouse to see the pop-up menu.

115

The pop-up menu is displayed over the Task List.

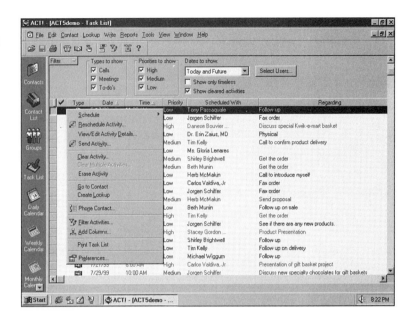

As you can see, one of the options is to go to the contact record. Once there, you can click the Dialer button to start the call. If you would rather make the call while viewing your Task List, you can do that from this menu by selecting the **Phone Contact** option. In either case, the dialog box appears with a list of phone numbers.

The Dialer dialog box lists the available phone numbers.

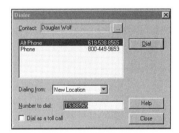

3. Click the number you want to dial. You also can select a location, so if you make calls from home and office locations, you can record the steps to dial from either. See the section on preferences for details.

4. Click the **Dial** button.

Depending upon the type of phone set you have, ACT! will dial the phone; when you hear the called party answer, click the **Speak** button. If you have the advantage of having a TAPI phone system, ACT! uses its software to handle the call. (The foregoing assumes that you have a modem in your computer and you have configured it for ACT!. If you have not done so, read the next section on installing the modem and dialing preferences.)

116

5. After the Speak button is selected, the Timer dialog box appears (unless you have turned it off).

The Timer dialog box appears after the called party answers.

You can start and restart the timer at will. When you have completed the call, and selected **Stop**, ACT! opens a dialog box to create a history record which includes the length of the call. You have the opportunity to enter text in the Regarding field.

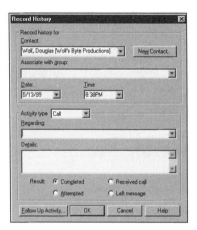

The Record History dialog box allows you to record the results of a call.

After making the entries in this dialog box, ACT! creates a history entry in the contact record. Here you can see the history record for your sample call.

So, if you are a consultant or attorney who bills by time, this is an invaluable record for creating invoices.

Some Dialing Options

When you start the Dialer, ACT! assumes that you want to call the contact onscreen. However, you can select a different contact by clicking the gray box at the end of the person's name and selecting another name. Or, you can have ACT! dial any number you want, by entering it into the Number to Dial field. You must include all numbers if you choose to make a call in this manner, as ACT! will not know if the number is long distance or international.

The Dial as a Toll Call check box is for those calls that are local—that is, the same area code, but require a 1 before dialing.

*ACT! Adds the History
entry for a phone call
with the duration for you.*

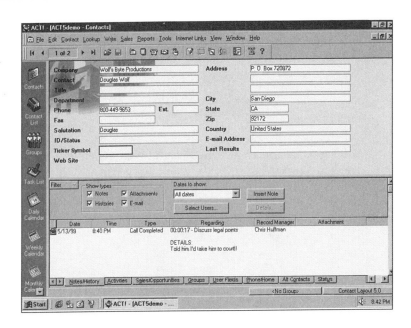

Installing the Modem and Setting Preferences

One of the joys of Windows 95/98 is that it looks at what hardware is installed on
your system and configures itself accordingly.

1. Open the **Edit** menu and select the **Preferences** option.

2. Click the **Dialer** tab.

*Select the Dialer tab from
the Preferences dialog
box.*

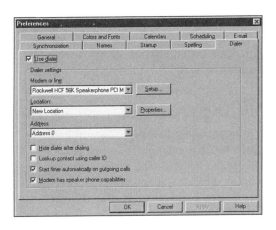

Windows 95/98 should have inserted the name of the modem it found installed
on your machine. If not, click the drop-down list box and type the name of the
modem and the model.

3. Click the **Setup** button. The Setup dialog box appears.

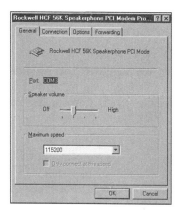

The dialog box for setting up the modem appears.

There are three tabs that you can select to add more setup data for the modem. Generally, the modem uses COM 1 unless you have selected a different port. You also can select the speaker level and the modem's maximum speed.

To see the other options, click the **Connection** tab, which allows you to specify the time-out setting. The Options tab has more settings. However, you should not have to change any of these settings if Windows 95 or 98 has recognized the modem.

Properties

You may use ACT! from several different locations—home, office, and so on. To configure the individual dialing settings for each, click the **Properties** button and the Dialing Properties dialog box appears.

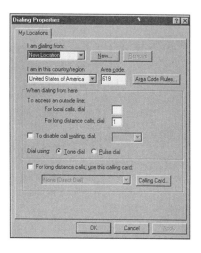

The Dialing Properties dialog box for specifying the dialing location appears.

The I Am Dialing From setting allows you to create multiple locations from which to call. That way, if your office and home dialing conditions are different—such as the area code or code for accessing an outside line—you can create the settings. Simply click **New**, add a location name, and fill in the blanks.

The For Long Distance Calls, Use This Calling Card option allows you to select the card you have or to create an entirely new set of calling card directions. You also can designate whether or not the phone system has call waiting. You must turn call waiting off if you use the modem to dial; otherwise, the interrupt feature of call waiting will disconnect your phone conversation if another call comes in.

After making these entries, go back to the Preferences dialog box. It has a few more settings of which you should be aware:

➤ **Hide Dialer After Dialing**   Unless you are TAPI enabled, you will want this dialog box to close after dialing is completed.

➤ **Lookup Contact Using Caller ID**   If you use your modem on a phone system that allows caller ID, ACT! can automatically retrieve a contact record by identifying the number as the phone rings!

➤ **Start Timer Automatically on Outgoing Calls**   If you make a call with the dialer, this option starts the timer for you. I recommend you activate this option.

➤ **Modem Has Speaker Phone Capabilities**   For those of you with a speaker phone built into your modem, this setting allows you to speak via that system when calling or receiving a call.

By using the Dialer every time you make a call, you begin to build a history of your business activities that is invaluable for charting the future. After all, how can you decide where you are going if you do not know where you have been?

Clearing an Activity

Even if you use the dialer to make a call, you need to take the steps to clear the activity from your schedule, as ACT! has no way of knowing the final disposition of the call. This is true for all activities, not only calls.

There are three ways to clear activities, either from the Task List or from the contact record. To clear an activity from the Task List:

1. Click the gray box to the left of the activity you want to clear.
2. Right-click the mouse. .
3. From the menu that appears, select **Clear Activity**.

The Clear Activity dialog box lets you remove a completed call from your schedule.

In this dialog box, you can accept the defaults or, if you need to, modify the Regarding field and the date and time that the activity was cleared. The Add Details to History field allows you to enter the exact disposition of the activity.

To clear an activity from the contact record, lookup the record, click the **Activities** tab, and right-click the activity. From the menu, select **Clear Activity**.

The third way to clear an activity is from the Task List. Click directly in front of the activity, below where the check mark is, but *not* on the gray box. ACT! opens the Clear Activity dialog box and, after making your entries, inserts a check mark in front of the activity.

Creating a Follow-up Activity

If the result of clearing the current activity is that you need to schedule another activity, click the **Follow Up Activity** button and the Schedule Activity dialog box appears, allowing you to do so.

Erasing an Activity

Instead of clearing an activity, use the same right-click procedure to erase an activity. When you do, it is as if the activity was never scheduled and no history is created.

Modifying an Activity

All the aspects of an activity are subject to modification. Click the particular aspect that you want to change. ACT! opens a drop-down list and allows you to make any change you want. Here you can see the drop-down list for the Time value.

The Time setting drop-down list in Task List is ready for modification.

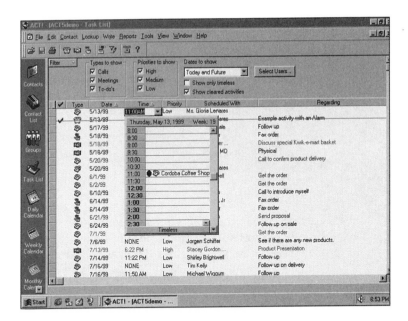

Printing the Task List

You have two ways to print the Task List. ACT! can print in the formats of the popular paper planners; however, you need the special paper for your printer. Fortunately, the paper forms have become ubiquitous and any office supply store carries them. To print to a form:

1. Click the printer icon. ACT! opens the Print dialog box.

2. From the list of forms presented, select the form you have.

3. To set options you want for the printed data, click the **Options** button. You can print the specific activities you want and in a time frame desired. You also can have only the person's name or both the name and company name. The best advice for this process is to waste some plain paper and try different options before actually printing on the expensive form paper.

The second option is to print on plain paper. The steps to do that are as follows:

1. Click the **Reports** menu and select **Task List**.

2. The Run Report dialog box appears.

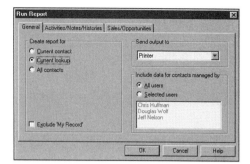

The Run Report dialog box appears.

Again, you have a range of options in terms of what to print, and to which output device. If you desire, you can print to a fax (provided you have fax software configured) or to an email message. The Preview option prints the report to the screen, and you can view the report before printing.

3. Click the **Filter** button to set more parameters. As you can see here, I've selected several filter options. I've also selected the Activities/Notes/Histories tab.

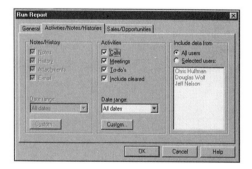

This Run Report dialog box has a variety of filter options already selected.

The salient option here is Date Range. Clicking the drop-down list offers you a wide variety of date settings. You can also select the Custom button to choose a special range from the calendar that appears.

If you are on a network, you can select the users to be included in the report.

Taking Notes

Another feature of ACT! that I appreciate more and more as I use it is the fact that I can see my notes on a contact without having to open a window. Simply clicking the tab presents the notes to me. The combination of the Notes and History together creates a synergistic tool for keeping track of projects. To add a note to a contact:

1. Look up the contact to which you want to add a note.

2. Click the **Notes/History** tab.

3. If you want, turn off the History portion of the window by clicking the **Histories** check box.

   Because the Notes/History window is a columnar report, the myriad of column options is in effect. You can resize the columns, move the columns, and add new columns. You also might sort the entries by clicking the column name or re-sort by pressing Shift and clicking the column name.

   The Notes field is dynamic, which means that you can type a note as long as you want, and ACT! wraps it into the space allowed.

4. Click the **Insert Note** button. ACT! inserts the date, time, and the type of entry it is. The Regarding field has an outline and you can begin typing. The text is editable, the same as any word processing document.

Other Stuff You Can Do in Notes/History

By right-clicking in the Notes window, you open a menu that allows you to add columns, attach files, and so on.

Right-clicking opens a menu in the Notes window.

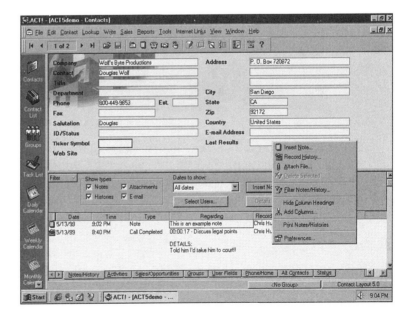

Attaching a File to a Contact Record

One of the more intriguing options on this menu is Attach File. This option allows you to do exactly what it says—attach a file link to a record. For example, you might have a JPG-format electronic picture of your contact, perhaps obtained from his or her Web page. You can attach this file to remind you what your contact looks like.

To attach a file, follow these steps:

1. Look up the record to which you want a file attached.
2. Open the **Contact** menu.
3. Select **Attach File**. ACT! opens the file dialog box.
4. Locate the file by using the dialog box's built-in file navigation system. So, if you have an email that you created as a document and saved, you can attach it to the notes/history.

Return to Visibility

When you create an attachment, you might not see it listed until you turn the attachment option off and then back on. Or, you could move to another record and then return.

Details

When you select a history entry, the Details button becomes active. Clicking it reveals more information on that particular entry.

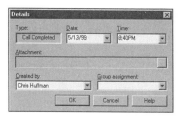

You've clicked the Details button on a record.

Changing Fonts

The font size and style can be modified for both notes and history records. The default size is quite small. This might be okay for a desktop computer, but on a laptop, it can be tough to read. To change the character style:

1. Click the **Edit** menu and select **Preferences**.
2. Click the **Colors and Fonts** tab.

The Colors and Fonts tab is selected.

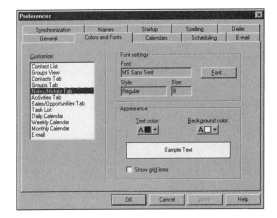

3. Click **Font**. The Font dialog box appears.

The Font dialog box appears.

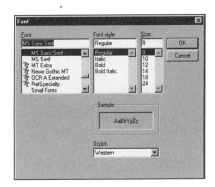

Select the size and style you desire. ACT! gives you a preview of how the font will appear as you make your choices.

After the size and style choices are made, you also can select the color of the text and the background for the Notes/History tab. Finally, you can select the Show Grid Lines option, which makes it easier to see each individual entry.

4. Click **Apply** to see the effect of the changes you have selected. If you are satisfied, click **OK**. Here you can see the text enlarged to 14 points.

As you have undoubtedly noticed, you can effect the same changes to text in all the tabs, in email, and in the contact list. One aspect that I wish would be added to this option is that the tab itself at the bottom of the window also change colors as set by me. That way, I could recognize the tab I want by the color. Maybe in a future release?

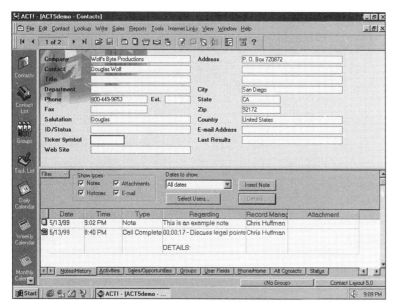

The Notes/History tab appears with enlarged text.

Printing Notes/History

Printing the contents of the Notes/History tab is similar to printing the Task List report:

1. Click the **Reports** menu and select **Notes/History**.

2. In the Run Report dialog box, select the contacts you want to include and the output device.

3. Click the appropriate tabs to set the filters for the report.

The Least You Need to Know

➤ To see all of your activities with every contact record, open the Task List by clicking the Task List button to the left of the screen.

➤ If your computer is connected to a modem, you can dial your contacts directly from ACT!.

➤ Once you've completed a scheduled activity, you should clear it.

➤ You can check the history of activities with a contact.

"If you cannot annoy somebody, there is little point in writing."

Kingsley Amis

127

Checking Your Calendar

"The exact contrary of what is generally believed is often the truth."

Bruyere

Calendars in General

ACT! provides three main calendars—Daily, Weekly, and Monthly—and a special calendar called the Mini-calendar, which is a nostalgia feature from the DOS days of ACT!. It still has some use, but it has diminished as a central feature of ACT!. The Daily, Weekly, and Monthly calendars can be printed in a variety of formats, and activities can be scheduled or modified directly in any calendar.

Opening a Calendar

New to ACT! 2000 are the icons that appear to the left of the contact record window. In Chapter 8, "Tackling Activities," I discussed the Task List. Assuming you read that chapter, you can see how the calendars and the Task List in ACT! are interrelated.

To open a calendar, click the appropriate icon (**Daily**, **Weekly**, or **Monthly**) to the left of the contact record window. To return the contact record, close the calendar by clicking the **x** in the upper-right corner of the window, or open the **Window** menu and select **XXX Contacts**, where *XXX* is the name of the database. If you are working in the ACT5demo database, the window is listed as ACT5demo-Contacts.

Company Name Versus Person on the Calendar

One of the disputes that arises among users of ACT! is whether a person primarily deals with a company or a person at that company. The dispute is not an academic exercise. Because ACT! is oriented toward people, the default setting for displaying activities on your calendar is by the name of the person with whom you have scheduled the activity. This is fine for most, but the argument is made that it is just as important to know which activity pertains to which company. ACT! does not show both, so you are going to have to make a choice. I suggest that you try the default of having the contact name and see if it is effective. To see the difference, open your database or the ACT5demo database and take a look at the Monthly calendar.

The Monthly calendar display in ACT! shows the contact name and scheduled activities.

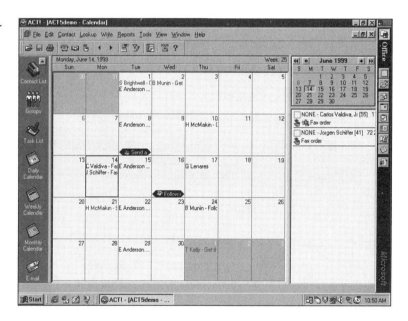

In the figure, a date has been selected and so more details are shown in the far-right column of that day's activities. To see the difference the company name makes:

1. Open the **Edit** menu.
2. Select the **Preferences** item. The Edit Preferences dialog box appears.
3. Click the **Calendars** tab.

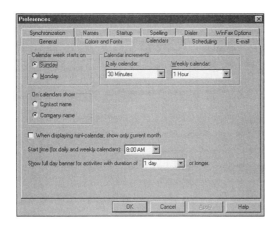

You've selected the Calendars tab in the Preferences dialog box.

4. On the left portion of this dialog box, there is the option On Calendars Show. Click the radio button in front of **Company Name**.

5. Click **OK** to close the dialog box.

The following illustration shows the results of the change. As I said, it is a matter of personal preference how you want to view the calendar. If you are on a network, the setting you make here affects only your view of the calendar—no one else's.

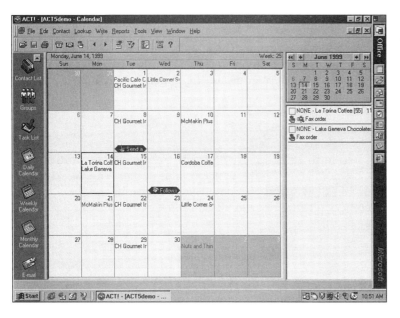

You can display the Monthly calendar with the company name and activities displayed.

Daily Calendar

Take a moment to look at the Daily calendar. If the Monthly calendar is open, you don't have to close it; ACT! replaces the current calendar with the selected calendar.

This Daily calendar lists company names with activities.

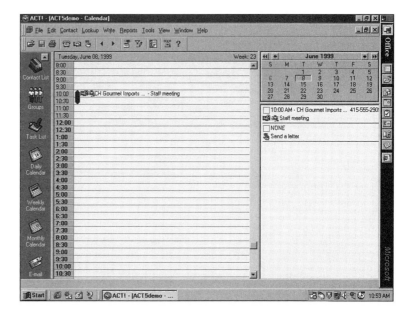

The length of the colored vertical bar preceding the activity indicates the time duration that has been allotted, a feature not available on the Monthly calendar. To see a specific date, click it on the small month calendar in the upper-right corner of the calendar window.

Weekly Calendar

The Weekly calendar is shown in the accompanying figure. As you can see in this figure and the ones preceding, the calendars have a very similar design. The Weekly calendar assumes that your week begins on Monday. This date can be modified to Sunday by using the Preferences setting for Calendars.

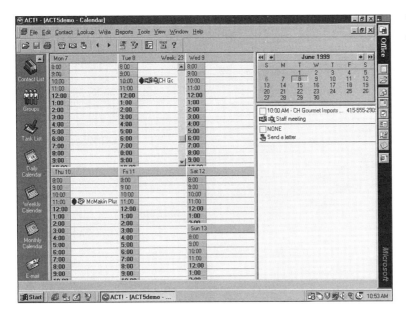

The ACT! Weekly calendar looks like this.

Modifying an Activity

In all of the calendars, you can change a scheduled activity. For example, you can click and drag an activity from one date to another to change the date on which the activity is to occur. When your mouse pointer is poised on an activity, the pointer is transformed into a four-headed pointer. At that point, pressing and holding the left mouse button allows you to drag the activity from date to date.

➤ In the Monthly calendar, dragging an activity to a different day maintains all the other activity settings, such as time of the activity.

➤ In the Weekly calendar, the activity can be dragged to a new date and time within the same week.

➤ In the Daily calendar, the activity can be dragged to a new time.

To further modify an activity, you can use a handy pop-up menu to make the additional changes:

1. Right-click the activity you want to modify. A pop-up menu appears.

2. Click the **Reschedule Activity** option. The Schedule Activity dialog box appears. At this point, make the changes as needed. (Refer to Chapter 7, "Scheduling Activities," for more information on scheduling.)

3. Click **OK** to finish the change.

When you right-click an activity, this pop-up menu appears, allowing activity modification.

Scheduling an Activity

While Chapter 7 covers scheduling activities in detail, the important point from the calendar perspective is that clicking a date and then right-clicking the mouse opens the pop-up menu. Select **Schedule** from the menu and then the type of activity: a call, meeting, or to-do. ACT! responds with the Schedule Activity dialog box. The current contact record is inserted into the With field, from which you can select a different contact record.

Clearing an Activity

To clear an activity from any of the calendars, right-click the activity and select **Clear Activity** from the pop-up menu. The Clear Activity dialog box appears.

The Clear Activity dialog box is for disposing of an activity.

The clearing action you can take depends on the activity and what has happened. All of the choices add the results of the activity to the History tab, *unless* you choose the Erase option. To add a new activity, click the **Follow Up Activity** button and ACT! displays the Schedule Activity dialog box.

Sending an Activity to Another Person

ACT! has the ability to send an activity that is scheduled with that person, to the other ACT! user, or to an Outlook 98 user. The activity is attached to an email message and added to the receiver's database. To send an activity:

1. Right-click the activity. The pop-up menu appears.

2. Click the **Send Activity** option. The Format Options dialog box appears.

   The choices in this dialog box are straightforward. It helps to know which system the receiver has, but it is not crucial.

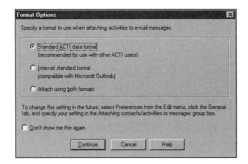

The Format Options dialog box appears when you are sending an activity to another ACT! user or Outlook 98 user.

3. Select the format.

4. Click **Continue**. The ACT! email Create Message window appears, if that is the email system you have selected for your default email system. Otherwise, the email system you have selected appears.

Complete the email and send it, or cancel.

ACT! email Create Message window with an activity ready to send.

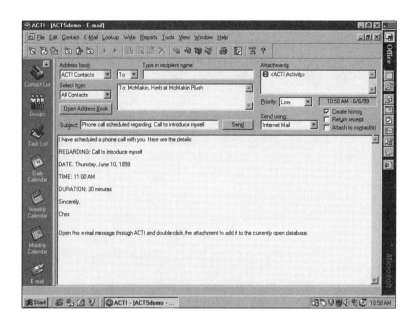

Going Directly to the Contact Record

This is a very handy option on the calendar pop-up menu—especially if you have forgotten why you have an item on your calendar. From any calendar, right-click and, from the pop-up menu, select **Go To Contact**. ACT! closes the calendar and displays the contact record for whom the activity is scheduled.

Clearing Multiple Activities

This option is not active in any of the calendar views. The only way you can clear more than one activity at a time is to go to the Activities tab of the contact, or via the Task List.

Phone Contact Record

This option is covered in detail in Chapter 8. Select this option if you want to start the dialer and place a call to the person with whom the activity is scheduled.

Creating a Lookup from the Calendar

There might be times when you want to create a lookup of contact records that have activities scheduled for the displayed day, the displayed week, or displayed month. Right-click and select the **Create Lookup** option. ACT! closes the calendar view and shows you a lookup of those contact records.

Filtering the Calendar, or How to Legitimately Snoop on Your Co-workers

This topic is important if you are on a network version of ACT!. Because multiple users are logging in to the ACT! database, each user has his own set of activities with various contact records. When you look at any of the calendars, the default setting is to show only the activities that you have scheduled (or someone has scheduled for you). But, suppose that you are an administrative assistant (you might not have to suppose!), and you schedule activities for your boss. When you schedule an activity, you will not see it on your calendar—because it is not for you. But by changing the filter setting, you can see his activities. A second example is the fun of trying to schedule a meeting for a group of people who are perpetually in and out of the office. By using the filter, you can select the people with whom you want to meet and scan for an open date and time. If you are lucky, they might even come to the meeting—but that's your problem.

To change the filter settings for a calendar:

1. Click the **Filter Calendar** button. (It's fourth from the right on the toolbar.) The Filter Calendar dialog box appears.

The Filter Calendar dialog box is ready for removing debris.

2. Click the **Selected Users** radio button—if you are on a network, it should already be selected.

3. From the list of login users, click the names of the people whose calendar items you want to add.

4. If you want, choose which activity types and the level of priority you want displayed.

5. Click **Apply**, because you can see the effect of the changes without closing the dialog box.

6. If the results are what you expected, click **OK**. Otherwise, make changes and then click **Apply** until you are satisfied, and then click **OK**.

The filter settings remain in place until you change them. If you close ACT! and then restart, the default setting of showing you just your calendar returns.

Printing Calendars

ACT! can print to many formats that are identical to paper planners, such Day Runner or Franklin. You purchase the blank paper from your handy-dandy stationery store (the one that is not moving) and insert it into your printer. Choose **Print** from the **File** menu. The Print dialog box opens and displays a list of the types of printer forms. On the right of the dialog box, ACT! displays a graphic of the way the selected format prints. On a slower machine, you can speed up this dialog box by turning off the **Show Preview** setting. No matter which calendar was open on the screen when you opened the Print dialog box, you can select to print the Daily, Weekly, or Monthly calendar, by pulling down the **Types** list.

You displayed the Monthly calendar selections in the Print dialog box.

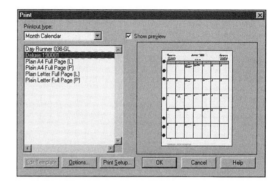

Calendar Printing Options

The Options button is nestled at the bottom of the Print dialog box. Click it to see what other options you have when printing—in this example, monthly calendars.

This Calendar Options dialog box contains a variety of ways to print the calendar information.

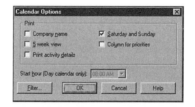

Setting a Filter

The Filter button in the Calendar Options dialog box gives you another level of control (and control is what we crave in the chaos that abounds in nature), allowing you to print a monthly calendar for a selected set of users. You can print only the activities desired in a restricted date range. Yes, you can even print a monthly calendar, but only include three of the four weeks.

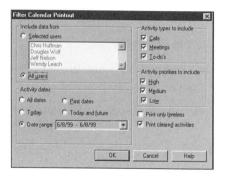

The Filter Calendar Printout dialog box offers many controllable options.

Click **OK** to close the dialog box. You are now ready to print. Select the destination and the paper orientation. ACT! prints the options that you have selected on the border of the calendar, so you always know what the printed calendar contains.

The Mini-Calendar and Your Life

The legacy of DOS lives on in ACT!. In the olden days before Windows, the only way to see a calendar pop up in ACT! was using the Mini-calendar. Now, the Mini-calendar remains in ACT! for those antediluvian users who cannot let go of the F4 key. The thing most users like about the Mini-calendar is that they can display it anywhere in ACT! except the word processor.

The Mini-calendar is in synch with any calendar you might display. So, if the Monthly calendar window is open, and you press F4, the Mini-calendar reflects the same date. Moving to another date in either calendar moves both displays. The Mini-calendar can be set to show three months at a time or only one month, in the Preferences setting as described in Chapter 10, "Setting Your Preferences." If you right-click the date in the Mini-calendar, ACT! displays the schedule of activities for that date.

Close the Mini-calendar by pressing **F4** again!

The Least You Need to Know

➤ To see your calendar, click the calendar type you want to view. The calendar icons are visible at the left of the contact form window.

➤ You can customize the ACT! calendars to display Daily, Weekly, or Monthly time spans.

➤ Adding an activity to a calendar is simple.

➤ You can filter calendars to display only appointments with certain contacts, a certain date range, or other restrictions.

"Every man is the creature of the age in which he lives; very few are able to raise themselves above the ideas of their times."

Voltaire

Part 3

I Know I Sent That Bid Update to Our Customer

Now that you know where you are going, you can communicate with the outside world via the written word, fax, or email. ACT! tracks what you have sent so that you can be certain you did what you told your customer you were going to do. Chapters 10–14 show you how to get your messages out.

So, whadda ya' like?

Chapter 10

Setting Your Preferences

In This Chapter

➤ Choosing the colors and fonts

➤ Customized scheduling

➤ Adding your words to the dictionary

"I am opposed to millionaires, but it would be dangerous to offer me the position."

Mark Twain

As you've learned, you can run ACT! either on a single computer or as part of a network. Running ACT! on a network allows users to share contact information and offers other advantages. You'll learn the differences in this chapter.

Network Versus Standalone

The preferences settings in ACT! allow you to customize many aspects of the ACT! program. Most of the settings are particular to your login name—that is to say, on a network, you can log in on any machine and ACT! remembers your preferences. If you are the administrator of the ACT! database, you can modify some preferences that affect all users of the database.

To see the Preferences settings, open the **Edit** menu and select **Preferences**. The Preferences dialog box appears and the General tab is automatically displayed.

The Preferences dialog box displays the General tab by default when you open it from the Edit menu.

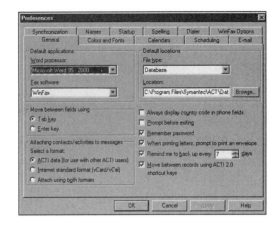

Looking at the General Tab

Some of the Preferences here were set when you installed ACT!. Most prominent is the selection of the default word processor. You have your choice of ACT!'s word processor or the popular, yet resource-hungry, Microsoft Word. The difference between the two programs is in scale: Word is the industrial-strength program with all the features, including the kitchen sink. ACT!'s word processor is very serviceable for 90% of the documents you are likely to create, and being more compact, is much faster. Any document you create in the ACT! word processor can be saved or exported to an ASCII or RTF file type, allowing any word processor to open it. Many companies insist that you use Word; if yours is one of them, you might not have a choice.

ASCII

Short for the *American Standard Code for Information Interchange*, ASCII basically means plain text files consisting solely of characters found on the keyboard, with no formatting or graphics. Their advantage is that, since all computers refer to the characters by a standard set of numeric codes, ASCII files are readable by any system.

RTF

Short for *Rich Text Format*, this standard, developed by Microsoft, is a step up from ASCII. It allows special formatting, such as **bold** and *italic* text. The files are readable by almost all Windows–based word processors and many other programs.

Using Faxing Software

The next choice in establishing preferences is for faxing software. ACT! is published by Symantec, and the best faxing software is WinFax, also published by Symantec and tightly integrated with ACT!. In fact, it is so tightly integrated that you can edit an ACT! record directly from WinFax. If WinFax is installed, ACT! displays it as the default software. Chapter 11, "Creating Documents," describes how to send documents created in ACT! via WinFax.

Move Between Fields Using the Tab or Enter Key

Many DOS users are still wedded to the Enter key as the one to press when moving between fields. Because of this, the default setting is set to Tab, the Windows standard, but you can switch to Enter. In Chapter 16, "Customizing your Layout," I discuss the way in which you can optimize using both the Tab key and the Enter key for data entry.

Attaching Contacts/Activities to Messages

ACT! 2000 allows you to send contacts and activities to other ACT! users, or to Outlook 98 users, via email. The recipient can then add the contact or activity to his or her own database. The default is to send in ACT! format, but if you are sharing data with Outlook users, you can make that choice. At the time you send email, you have the opportunity to change the format.

Always Display Country Codes in Phone Fields

On the right half of the dialog box, beneath the Default Locations section, this option appears. If your firm deals with many companies or individuals that are from other countries, this setting specifies that the country code is displayed with the number. This is a time-saver when you are dialing the phone manually, as you do not have to look up the country code to place the call.

Prompt Before Exiting

Select this option if you want ACT! to alert you that you are closing the program, at which point you can decide to keep it open. Frankly, unless you are prone to clicking the Close box in the upper-right corner of the ACT! program window, you can let ACT! assume you want to quit when you tell it to.

Never Fear, Your Data's Here!

Many programs prompt you to save your data when you click the Close box. Act doesn't bother you with such a prompt. Since ACT! automatically saves your data, you never have to worry about losing your work when you exit.

Remember Password

The password entry (displayed in asterisks) will remain in the logon dialog box unless you turn this setting off. You might want ACT! to require a password every time if your computer is in an area where others could gain access.

When Printing Letters, Prompt to Print an Envelope

When you create and print a letter, you can have ACT! ask you if you also want to print an envelope.

Remind Me to Back Up Every X Days

Turn this setting off for all users who are on a network. Leave it on if you are a stand-alone user. The question is, how often to back up? Do it *every* day.

Move Between Records by Using ACT! 2.0 Keys

The shortcut keys you can choose to invoke are Page Up and Page Down to move from record to record, and Control+Home to the first record in the lookup and Control+End for the last record in the lookup.

Default File Locations

When you installed ACT!, it created the subfolders it needed for databases, documents, layouts, reports, and so on. For a standalone installation, the default choices should be quite adequate.

On a network with a shared database, the default locations must be changed. Assuming that you are the person in charge of ACT!, you need to be able to create folders on the network server. This task is not difficult, but you might need the help of the network administrator. The folders must allow for read, write, and delete capabilities. My recommendation is that you create a minimum of two folders, one for the database and one for customized layouts. If you want all ACT! users to use the same document, fax, and memo templates, then a folder for those is in order as well. After creating the folders, you need to go to each computer that will be accessing the database and open the Preferences dialog box and make the changes as follows:

1. In the Preferences dialog box, on the General tab, click the drop-down arrow to select the file type. For the database, select the database file type.
2. Click the **Browse** button.
3. Navigate to the folder that has or will contain the matching file type. For example, if the file type is database and you have created a folder on the network server named ACTDATABASE, navigate to that folder.
4. Click **OK**.

After doing so, when the user opens the File menu and selects Open, this is the folder that ACT! looks in for database files. Repeat the steps for each type of file that you want shared by all ACT! users on the network.

ACT! is programmed to open the last accessed database every time you start. So, if you opened the SALES database on your C drive, and then shut down ACT!, the next time you start ACT! it opens the SALES database. In order for the users to have ACT! open the shared database, the next step is to open the **File** menu, and then select **Open**. Because you have changed which folder ACT! is to look in when opening a database, the shared database should be visible. Select the shared database and open it. Next, exit ACT!. Now, reopen ACT!, and the shared database is opened automatically. There are several other settings in preferences that are integral to ensuring that the user always opens the shared database and these are discussed under the Startup tab.

Captain's Login

You must first log in to the network system in order to access a shared database. Usually, to do so, you are asked to enter a username and password when you start your computer. Of course, you can choose to log in to your computer without accessing the network, but if you aren't logged in to the network, you can't access the database files located there.

Colors and Fonts

One of the first things I do for my clients is change the display for Notes. Why? Because people refer to them almost every time they look up a record, and the default font setting for notes is so tiny that eyestrain is inevitable. So, make the font larger and add grid lines as I'll describe in a moment. The instructions work for all the choices under Customize on the left side of this dialog box.

Select the Colors and Fonts tab in the Preferences dialog box.

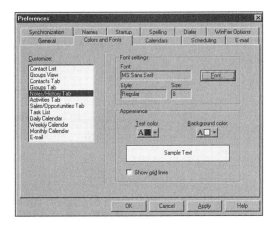

1. Click **Notes/History Tab** in the Customize list box.
2. On the right side, click the **Font** button. The Font dialog box appears.

The Font dialog box displayed.

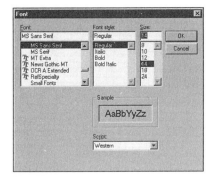

3. It seems the older you get, the less your eyes focus on close objects, so at this point in time, suffering middle-age myopia, 14 point is my favorite. If you are so inclined, change the font style and the font, too. By customizing all the tabs in ACT!, you can tell at a glance which tab is selected by the fonts selected. Note that you see a preview of the change before you apply it.

4. Click **OK**.

5. Click the check box in front of **Show Grid Lines**.

148

The results of changing the font for the Notes/History tab are shown here.

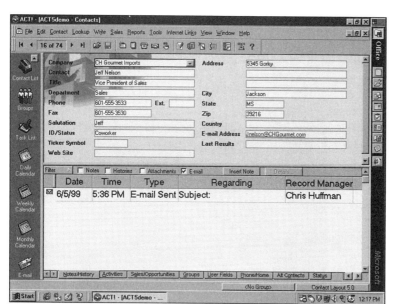

The 14-point font for myopic folks is available in the Notes/History tab.

The grid lines make it easier for the eye to follow the entries. However, the columns do not automatically expand to accommodate the new size, so you might have to move the mouse pointer to the column border and drag it to the right to make more room for the entries.

These settings for the Colors and Fonts tab are specific to the individual user. So, on a network, each person may have his or her own look and feel to ACT!.

Calendars

The Calendar tab has one crucial setting, that being the choice to display the contact name or the company name on the calendars. The distinction is whether you want to see the name of the person with whom you have an activity scheduled, or the name of the company. If you choose the company name, and the person with whom the activity is scheduled does not have an entry in the Company field, the contact name appears.

The other settings are whether or not to have the Weekly calendar start on Sunday or Monday, what time increment to use for the Daily and Weekly calendars, and what time to show for the start of day. The full day banner runs across the bottom of the individual day for any activity that meets the specified duration. The final setting is for the Mini-calendar, with three months being the default.

Scheduling

The settings for scheduling are the defaults that appear when you begin scheduling an activity. The preferences for all three types of activities are accessible by pulling down the list in the Settings For field. You might want to try scheduling a few different activities prior to deciding what the defaults should be—remembering that you can always change any of the attributes for the particular activity at the time you actually schedule.

Select Calls from the Scheduling tab in the Preferences dialog box.

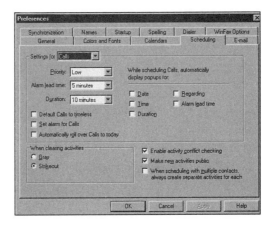

For your activity defaults, the salient settings are the ones for the pop-ups and the "rolling over" of the activity. The pop-ups are handy for speed in scheduling a new activity, but they can be clumsy when rescheduling an activity. For example, when you schedule a call, you might want to see the Monthly calendar pop-up so as to pick a date, but you might not want the time menu to appear. For meetings, you probably want the date and time pop-ups to open.

More important is ACT!'s rolling over feature. I strongly urge that you have all calls and to-dos automatically roll over to the next day if you don't clear them. That way, ACT! continues to remind you of the activity. Also, make sure that an alarm is set for all your activities to remind you when the time approaches.

The only drawback to this is if you fail to clear the activities as you should, or, if you have been using ACT! for some time and have not been clearing activities. Changing this setting causes ACT! to go back and get all the activities that have not been cleared and roll them over immediately. If you have been negligent in this area, you might find hundreds of uncleared activities—which can take hours to clean up. Proceed with caution.

The When Clearing Activities setting lets you determine how to display completed activities. The best time management experts recommend that a line should be struck through the item. In a world in which we mostly manipulate information, not objects, it is satisfying to look at your Task List and see a series of scheduled activities crossed off. As you might expect, then, ~~strikethrough~~ text is ACT!'s default for displaying completed tasks.

This dialog box contains several more settings of note. The Enable Activity Conflict Checking option alerts you when you try to schedule more than one activity at a time. It should be set to On. When ACT! recognizes the conflict, the dialog box alerts you to the fact—but you can ignore the conflict at that point or reschedule the new activity. The Make New Activities Public setting is for network use. The default is that all activities are public—that is, anyone using the shared database can see what you are up to. Any individual activity you schedule can be made private, so accept the default.

There's one more setting, with a long moniker: When Scheduling with Multiple Contacts, Always Create Separate Activities for Each. This setting is there to let you invite more than one person to the same appointment. If you are scheduling a meeting with several people, at the same time, the choice is to have ACT! add the activity to the calendars with each of the members of the meeting, or only to the initial member of the meeting. So, instead of your calendar being crowded with a host of names at the 2 p.m. time slot, only a single name appears. The default, to create a single activity, is the superior way.

Email

Take a peek at Chapter 14, "Internet and Email," for the steps to set up email. If you have already done the setup and are having problems, this section of the Preferences dialog box is where you can look to see if the settings are correct.

Synchronization

Synchronization is the process whereby two or more databases are updated so that all data is identical in all databases. The common scenario is where a company has a master database of all its customers and one or more remote users that work with records that are in the main database. The remote user might make a change to the ABC company record and the record might be changed in the master database. The trick is to get the data in synch so that both have identical information.

This tab reflects the settings that have been made when synchronization is set up. Because of the complexity of the subject, see Chapter 25, "Synchronizing with Remote Users," for a complete discussion.

Names

Due to the wide variety in people's names, when you enter a person's name as part of a contact record, ACT! does its best to determine which entries are the first and last names. In this tab, you can see what ACT! recognizes as first name prefixes, last name prefixes, and last name suffixes. So, if you enter a name such Dr. Kris van Lom Sr., ACT! knows that the *Dr.* is not the first name and that the last name is not *Sr.*

If you commonly enter names with unusual prefixes, add them to the list. ACT! automatically opens the definition dialog box for unusual names—but you can set this default to off.

Note that if you import records that have name suffixes, and so on, as part of the name, ACT! will not correctly recognize the first and last names, so you will have to manually identify the names. I described this process in Chapter 3, "Entering Records."

The Salutation setting also is determined on this tab. When you enter a name, ACT! selects the first name, last name, or no entry into the salutation field as directed here. You can always edit the entry you want into the salutation field.

Startup

The settings on this tab work with the settings for the default file locations. The default contact layout is the place that is used to make certain that every user on a shared database has the same layout. To do so, click the gray box with the small dots to the right of the field. This opens the Browse window, from which you can locate the folder that has the layout you want the user to see. Similarly, the group layout can be set up the same way. By making these entries, you can feel confident that the layout you have painstakingly designed is actually in use!

The next most important setting is Startup Database. Here, you can browse to the database that you want every user to access when he or she starts ACT!. As you can see, the default is that ACT! opens the last opened database, which will work most of the time. But, you can't predict what users are going to do, so I recommend that you select the **Named Database** setting, and then click the **Browse** button to select the database you want opened. The database does not have to be in the folder you set as the location in the General tab, but that is where you should store the database.

The last two settings of note are the making of new records or groups private. Use these settings when you plan to enter multiple records into a shared database that you want marked as private. So too, with a group. Suppose that you want to create several groups that are important to you, like the tennis players from your club, your euchre partners, and your PTA roster, into a shared database. The records should be entered as private and the group should be accessible only by you. This is the place to make those settings.

You also can run a macro when you open ACT!. As an idea, you could have ACT! download your email when ACT! starts. See Chapter 18, "Forecasting Sales," for information on creating macros.

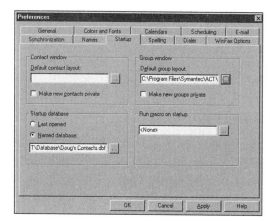

The Preferences dialog box's Startup tab lets you assign a database for users to access when they launch ACT!.

Spelling

This tab pertains to creating documents. ACT!'s word processor has a built-in spell checker, but you may want to customize it with words that are specific to your profession so that ACT! does not stop on those words. Or, you can create industry-specific dictionaries that you can access when you are spell checking—thereby allowing words that in one instance would be incorrect, but in another, appropriate.

ACT! also has choices for dialect—English being the common language that separates the British, Americans, and Australians—so you can select the dialect that fits your country.

To add a new word to the new user dictionary, follow these steps:

1. Click the **User Dictionary** field.
2. Click the **Modify** button.
3. The User Dictionary dialog box appears.
4. Click **Add**. The Add Word dialog box appears.

The Add Word dialog box appears here stacked atop the User Dictionary dialog box and the Preferences dialog box.

5. Type the word that you want to add.
6. Click **OK** twice.

The next time you spell check a document using ACT!'s word processor, the word is ignored and considered correct. If you are forced to use Word, you must modify its dictionary to change the spell checker.

The Auto-Suggest attribute is set to on, and you initiate a spell check, ACT! pops up a dialog box with suggestions for the correct spelling if it doesn't recognize a word. For example, if you type *thier*, ACT! might suggest *their* instead.

Dialer

The dialer is a terrific feature in ACT! and can increase your productivity when used properly. You can use these settings to ensure optimum efficiency. For example, ACT! never misdials the number. Using the dialer starts the recording process for the call—making the Date and Time History entry and prompting you to record what happened in the call. On a laptop, you can designate different locations from which to dial, home or office, for example.

To begin, click the **Dialer** tab.

The Dialer tab is selected in the Preferences dialog box.

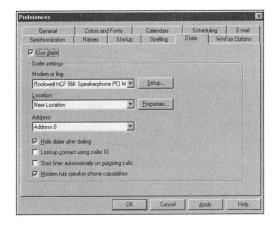

Click the **Use Dialer** check box. This might be all you have to do, as ACT! looks at the Windows settings to determine if you have a modem. If it finds one, then ACT! inserts the pertinent information into the fields.

Setup

To change the settings for the modem, click the **Setup** button. Each modem has its own characteristics, so you might have to refer to the information supplied by the modem manufacturer to make changes. Usually, Windows handles all this for you.

Setting Up Different Dialing Locations

Suppose that you have a laptop and want to be able to use ACT! to dial from your office and also from home. Because the dialing sequence is likely to be different in each location, ACT! needs to know the differences.

1. Click the **Properties** button. The Dialing Properties dialog box appears.

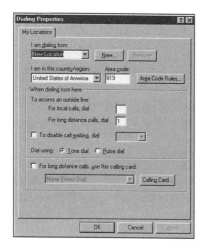

Use the Dialing Properties dialog box for creating unique dialing locations.

2. In the I Am Dialing From text box, enter the name of the location, such as Office.
3. Open the drop-down list to select the country from which you are dialing.
4. Enter the area code, if appropriate.
5. Click the **Area Code Rules** button, and you see the Area Code Rules dialog box.

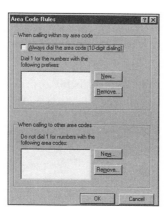

Use the Area Code Rules dialog box to establish whether certain area codes require a 1 prefix.

The demand for new phone numbers has created a proliferation of new area codes. Ergo, the need for fancy ways to cram more numbers into an established area. Ten-digit dialing is one method and your area might have been overrun by this technique. A refinement of the phone company dialing confusion is to dial

155

a 1 for some prefixes, and not others! So, you can enter the prefixes that require a 1 and those that do not. If you are lucky, you will only have to do this once a year or so.

6. Click **OK**.

To create a second dialing location, such as home or a satellite office, click the **New** button and you can enter the new dialing location.

The next section of this dialog box is simple. Enter the initial numbers for local calls and long distance. Call waiting is next; you want it disabled for email access and Web browsing.

Although long-distance calling has gotten cheaper, it is not yet free, and many companies require that you use a credit card to track calls. ACT! provides a painless way to use a calling card or alternative phone service. Click the **For Long Distance Calls, Use This Calling Card** check box, and then open the drop-down list that includes many carriers' access codes. For credit cards, click the **Calling Card** button, and then **New**, and finish by entering the numbers as required. This is one example of where computers are much more efficient than humans.

WinFax Options

If you have WinFax on your computer, this tab is available. First, you can make the ACT! database a phonebook for WinFax, which means that all your contacts can be faxed directly from ACT! or directly from WinFax—even if ACT! is not running! The logging features are very valuable and I would recommend that you check all the boxes unless you fax to clients so frequently that History entries will become overwhelming. Particularly inviting is the option to have an activity created to re-send a fax when a scheduled fax fails.

Finally, you can have a link created to the fax that is visible on the Notes/History tab that allows you to click the link and open the fax itself, directly from ACT!.

The WinFax tab appears with a variety of setup options regarding ACT!

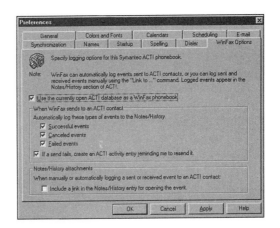

Another bit of advice. Sending more than 200 faxes as a mail merge is likely to over-burden your system. When clients ask what to do, I point them to a third-party fax-ing service that will take your ACT! information and the document and send it for you. Check Chapter 25 for information on the fax service.

The Least You Need to Know

➤ The Preferences dialog box lets you establish ACT!'s default settings the way you like them.

➤ One of the changes you can make to the defaults is the color and font ACT! uses to display text.

➤ You can configure the Dialer to place your phone calls for you—but you still need to do the talking!

"Idealism increases in direct proportion to one's distance from the problem."

John Galsworthy

Creating Documents

"A very great part of the mischiefs that vex this world arises from words."

Edmund Burke

In the early 1980s, the business gurus were boldly predicting that the paperless office was just around the corner. They believed that sending electronic messages and files on disks would obviate the need for printed material.

As is true with most predictions, however, the experts were wrong. Computers have actually increased the amount of paper generated by businesses. Successful people consistently keep in touch with their clients, customers, fellow workers, friends, and prospects by sending thank-you notes, update memos, and other pieces of written information.

The problem is the process. First, you have to write the letter or memo, then you have to dig through an address book to find the recipient's address, and finally you have to find an envelope and get it in the mail. ACT! makes it easy to do the first two parts: writing the letter or memo and getting the correct address. (You still have to supply the envelope and stamp.)

ACT! generates letters, personalized form letters, memos, fax covers, email, and documents that you design. ACT! then prints the accompanying mailing labels or envelopes. In short, ACT! can be used as a mass-mailing machine that one person can easily operate. This chapter is devoted to the word processor and the enhancements that make it easy to send 1 or 100 letters.

Creating a Letter

Creating a standard business letter in ACT! is simple:

1. Look up the contact record for whom you want to send a letter.

2. Open the **Write** menu and select **Letter**.

Choose Letter from the Write menu to begin a letter to your contact.

ACT! opens the word processor you selected when you installed ACT! and then inserts the inside address information from the contact record. Also, ACT! includes a salutation based on the entry in the Dear field of the contact record, and a closing based on the name entered in the My Record dialog box. (Remember, you entered your name in My Record when you installed ACT!.)

ACT! inserts the contact record information to complete the inside address.

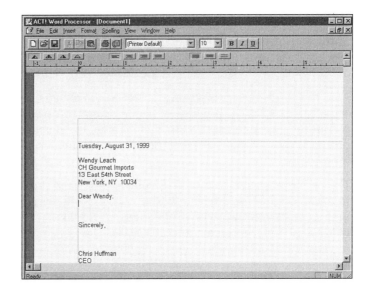

The insertion point is the vertical flashing bar that indicates where characters appear as they are typed. The mouse pointer is no longer shaped like an arrow, but is an oversized capital I. Note, too, that the letter body is surrounded by an outline that indicates the borders of the text in relation to the paper dimensions.

The menu names and icons have changed to reflect word-processing functions. In the border at the top of the window is the title of the letter. At this point, however, there's no title (because you haven't saved the document), so the word *Document1* appears. Had you retrieved a saved letter, the title would appear. ACT! enables you to have many open word-processing windows and switch among them, and even move back and forth between the contact record window and the word-processing windows. At the top of the word processing window, underneath the border, is the ruler.

Look at the position of the scroll boxes in the scrollbars. Click the horizontal scroll box and drag it to the far right edge of the scrollbar. Click the vertical scroll box and drag it to the bottom of the scrollbar. This gives you an idea of the electronic sheet of paper concept. The default left margin is 1.25 inches and the top margin is 1 inch.

Entering and Working with Text

The word-processing window is an electronic sheet of paper that is extremely long—infinitely long, in fact. The words you type are stored temporarily in memory, and you can manipulate them by cutting and pasting. When you type a line of text, ACT! automatically determines the number of characters, including spaces, that can fit on a single line. ACT! "wraps" any word that won't fit onto the next line, creating what's known as a soft carriage return. So you don't have to (and shouldn't) press the Enter key when you come to the end of a line. Pressing the Enter key creates a hard carriage return, which you should use only when you want to create a new paragraph.

If you are new to word processing, try entering the following practice letter. I included several intentional errors to illustrate the spell checker and editing functions. Use any contact you want—form the sample database, if necessary. The insertion point should be beneath the salutation. Type the following:

```
Thank you for taking the time to meet with me today. As you
requested, I will be sending you a sample of my product, prior to
our next meeting. You should recieve them shortly.

I would like to invite you to visit our booth at the Consumer
Electronics Show. It is booth #333, and we will be exhibiting all of
our new products. I have enclosed a guest pass for your use.

I hope your dog is feeling better!
```

Saving a Letter

Before editing or enhancing the letter, it's best to save it. That way, if you decide the original text was superior, it's retrievable. ACT! won't let you exit the program if you haven't saved a letter, but computers do shut off accidentally or crash when you least expect it, so it's a good idea to save a letter periodically, even before finishing it. To do so, follow these steps:

1. Click the **File** menu and select **Save**.
2. If this is the first time you've saved the document, the Save As dialog box appears.

The word processor's Save As dialog box looks like any other in ACT!—or Windows, for that matter.

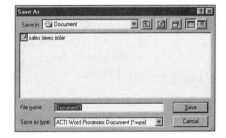

In the File Name field, ACT! inserts the current name of the letter. In this case, the default entry is Document1 because the letter doesn't have a name yet. By default, ACT! saves letters in the ACT\DOCUMENT folder. At the bottom of the dialog box is the Save as Type field.

3. Press the **Backspace** key. ACT! erases the Document1 entry from the File Name field.
4. Type **Thanks** in the **File Name** field.
5. Click **Save**.

Unless you've saved a different letter under the name THANKS, ACT! saves the letter and returns you to the word-processing window. Notice that the name THANKS now appears in the window border at the top.

Spell-Checking and Editing the Letter

Let's start editing by checking the spelling. Click the **Spelling** menu.

The Spelling menu allows you to begin checking a document, or create/modify user dictionaries.

Click the **Check Document** option, and ACT! starts checking both spelling and basic grammar at the beginning of the document. The ACT! Spell Check dialog box appears.

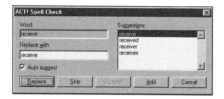

The ACT! Spell Check dialog finds suspect words and suggests an alternative spelling.

ACT! begins by checking and stopping on the names and addresses in the inside address. To avoid this, you can highlight the body of the letter before starting the spell checker and then select the **Check Selection** option. The spell checker only checks the spelling for the material you have selected.

In the sample letter, the word that's being questioned in the dialog box is one that has bedeviled school children (and adults) forever. *Receive* is one of the words whose spelling is governed by the *i before e except after c* rule. Well, ACT! has correctly identified it as being misspelled in the letter.

ACT! suggests what it believes to be the correct spelling in the Replace With box, and also displays a list of other possible correct spellings. The list is provided because the Auto Suggest function is set to On, which is the default.

Click the **Replace** button. ACT! inserts the corrected spelling and finishes the spell check. Click **OK** to continue, and the insertion point is positioned after the last word that was checked.

Rereading the letter reveals a grammatical error. The letter specifies that the customer is being sent a sample of a product, which is referred to in the next sentence as *them*. You need to replace the word *them* with the word *it*.

1. Position the mouse pointer on the word *them*.
2. Double-click the word. The entire word should be highlighted.

The entire word is highlighted when you double-click it.

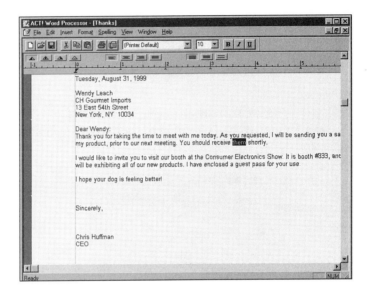

3. Type it, and the newly typed text replaces the highlighted word.

Checking a Word or Group of Words

If you want to check the spelling of a particular word, double-click the word so that it's highlighted and then click the **Spelling** menu and the **Check Selection** option. Or highlight a phrase, sentence, or paragraph, and click **Spelling** and **Check Selection**. ACT! then checks just the highlighted word or words.

Adding Specialized Words to the Dictionary

Many businesses have specialized language, or jargon, that might violate the normal rules of the spell checker. You have two choices on how to deal with this. You can add your specific words to the main dictionary of ACT! or you can create a dictionary with specialized terms:

1. Click the **Spelling** menu and choose **Create User Dictionary**.
2. Type a name for the dictionary. ACT! adds the .USR extension.
3. Click **Open**.

   Now that the file exists, the rest of these steps enable you to add your terms.

4. Click the **Spelling** menu and choose **Modify User Dictionary**. The User Dictionary dialog box appears.

The User Dictionary dialog box is for adding specialized words to the spell-checking process.

5. Click **Add** and type the word that's special to your industry. In the illustration, I added a strange name to the user dictionary.

The name "Tsongas" is added to the user dictionary.

There's no limit to the number of entries you can make to a user dictionary, nor to the number of specialized dictionaries you can create.

Turning Off Auto Suggest

If you're running ACT! on a laptop, as I often do, you'll find that the Auto Suggest feature slows down the process of spell checking significantly. With it turned off, you can still spell check. ACT! locates a questionable word and you can either figure out the correct spelling or click the Suggest option in the dialog box. ACT! dutifully finds what it thinks to be the correct word. To turn off Auto Suggest, follow these steps:

1. Click the **Edit** menu and choose **Preferences**.
2. Click the **Spelling** tab.
3. At the bottom, deselect the **Auto Suggest** check box.
4. Click **OK**.

From this point forward, Auto Suggest is off. You can turn it on manually when you run the spell checker.

Erasing an Entire Line

You may decide that the final line of the text of the letter is a little too cute, so you want to cut it. To do so, click and drag so that the entire line of text is highlighted. Press the **Delete** key, and the line is erased. (You could have used the **Edit** menu and **Cut** option, too.)

165

Undoing a Mistake

If you make a mistake while deleting, you can retrieve the deleted text if you immediately access the Edit menu and click the Undo option. Let's give it a try to see how it works:

1. Click and drag so that the body of the letter is highlighted.

2. Click the **Edit** menu and select **Cut**. Your screen should be blank.

3. Click the **Edit** menu again and the menu appears.

The Edit menu appears with Undo Cut as the first option.

4. Click the **Undo Cut** option. ACT! replaces the deleted text. The highlighting remains on so that you can further manipulate the text if necessary.

5. Click the mouse button to turn off the highlight.

The important thing to remember about using the Undelete option is that only the text most recently deleted can be retrieved. So if you delete the first line of a letter, and then delete a paragraph at the end of the letter, you can retrieve only the paragraph.

Finding and Replacing

Suppose your company changes the name of a product that you've used repeatedly in a long document. Sure, you could sit down, read through the document, and try to find every instance of the change, but that's what computers are supposed to do!

1. Open the document you want to change.

2. Click the **Edit** menu and select **Find and Replace**. The Find and Replace dialog appears.

The Find and Replace dialog box lets you make global changes to your documents.

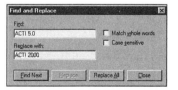

Use the settings as described here:

➤ **Find**   Enter a word, phrase, or just a couple of characters for the match you want to find.

➤ **Replace With**   This is an optional entry. If you want to find only a certain piece of text, skip this entry and click **OK**. If you're certain of the replacement, enter the text or characters here.

➤ **Match Whole Words**   If you want ACT! to locate only characters surrounded by spaces or punctuation, click this box. Otherwise, if you enter the letters <u>act</u> as the match, words such as <u>act</u>ive, <u>act</u>ion, and tr<u>act</u> will be found as possible replacements.

➤ **Case Sensitive**   This is a great feature for finding and replacing words that should or should not be capitalized. When this box is checked, ACT! matches not only the characters in the Find box, but the capitalization, too.

If you click the **Find Next** button, ACT! locates the first matching entry and high-lights it. At that point you can click the **Find Next** button again, click **Replace**, and the change is made. Or you can click **Replace All** and every occurrence is changed.

Use the **Find Next** button to check that your parameters for the change are correct. Then go with the **Replace All** button. If you mess up, click the **Edit** menu and the **Undo** option and all will be well again.

Changing Text Styles

Because of the capabilities of Windows, changing the format of text is as easy as can be. You can change the style (regular, bold, italic, and so on) of a word, sentence, or paragraph, or change the font for the entire letter. ACT! always leaves the highlight-ing on after you make an adjustment, allowing you to make as many changes as you want without having to click and drag the same text over and over. Follow these steps to change specific text:

1. Click and drag over the text that you want to change. In the sample letter, the words Consumer Electronics Show are selected.

2. Click the **Format** menu and select **Font**.

3. Click **1 pt.**; the words are increased in size to 1 point and remain highlighted.

4. You can make other text enhancements as well. For instance, you might decide to make the words bold, too, so you click the **Bold** option.

*To make the words bold, choose **Bold** from the **Font Style** drop-down list.*

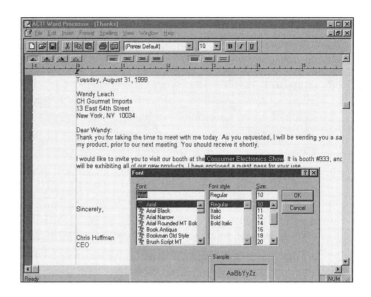

For display purposes, you can also change the color of specific text. (And someday, when we all have color laser printers, it will print in color.)

The finished text is shown here after you've made your text style changes.

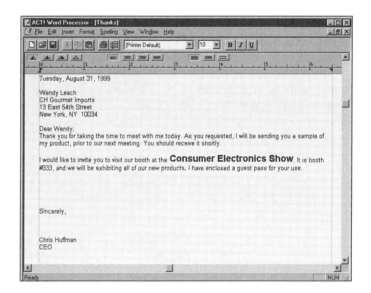

Resaving the Edited Letter

You can save the letter so that you can recall it later. Click the **File** menu and choose **Save**. ACT! assumes that you want to save the letter under the same filename. If you want to save under a different name, click **File** and **Save As**, and type a different filename.

Saving a Letter to a Different Drive or Directory

ACT!'s installation program creates 10 folders for different file types. One of those folders is called Documents and it is the default folder for all your letter correspondence. To save a letter to a drive or folder other than the default, follow these steps:

1. Click the **File** menu and select **Save As**.
2. At the top of the dialog box is a small folder icon. Every time you click the folder icon, you move up one directory level and you see different folders, until you get to the main directory, which lists My Computer and any disk drives you have.
3. Click the folder to which you want to save the file, or click the disk drive.
4. Click **Save**.

Saving a Document as an RTF File

Every Windows-based word processor can open a Rich Text Format (RTF) file. This format removes some complex document formatting, such as tables and embedded graphics, but retains bolding, underlining, font color, and so on. So, if you want share a document with other users, save it in RTF format.

1. Click the **File** menu and select **Save As**.
2. If you need to save the file to a different drive or folder, make the necessary entries.
3. Type in a filename.
4. Click the **Save as Type** box.
5. One of the types listed is Rich Text Format (rtf); click it.
6. Click **Save**.

Changing Margins, Layout, and Line Spacing

Using the Thanks letter, let's look at how we can change the page-layout features. Click the **Format** menu to begin.

The Format menu includes options for setting page margins, paragraph attributes, and more.

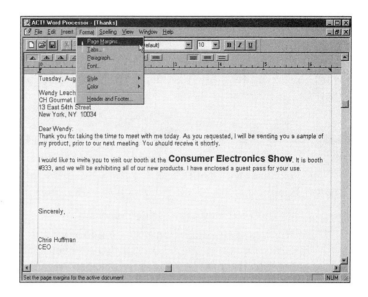

Formatting the Letter

Along the top of the ruler are symbols that are used to adjust tabs, justification, and line spacing. You can also adjust these settings from the Format menu, but it's easier in most cases to use the mouse and the ruler. When you click one of the buttons, text you subsequently type is affected by the new setting. Or, you can highlight text and then click the appropriate button to make the change.

Setting Page Margins

Clicking the Page Margins option opens the dialog box in which you can set the margins for the top, bottom, left, and right edges of the document. The default measure is set in inches, but you can change that by opening the Edit menu and selecting the Preferences option. In the Preferences dialog box, select the measure you prefer. You can also access this dialog box by right-clicking and selecting Preferences from the shortcut menu.

Setting Tabs

The symbol on the far left of the ruler is the left tab, which is the default tab setting. The next symbol is the center tab, which centers text on the tab. The next symbol is the right tab. This aligns text on the right.

The last button is the decimal tab. Use this to build columns of numbers that are lined up based on the position of the decimal point. The decimal tab is great for aligning a column of numbers in a letter. This illustration shows an example of a decimal tab.

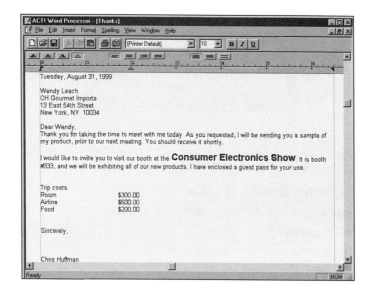

A decimal tab makes sense for dollar figures.

A decimal tab lines up each item in a list based on the position of the decimal. To set a decimal tab, take these steps:

1. Click the decimal tab button.
2. Position the mouse pointer on the ruler where you want the tab set.
3. Click the mouse button. The decimal tab symbol appears on the ruler line.

In the sample letter, I inserted the numbers by pressing the Tab key and then typing the numbers with a decimal point. I continued to press the Tab key and add numbers. The tab symbol on the ruler line reflects the line in which the insertion point is positioned. After a decimal tab has been set, to have the tab (or any special tab format) carry over to the next line of the letter, you must press **Enter** at the end of the line. If you use the mouse to move to a different line and then begin typing, the decimal tab is turned off. ACT! assumes that you want to continue using the format as long as you press **Enter** or continue typing, so ACT! word-wraps to the next line. Then, when you're in the column of numbers, the decimal tab appears on the ruler; when it's in a different paragraph and no special tab has been set, it doesn't appear.

Many people like to add a leader (dotted or dashed lines, for instance) in front of tab stops—especially on a column of numbers, so it's easier to tell which number fits each category.

Select your tab stops and any leader in the Tabs dialog box.

Click the tab setting you want and click **OK**. In the sample decimal tab setting, no leader type was included in the format. To add fill, follow these steps:

1. Highlight the lines of text that have the tab formatting.
2. Click the **Format** menu and select the **Tabs** option.
3. Click the Leader option you want.
4. Click **OK**. The leader type should be applied, as shown here.

Decimal tabs with leading are easy for your eye to follow.

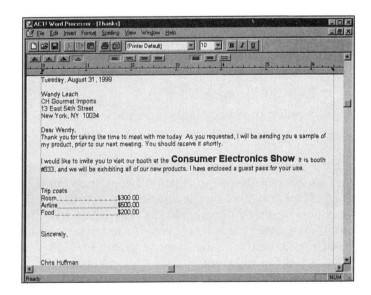

Removing a Tab Setting

Click the tab and drag it down and to the right, off the ruler. The tab is removed. Keep in mind that when a tab is removed, it's removed for only the active line—that is, the line in which the insertion point is located. No other existing tabs are affected.

Aligning Text

The next set of buttons on the ruler is the text-justification buttons. The first button—left align—is the default. That means that the text is lined up on the left edge of the document and ragged on the right. The second button centers text on the page. The third button right-aligns the text so that the right edge is lined up with the right margin and the left edge is ragged. The last button is the full-justification button. Full justification adjusts the text as it appears in a newspaper column, lined up on both margins, and should be applied before typing in the text for the best results. Using the Thanks letter, let's apply some of the ruler options:

1. Click and drag over the inside address.
2. Click the center-align button. The text moves to the center of the page.

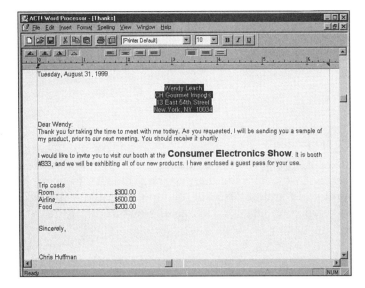

The inside address is center aligned.

Changing the Line Spacing

The last three buttons on the ruler are for changing the spacing of lines in the document. The default is single spacing, and you can change it by opening the **Format** menu and selecting the **Paragraph** option. From the Paragraph dialog box, select the spacing option you want. The other way to change the spacing is to type the text and then click and drag over the paragraph(s) that you want to change. Using the sample THANKS letter again, try these changes:

1. Click and drag over the first paragraph of the letter, highlighting it.
2. Click the **One and a Half** option button in the Spacing area of the dialog box. ACT! inserts the extra half space between the lines of text.
3. Click the **Double** option button. The text is separated again.

173

The text of the first paragraph is double spaced.

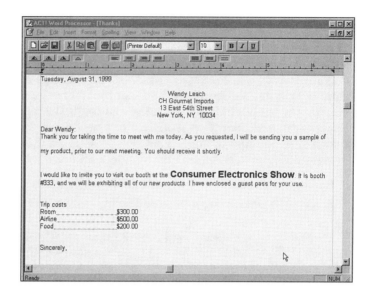

If you don't like the way the text looks, click the spacing you want.

Changing Page Margins

Under the 0 and the 6.5 on the ruler line is a tipped triangle. This symbol represents the left- and right-margin settings. To adjust the margins, click the triangle, drag it along the ruler to the position you want, and release the mouse button. If the insertion point is in a paragraph when you make the change, the text in the entire paragraph is reformatted to the new margin.

Changing the Paragraph Indent

If you prefer to indent the initial line of a paragraph, ACT! allows you to apply such a style. On the ruler at the left margin marker is a symbol that looks like an upside down T. Position the mouse pointer on the bottom of the symbol and drag it to the indent position. If the insertion point is positioned in a line of text, the text is reformatted.

Inserting the Date or Time

If you need a date or time stamp when a document is printed, open the **Insert** menu and select the appropriate option. If you also select Always Update, ACT! updates the stamp every time you print the document. That way, you can create several drafts of a document and be confident that you're working with the latest draft.

Adding a Header or Footer

The default top margin in ACT! letters is one inch. When you add a header, rather than using part of the margin space for the header, ACT! adds an additional half inch at the top of the document for the header. The insertion point moves to the header space, allowing you to enter the text you want printed on every page. The half-inch of space is good for three lines of text in the default type size of 10 points. You can use the date/time stamp in the header, too.

Click the **Format** menu and click **Header and Footer**. From the dialog box, select **Header** or **Footer** or both. ACT! adds the header/footer outline. After you're finished making the header entry, click the body of the letter to resume editing. All the formatting features, such as bold style, different fonts, and type size, can be used in the header the same way they are used in the body of the text.

You can also add a header/footer to a document to print text or page numbering. To add page numbers to a header/footer, open the **Insert** menu and click **Page Number**.

To delete a header or footer, open the **Format** menu, select the **Header and Footer** item, and click the option's check mark to deselect it.

Inserting a Hard Page Break

As you type a long document, ACT! automatically breaks the pages at the standard 66 lines per page. A gray bar appears on the screen and the insertion point jumps to the next page, allowing you to continue typing. With some documents, however, you might want to end a page before the automatic page break.

To insert a page break, position the insertion point where you want the new page to begin, click the **Insert** menu, and click the **Page Break** option.

Page Break Shortcut

To insert a page break quickly, just press **Shift+Enter**.

To delete a page break, point to the page break in the text and press the **Backspace** key. If a page break occurs within a sentence or paragraph that you want to keep together on one page, you can tell ACT! to format the document so that the items are kept together:

1. Click and drag over the sentence or paragraph that you want to keep with the following page.

2. Click the **Format** menu and select the **Paragraph** option. The Paragraph dialog box appears.

You can make changes to the paragraph formatting in the Paragraph dialog box.

3. Click the **Keep with Next** check box.

4. Click **OK**.

Printing Documents

After creating the letter, memo, or other document, printing it is a snap. Because you're working in the Windows environment, any document you want to print is sent to the Windows Print Manager. The Print Manager not only controls the printing, but acts as a buffer, allowing you to designate a long document for printing and then continue working while the Print Manager takes over the printing chore.

With the printer set up, turn your printer on and follow these steps:

1. Click the **File** menu and choose **Print**. The Print dialog box appears.

2. If you want to print selected pages in a document, click the **Page** button, click the **From** box, and enter the beginning page number. Then click the **To** box and specify the ending page number.

3. If the document is a draft, you can reduce the print quality and thereby the printing time by clicking the **Properties** button and specifying a lower dpi (dots per inch) setting.

4. If you want to print multiple copies, click the **Number of Copies** box and enter the number you want.

5. Click **OK**.

Decide how many copies you need in the Print dialog box.

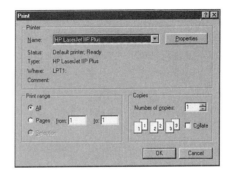

Attaching the Letter to the Contact Record

Besides asking if you want to print an envelope, ACT! prompts you to record a history for the letter and asks if the letter should be attached to the contact record. The Create History dialog box appears, as shown here.

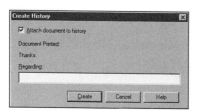

This dialog box appears after you print a letter.

Creating a history is always a good idea. Let ACT! remember what you have sent and when by typing a short note in the Regarding field. Attaching the letter to the contact record takes a further step. Clicking the Create button requires that you give the letter a name to save it as a file. The document is saved in the DOCUMENTS folder and the link is added to the Notes/History tab.

Because of this capability, and the long filenames that can be used to name a document, you don't have to create multiple folders for different types of documents.

This illustration shows the link on the Notes/History tab. Double-clicking the link opens the word processor and the document. If you are using Word to create a letter, the link is a small Word icon.

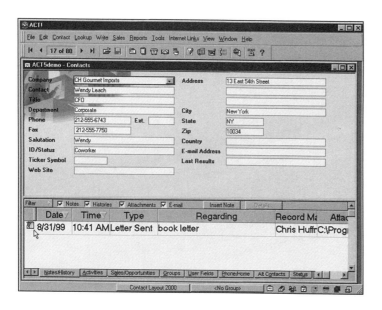

A Word attachment link on the Notes/History tab looks like this.

The Least You Need to Know

➤ To write a letter, open **Write** and select **Letter**.

➤ To send a fax to the current contact, click the **Quick Fax** icon.

➤ To send a mail-merged letter, open **Write** and select **Mail Merge**.

➤ Spell check a letter with the Spelling menu.

➤ To use Word as your default word processor, open the **Edit** menu and select **Preferences**.

"Experience is the name everyone gives to their mistakes."

Oscar Wilde

Chapter 12

Mail Merge, a.k.a. Form Letters

In This Chapter

➤ Creating a mail merge

➤ Printing mailing labels

➤ Opening an attached document

➤ Adding a template to the Write menu

Form letters are one of those tasks that computers are supposed to do so much more easily than people can. But for all their power, many word processors make you jump through lots of hoops before printing a batch of form letters. But since ACT!'s word processor is part of the program in which you keep your database, the process is fairly simple. In this chapter, you'll see how to create form letters, faxes, and email messages.

Creating a Mail Merge

If you've ever tried to create form letters with a word processor and a database, you know that you have to be a computer programmer to do so. Creating and printing a form letter using ACT! is the same as creating any other type of letter, except that you first create a form letter template, and then select the contacts to be included in the mailing. You can start a form letter by using an existing template, or start completely from scratch. The following steps use an existing template as a model:

1. Click the **Write** menu and select **Edit Document Template**. The dialog box with document templates appears.

Choose a document template from the Open dialog box.

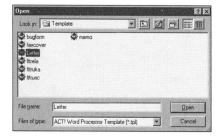

2. From the list of templates displayed, click **Letter** and click **Open**. The template appears.

The Letter template lets you whip up a quick form letter.

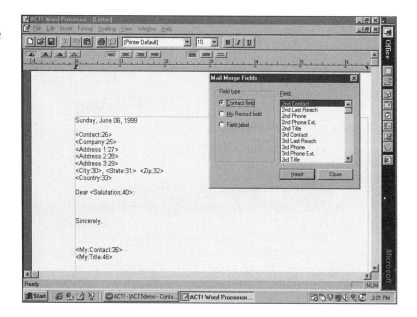

As you can see, ACT! inserts the current date and the names of the fields from which data is pulled from the contact record. At this point, you can type the text you want in the form letter. The Mail Merge Fields dialog box allows you to add a Contact Field, Field Label, or My Record Field into the letter. For example, if you were a participant at a trade show and wanted to send a letter to all the contacts you met, you could easily do so. The letter would be much better if you included the product or service that the contact was interested in (called inserting a variable). Using the Mail Merge Fields dialog box, you can specify that information from a field in the contact record is inserted when the letter is printed. Scroll through the field names in the dialog box to locate the field name that has the information you want inserted into the letter. For example, if you want the name of a product that the prospect was interested in, and the product name was typed into User 1, click **User 1**. The field name appears at the insertion point. Here, you can see a sample form letter.

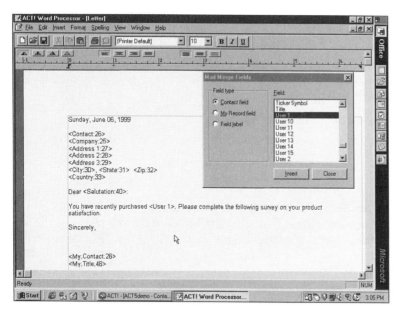

Sample letter with variables inserted for the contact, address, and product.

Field Names and Mail Merging

When you change a field name, for example, User 1 to Product, ACT! shows you the new name in the Mail Merge Fields dialog box. This makes it easy to find the field you want. Read more in Chapters 16, "Customizing Your Layout," and 17, "Creating New Fields," for modifying and creating fields.

Body text and a variable have been added. The information in User 1 is the product the client expressed interest in. When the letter is printed, the name of the product is inserted and properly formatted. In addition, the phone and fax numbers of the sender are inserted. This is accomplished by clicking the **My Record Field** option button in the Mail Merge Fields dialog box and inserting the field names.

When you type the form letter, you might want to move the Mail Merge Fields dialog box or remove it from view. Move it by clicking the title bar and dragging the dialog box out of the way. Or click the **Close** (×) button in the upper-right corner of the dialog box to remove it completely. Reopen the dialog box by choosing **Insert** and selecting the **Mail Merge** option.

Saving the New Template

Before saving the new letter template, take a moment to spell-check the text. ACT! stops on the user-field variables you've inserted. *Save the template using a new filename!* This is important. If you save the template as LETTER.TPL, every time you want to write a letter, this document will appear.

1. Click the **File** menu and choose **Save As**.
2. In the Save As dialog box, enter a name. In this example, the name is CON-SUMER.
3. Click **Save**.

ACT! automatically adds the TPL extension. The original template, LETTER.TPL, is undisturbed because you saved the modified template with a different filename. When you're ready to actually print the form letters, the CUSTOMER.TPL file is available, too.

Testing the Form Letter

Before you actually print all the form letters, give the template a spin around the block by merging it with the current contact record:

1. Click the **File** menu and choose **Mail Merge**. The Mail Merge dialog box appears.

The Mail Merge dialog box has options for the destination of the document, who is going to receive it, and which template is to be used.

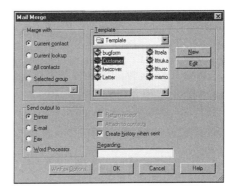

2. Click **Current Contact** to create a single copy of the letter.
3. Click **Printer** as the destination.
4. Click **OK**.

ACT! inserts the field information from the current contact into the template. Read the letter. If it is acceptable, you are finished. If not, use the **Write** menu to select the template and make changes. Do not forget to save it again.

Printing a Form Letter

You've already created the template. The next step is to look up those contacts to whom you want to send the form letter:

1. Use the **Lookup** menu to create a subset of contacts.
2. Open the **Write** menu and select **Mail Merge**. The Open File dialog box appears with Templates as the file type.
3. Select the template you want to use and click **Open**.
4. In the Mail Merge dialog box, click **Current Lookup** and select **Printer**.
5. Click **OK**.

To print envelopes or labels for the letters, see the "Creating Mailing Labels" section in this chapter.

Printing a Form Letter as Email

One of the irritating things about email is that, when you forward a message, the entire list of recipients is included in the header of the email you receive. But, by using a word processing template in ACT!, the email looks personalized in the same way a letter does.

To send mass email, prepare the document template just as you did for a letter. The only difference is at printing time. In the Mail Merge dialog box, select **E-mail** for the output. The other options are active as well: Return Receipt, which lets you know the email was delivered; Attach to Contacts, which actually attaches the entire text to each contact record; Create History When Sent, which records that the email was sent; and the Regarding field into which you should type the gist of the email (this Regarding field information is included in the History entry).

Printing a Form Letter to WinFax

To print mass faxes, you must have faxing software installed, preferably WinFax. I recommend 200 faxes as the top limit for mass faxing, because of the time involved with sending that many. A third-party service, listed in Chapter 26, "ACT! Add-on Products," can send faxes in greater quantities at an affordable price, using the document you create and your list of contact records.

When you select fax as the output, the WinFax option becomes active. Click the **WinFax Options** button to see the WinFax Options dialog box. Select a cover page if desired, and then click the **Schedule** button to choose a time for the send.

Printing to a Word Processor

The Word Processor output option in the Mail Merge dialog box is designed for the situation in which you want to preview each individual document before sending it.

After clicking **OK**, the word processor appears and shows each individual document, one after another so that you must scroll down to see them.

Creating Mailing Labels

To print the mailing labels for your form letters, you must first return to the contact screen. Assuming that you still have the same lookup of contacts selected, follow these steps:

1. Open the **File** menu and click the **Print** option. A dialog box appears that gives you the opportunity to print address books, labels, and reports.

2. Choose **Labels** from the **Printout Type** drop-down list. When you do, ACT! lists the label templates available. The most common is the three-up Avery 5160 label, but you can choose whatever label type you have.

3. Click **OK**.

4. Next, ACT! presents you with the Run Labels dialog box, which you can use to filter the labels. Two things to note at this point: If you are printing labels to go with a mail merge, you should have created the same lookup as when you created the letters. So, you would naturally choose the **Current Lookup** as the report to print. Second, you can begin printing the labels at any position on the paper. To set the start position, click the **Position** tab and select where ACT! should begin.

Adding a Template to the Write Menu

It's a simple task to add a template you've created to the Write menu:

1. Click the **Write** menu and select the **Modify Menu** option. The Custom dialog box appears.

2. Click the **Add Item** button. The Add Custom Menu Item dialog box appears.

3. Type in a description for the document. In this example, I used Response to Trade Show, and COSUMER.TPL for the filename. If you forget the name of the file, click the **Browse** button to see a list of the template files. The finished entry is shown here.

The Consumer letter file-name appears in the Add Custom Menu Item dialog box.

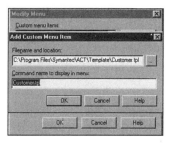

4. Click **OK**. The Custom dialog box reappears. If you want to, you can add a solid line to separate the custom items.

5. Click **OK**.

6. Click the **Write** menu. The new customized letter appears at the bottom of the menu.

To test the newly added menu option, select a contact, click the **Write** menu, and then select the **Customer.tpl** option. The word processor opens and the appropriate data is inserted into the letter. From there, print the letter.

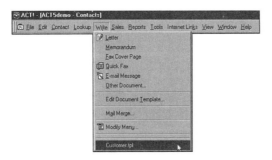

The Response to Trade Show letter item appears at the bottom of the Write menu.

This example of modifying an existing template barely scratches the surface of all the kinds of specialized documents you can design. Also, if you aren't satisfied with the templates that appear as the defaults, such as FAX.TPL, you can add or subtract what you want to the template and resave it. Then, when you open the **Write** menu and select the **Fax Cover** option, your templates appear.

Changing the Default Letter Template

The first change you should make is to increase the size of the type in the letter template to make it easier to read:

1. Click **Write** and choose **Edit Document Template**.

2. Select **Letter.**

3. With the letter template onscreen, open the **Edit** menu and choose the **Select All** option, and then from the toolbar, increase the point size to 14.

4. Click **File** and **Save**. When ACT! asks if you want to overwrite the file, click **Yes**.

Adding Your Company Logo to Letters and Faxes

Customize your documents with your company logo and eliminate the need to have expensive stationery in the printer at printing time.

1. Use any graphics program to open your logo file. For example, you can use the Paint program in Windows 98 that is listed under Accessories.

2. With the graphic open, select it by drawing a box around it with the graphics tools. Here, I have opened my logo and drawn a box around it.

A box has been drawn around the logo, ready for copying.

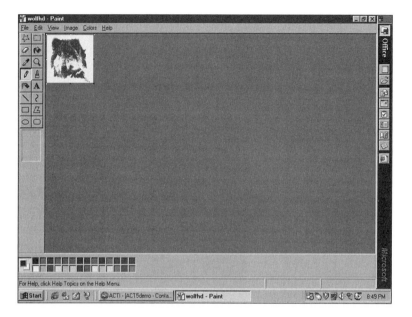

3. Use the **Copy** option to copy the logo onto the Windows Clipboard.
4. In ACT!, click the **Write** menu and select the **Edit Document Template** option.
5. Select **Letter**. When the template is onscreen, move the insertion point to the place you want the logo inserted.
6. Click the **Paste** button on the toolbar or select the **Edit** menu and click the **Paste** option.

I tried inserting my logo into the body of the letter above the inside address, which I moved down the page before placing the logo, and then decided to insert it into the header. This task is easy. Open the **Insert** menu and select **Header/Footer**. When the border indicating the header appears, click in the upper-left corner and then paste your logo. More likely than not, it won't fit, so you'll need to increase the size of the header. Click **Insert** and **Header/Footer** again and click the small up arrow until you have plenty of room. Another adjustment you will probably have to make is to decrease the size of the margin at the top of the page. In this illustration, the wolf logo has been placed and the business information added.

This technique works for all the templates and any documents you create. To add the logo to your fax cover, open the template and proceed.

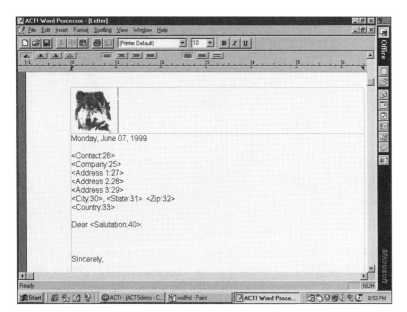

The Wolf logo and the business address have been placed in the header.

Printing Envelopes

Many users of ACT! have problems getting envelopes to print properly. Envelopes are printed via a report that's created by, and can be modified by, the ACT! Report Writer. When you print a letter, ACT! asks you if you want to print an envelope. ACT! then accesses the default ENVELOPE.ENV file. It should work with your printer. If it doesn't print the information you want or doesn't print on the envelope where you want it to, you need to modify the template:

1. Click the **File** menu and choose **Print**.
2. From the Print dialog box, pull down the **Printout Type** list and select **Envelopes**.
3. The most common envelope is a #10, so that is the report ACT! uses to print an envelope following the printing of a letter. Click **#10**.
4. Click **Edit Template**.
5. Click **OK**. With the template onscreen, adjust the margins by opening the **File** menu and selecting the **Page Setup** option. Change the printing orientation—from portrait to landscape—by clicking the **Printer Setup** button.

By comparing the output from the first envelope and the edited envelope, you should be able to get an idea of where the adjustments need to be made. Believe me, ACT! *does* print envelopes properly; it just takes a little fiddling to get there.

187

Attaching the Letter to the Contact Record, Later

Suppose you created a letter or other document and forgot to attach it at the time, or in the case of a memo, you are not prompted to attach it and now want that document linked to the contact record.

1. Look up the contact record to which you want to create a link.

2. Open the **Contact** menu and select **Attach File**. The Attach file dialog box opens.

3. At this point, you must browse to the folder that has the document. In ACT!'s case it is the C:\ProgramFiles\Symantec\ACT\Document folder.

4. Double-click the filename.

ACT! creates the link on the Notes/History tab.

As you may have guessed, the foregoing technique works with *any* type of file. You can attach spreadsheet files, PowerPoint presentation files, or any file that you want. But, you must have the program that you created the file with on your hard drive, for the link to work. So, if you attached a Lotus 1-2-3 spreadsheet file, but 1-2-3 is not on your hard drive anywhere, the link cannot work.

Creating a Memo

Creating a memo is identical to creating a letter. Look up the person to whom you want to send the memo, and then open the **Write** menu and select **Memo**. The word processor starts and the memo template is filled for you.

Creating a Fax Cover Page

In the past, everyone had standalone machines and it was deemed necessary to have a cover sheet that detailed the contents of the fax. Today this is archaic, but survives. When you want to send a fax in ACT!, open the **Write** menu and select **Fax Cover Page**. ACT! transfers the requisite information—whom the fax is from and to whom it is intended. Type the number of pages and the subject. If you have WinFax installed, you can fax directly from your desktop.

1. Click the **Fax** icon in the toolbar.

2. WinFax starts and takes over the process of actually sending the fax. The WinFax dialog box appears when you begin to send.

Enter the information that you want recorded. If you choose to attach the fax to the contact record, it can be saved as a word-processed file or as a WinFax file. If you save it as a WinFax file, it can be viewed later using the WinFax viewer.

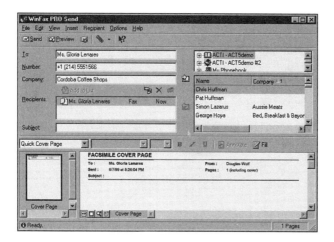

The WinFax dialog box appears, requesting information for the fax send.

Opening a Document That Is Attached to a Record

If you have created attachments to a record, the next step is to open the attachments. This process is simple:

1. Look up the contact record that has the attachment.

2. Click the **Notes History** tab.

3. Check the **Filter** button to make sure that the **Date Range** includes the time the fax was attached. If you still don't see the attachment, click the **Select Users** button to make sure your name (or the person who actually made the attachment) is selected.

4. Double-click the attachment's icon at the far left. The program that created the file starts and the document is shown.

Creating a QuickFax

QuickFax is used to open WinFax and send a fax to the current contact, or to the current contact and others in your ACT! database. WinFax opens on the desktop. (You must have WinFax installed for this option to work.) Open the **Write** menu and select **QuickFax**.

The current contact record's company name, contact name, and fax number are inserted. The list of the names and companies from the ACT! database appears on the right side of the WinFax window. Above the name and company is a list of the databases that ACT! can access as a phonebook.

The current contact infor-
mation appears in the
WinFax window when
you select QuickFax from
the Write menu.

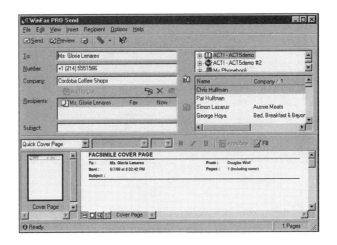

You can scroll the list to locate additional recipients of the fax. The default sort is by last name in ascending order (ABC...). Re-sort the list of names or companies by clicking the column header.

To add an additional recipient, click the name or company and click the words **Add to List** in the **Recipients** field.

Type text in the **Subject** field and it is automatically added to the fax page.

Next, type the text you want on the fax. To see the typing better, right-click and select a lower number, such as 50%, from the pop-up menu. The text processor in WinFax includes a spell checker and different fonts.

Send the QuickFax (or faxes) by clicking the **Send** button.

Accessing Other Document Templates

If you have a multitude of document templates, you cannot put them all on the **Write** menu. To access other templates, open the **Write** menu and select the **Other Document option**. ACT! opens the Open dialog box with a list of existing templates.

Opening a Saved Document

You cannot open a saved document directly from the Write menu. To open a saved document, use this method:

1. Open the **File** menu and select **Open**. The Open dialog box appears. The default type of file to open is a database.

2. Change the file type by pulling down the list in the **Files of Type** field.

3. Select **ACT! Word Processor Document**, if that is the word processor you are using, or choose **Microsoft Word**. ACT! automatically changes the folder it is searching to the Document folder.

4. Click the name of the document you want to open.

5. Click **Open**. The word processor opens and the document is displayed.

Using Microsoft Word as Your Default Word Processor

You may be in the position in which you are forced to use Word to create documents or maybe you simply prefer to use Word. If so, a couple of considerations are worth mentioning.

First, ACT! ships with Word-specific templates for a letter, fax, and memo. The key idea is that you cannot take existing templates in Word and make them the default templates for letters, memos, and faxes. You must use the templates that ACT! supplies as the starting point. So, if you already have Word documents that you want to use in ACT! as templates, use the Word letter template that ACT! provides, cut and paste your text into the template, and then use the **Save As** option on the **File** menu, to create a new name for the template.

When you are editing a template in Word via ACT!, you can access the fields from the ACT! database.

1. Open the **Write** menu and select **Edit Document Template**. Word starts and the template appears.

2. Open the **Insert** menu.

3. Choose **ACT! Mail-Merge Fields** at the bottom of the **Insert** menu. The Mail Merge fields dialog box opens. Insert the fields in the same way as you would for the ACT! word processor.

Microsoft Word Date Format Problems

If you are trying to write a letter in Word via ACT!, and the date field is printed as "Day of Week" "Month" "Day" "Year", you need to make the following change:

1. Close ACT!.

2. Click the Windows **Start** button, select **Settings**, and then select **Control Panel**.

3. From the Control Panel dialog box, double-click **Regional Settings**.

4. Click the **Date** Tab.

5. Change the format to read MMMM, dd, yyyy in the Long Date Format, and then click **OK**.

6. Open ACT!.

7. Open the **Write** menu, select **Edit Document Template**, select the letter template, and then click **OK**.

8. Highlight and delete the date line from the template.

9. Open the **Insert** menu, and then select **Date and Time**.

10. Check **Update Automatically** and choose the correct date format.

11. Click **OK**.

12. Open the **File** menu, select **Save**, and then exit the template document.

The History and Print Envelopes Dialog Boxes Do Not Appear

Have you written a letter from ACT! using Microsoft Word 97 and printed it, only to find that the dialog boxes prompting you to create a history and print an envelope do not appear? Does this happen even though you have enabled the option to print an envelope in ACT!'s Preferences? However, both boxes appear when printing in the ACT! word processor, right?

Follow these steps in Word:

1. Open the **Tools** menu, select **Templates**, and then choose **Add-ins**.

2. Under **Global Templates and Add-ins**, uncheck any checked items.

3. Click **OK**. You should now get the boxes after printing a letter.

Creating Forms Using ACT! and Microsoft Word

Many users have asked how they can attach a form to a contact record. The idea is to create a form letter with spaces for the reader to fill in requested information. You may also want to print the form with the merge fields underlined. That way, if any fields in the records are blank, an area will be created for someone to write in the information after the form has been printed. An example would be an order form. First, make a paper-and-pencil outline of what should be on the form.

Adding Underlining in a Word Form

In this procedure, there are two types of underlined fields: those that will be filled in by the customer, and those that contain information from your database. You might want spaces for database fields underlined, so if information is missing in your database, you or the customer could fill it in manually.

1. In ACT!, open the **File** menu and select **New**.
2. Select **Word 95-2000 Template** and click **OK**.
3. Save your new template using a unique filename.
4. Type any text that precedes a fill-in field.
5. At the point where a field begins, turn on underlining.
6. If you are inserting a field from your database, continue with step 7 and stop. If you are inserting a blank line for the customer to fill in, skip down to step 8.
7. Insert the desired field from the Mail Merge Fields dialog box.

Fitting the Fields with Long Names

If the field name is too long and you need to insert more than one database field on one line, delete only the field name from within the brackets. (Leave the brackets as well as the colon and field code.) For example: `[[City:30]]` `[[State:31]]` `[[Zip:32]]` would look like `[[:30]]` `[[:31]]` `[[:32]]` when the field names are removed.

8. (Remember: These steps are for inserting a blank line for the customer to fill in ONLY.) On the ruler, insert a tab where you want the underline to stop. Be sure you allow sufficient space for the information to be written in, if necessary.
9. Press the **Tab** key, and a line is drawn to the tab you just set.
10. Turn off underlining. You are finished with this field.
11. Continue with additional body text, and return to step 4 if you want to add a new field.
12. Save your changes.

When you merge this template, the document creates either the merged fields underlined or a blank line extended to the tab.

The Least You Need to Know

➤ You can aid your marketing campaigns by creating form letters, faxes, or emails.

➤ You can print mailing labels from your ACT! contact list.

➤ You can attach frequently used templates to ACT!'s Write menu for quick access.

"Experience is the name everyone gives to their mistakes."

Oscar Wilde

Chapter 13

Printing Labels, Envelopes, Address Books, and Calendars

"Even if you are on the right track, you will get run over if you just sit there."

Will Rogers

ACT!'s capability to send custom letters to the people in your contact database is a valuable business tool. It's also a time saver, because it inserts the contact's name and address for you in the body of the letter. ACT! uses that information in other ways, too.

Printing Labels

After creating a letter, ACT! asks you if you want to print an envelope. But, you might have a situation in which you need to print an individual label or a series of labels, as opposed to an envelope.

Labels for Mailing

The best businesses keep in regular touch with their customers via direct mail. In my ACT! consulting practice, I send a monthly newsletter to all my accounts. ACT! makes the printing of the labels easy. I have all my clients in a group (see Chapter 15, "Working with Groups"). I access the group and then print labels on the Avery 5160 form. My daughter earns her allowance by folding, labeling, and applying the postage to the newsletters.

1. Look up the name of the contact for whom you need to print a label.
2. Open the **File** menu and select **Print**.

The Run Label dialog box lets you print a label for a single contact, the current Lookup or all contacts in the database.

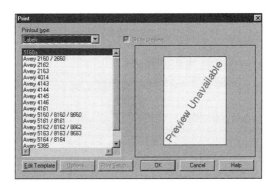

3. From the Print dialog box, pull down the list in the **Printout Type** field.
4. Select **Labels**.
5. ACT! displays the list of preformatted label types.
6. Select the label type that you have.
7. Click **OK**. The Run Label dialog box appears.
8. On the General tab, you want to choose whether to print labels for All Contacts, the Current Contact, or for the Current Lookup. You can send the output to the printer or to a screen preview of the labels. If you send output to the preview, you can then proceed to print after reviewing the labels. The Included Data for Contacts setting is not used in this situation; it is for reports. Last, the setting to Exclude the My Record should be left as is, unless you want to print a label for yourself.

9. Click **OK** and the label printing task is sent to Windows. You will see the Print dialog box, which gives you the opportunity to select the correct printer. Make sure you have loaded the printer with the correct label stock, and away you go.

Mail Merge Labels

The process for printing labels for a mail merge starts by creating the correct lookup—that is, the lookup you used to create the mail-merged letters. After that, when the Run dialog box appears, select **Current Lookup** as the set of records.

Customizing Labels

To make the labels work, ACT! does not allow you to make wholesale changes to the labels. But, you can add and delete fields from a label. To change the fields on a label:

1. Open the **File** menu.
2. Select **Print**.
3. From the dialog box, pull down the menu and select labels.
4. From the list of labels, select the one you want to modify.
5. Click the **Edit Template** button. The label editing window appears.

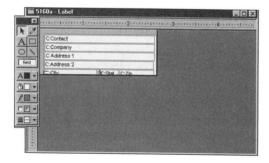

The label editing window includes a floating tool palette.

At this point, you can add or delete a field from the label and tinker with the label margins for the entire page, although I do not recommend that you change any margins unless you have a consistent problem with labels printing incorrectly. One of the changes that many ACT! users make to a label is to add the Address 2 field to the label, after the Address 1 field.

1. First, shorten the Address 1 field by clicking the right margin so that the mouse pointer is transformed into a two-headed arrow, pointing left and right.
2. Hold the left mouse button down and drag it to the right until the Address 1 field is two-thirds shorter.

3. Click the **Field** tool in the tool palette. This allows you to draw the new field.

4. At the right edge of the Address 1 field, click and drag so that the field drawing tool creates a rectangle that fills the space all the way to the right margin of the label.

5. Release the mouse button. ACT! opens the list of available fields.

With the new field drawn on the label, the Field List dialog box appears onscreen.

6. Scroll the list to locate the Address 2 field and select it.

7. Click **Add**.

8. Close the Field List dialog box.

9. Click the **Tool Palette** pointer tool, so the mouse is back to normal mode.

Test the results of adding the new field. If you are in the ACT! 2000 demo database, you can see a label in preview that has an entry in the Address 2 field that now appears on the label. The illustration shows the zoomed view of the new label.

Here's a zoomed view of the print preview for the modified label.

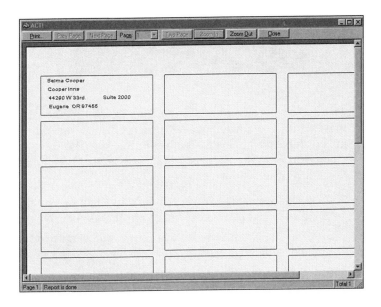

1. Open the **File** menu and select **Run**.

2. In the dialog box that appears, click the radio buttons for **Current Contact** and for **Send Output To**, select **Preview**, and then click **OK**.

3. Click the **Zoom In** button twice to see the results.

If you are satisfied with the modification, close the preview and open the **File** menu. Then, either select **Save**, to overwrite the old format, or **Save As**, to create a new label definition.

Changing the Field Properties

There are many properties that you can modify, but for this example, two are most relevant. To see how to modify a field property, close Print Preview from the previous example.

1. Click a field.

2. Right-click to open the pop-up menu. Take a look at the variety of attributes you can apply to a field.

3. From the menu, select **Properties**. The Properties dialog box appears.

The Object Properties dialog box allows you to modify the attributes to a particular field on the label.

There are four tabs in this dialog box. The Format tab is the default and the Close Up Blank Space attribute is your focus. Right-click the words **Close Up Blank Space** to open the help text.

Help! I Need Somebody!

In any dialog box, you can right-click your mouse to see a help menu with the words "What's This?" This menu can identify the various components of the dialog box and their function. However, not every part of every dialog box has a help topic associated with it.

This attribute adjusts the length of the field based upon the entry in the contact record. So, if the entry in the Address 1 field is 20 characters, ACT! allocates exactly that much space. If the entry is only 10 characters, then that is the allocated space. So the field following—in this example, Address 2—is shifted to the left, making the printed label more professional looking. In the sample label, the Address 2 field was pushed to the far right, leaving a good deal of blank space between the two entries. Turning this attribute on would cause ACT! to close that gap between the two pieces of data, which in this example would be a smart thing to do.

1. Click the check box in front of **Close Up Blank Space**.
2. Click **Apply,** and then **OK**.

Run Print Preview again and you can see the difference in the formatting. ACT! moves the characters from the field following to the left.

Printing Envelopes

Printing envelopes usually happens automatically. After printing a letter, ACT! asks if you want to print the envelope. This is a setting that you can turn off, by clicking the **Edit** menu, choosing the **Preferences** option, and deselecting the appropriate check box on the General tab. From that point on, ACT! won't ask you to print an envelope.

However, you might want to simply print an envelope without printing a letter. If you do, the steps are as follows:

1. Open the **File** menu and select **Print**. (Don't forget to insert an envelope in the printer tray.)
2. From the Print dialog box, pull down the list and select **Envelope**.
3. Select the type of envelope—#10 being the most common—and click **OK**.

4. The Run Envelope dialog box appears. Select **Current Contact** and the output should go the printer.

5. Click **OK**. The printing task is taken over by Windows, and you can select which printer you want to use.

Automating Envelope Printing

It is easy to add envelope printing to the Reports menu, but the procedure is not obvious. Printing an envelope is actually a specific type of report. But, unlike most reports in ACT!, the envelope reports are named with a different extension. To see this process in action, follow these steps:

1. Open the **Reports** menu.

2. Click the **Modify Menu** option. You get the Modify Menu dialog box.

3. Click the **Add Item** button. Your screen should resemble the one shown here.

Add Custom Menu Item dialog box.

4. At the far right of the Filename and Location field is a box with 3 tiny dots. Click the box.

5. You get the Open dialog box, which lists the report files in the Reports folder. Now here is where they really get clever. Do you see anything that might indicate an envelope-printing routine?

6. Click the drop-down arrow at the far right of the **Files of Type** field.

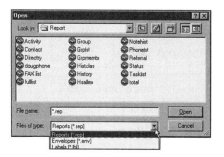

The Files of Type list opens in the Open dialog box.

7. Select the ***.env** option. The report files that print envelopes are yours.

8. Click the **10**, and then **Open**.

9. Returning to the Add Custom Menu Item dialog box, replace the name 10.env with something like Envelope # 10.

10. Click **OK** twice.

Now, open the **Reports** menu and select the new menu choice. The report will run until the Run Envelope dialog box appears, in which you make printing choices.

Maybe a Macro?

The foregoing process might be okay, but to make it even easier, you can record a macro to make printing an envelope a one-button exercise. Recording macros is easy in ACT!, but keeping them working can be a problem. As an example, I recently changed my video settings from small fonts to large. So when I tried to run my envelope printing macro, I was chagrined to find that I could not. Why? Because I had used mouse clicks as part of the macro and they are determined by the screen location of what I was selecting—the Print option on the file menu for example—which had now shifted screen location due to the change in font size.

Techno Talk

Macros Eliminate Repetition

Computers are supposed to make our lives easier and automate repetitive actions. A macro is simply a computer file that records the steps taken in a program to perform a task. So instead of clicking 15 times to print an envelope, you record the process in a macro file and then click one time to start the ball rolling.

To record an envelope-printing macro, take the following steps:

1. Open the **Tools** menu and select **Record Macro**. On a piece of paper, write the keystroke Alt+F5.

2. In the Record macro dialog box, type the name Envelope # 10.

3. In the **Description** field, type **Prints Envelope**.

4. In the **Record Events** field, select **Everything**.

5. At this point, repeat the steps you just covered that are needed to print an envelope, and ACT! will record them for later use. To avoid the problem I described a second ago, you'll want to use keystrokes wherever you can. For example, instead of clicking the File menu, open it by pressing **Alt+F**. Some printing steps require a mouse action, though—opening a pull-down menu, for example.

6. At the point where the envelope starts printing, press **Alt+F5** to stop the recording process. (I told you to write that down because the next time you want to record a macro, you might forget how to stop recording.)

7. To run the macro, open the **Tools** menu and select the **Run Macro** option. You are given a dialog box that lists any macros you created. Select **Prints Envelope** and sit back and let it run.

If everything goes as planned, you have a macro that obviates your having to click, click, click ad nauseaum simply to print an envelope.

Editing the Return Address on the Envelope

The return address on an envelope is pulled from the information on the My Record. On a network, the return address works the same way—the login username is used to create the return address. However, your company might have already gone to the expense of having company envelopes printed—and if so, they probably want them to be used. In that case, you can remove the return address. Even better, you could remove the return address, and then move your name so that it prints underneath the company information.

To remove or edit the return address on the envelope template, do the following:

1. Open the **File** menu and select **Print**.
2. Click the **Printout Type** drop-down list and select **Envelopes**.
3. The default envelope is #10. Select it, and then click the **Edit Template** button.

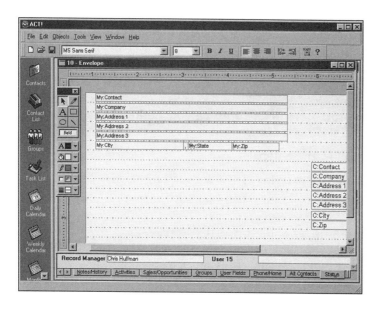

The number 10 Envelope Report template has place-holders for the various pieces of information that are pulled from the data-base record.

Note that the return address fields have the word *My* preceding each, indicating the information is drawn from the My Record. Similarly, the recipient address fields have a letter *C*, indicating that those fields are pulled from the contact record.

To remove a field, click it so that the small handles are visible, and then right-click to open the pop-up menu. Select the **Cut** option. After removing the extraneous fields, save the envelope with the **File** menu and **Save** option. If you accidentally deleted a field, right-click and select **Undo**.

Adding a Logo

If you operate a small company and want ACT! to print the return address because you are saving money on stationery, you can jazz up the envelope by adding your logo—provided it is saved as a bitmap file somewhere on your hard drive or a disk. Open the envelope template in ACT!. Open Windows' Paint program by clicking the Windows **Start** button, and then selecting **Programs**, **Accessories**, **Paint**. In Paint, open the file containing your logo. Use the **Edit** menu to select the logo image, and then select **Copy** from the **Edit** menu. The logo image is now saved in memory on the Windows Clipboard. Return to ACT!, right-click the mouse to open the pop-up menu, and select **Paste**. When the logo image appears, you can move and resize it as needed. Save the envelope and try printing. If the design is not enchanting, simply repeat the editing steps and modify the design.

Printing Address Books

In the paper-based world, it seems that every time you get the latest information on all your contacts, a phone number area code changes or somebody moves or gets promoted. The point is information is very malleable and very difficult to keep accurate. With ACT!, you can be as up to date as possible on paper, by printing directly from the database—provided that you have been diligent about keeping ACT! current. If you carry a day timer or other planner (but as soon as you read about the ACT! add-on products I describe Chapter 26, "ACT! Add-on Products," you won't), you need to purchase the concomitant paper stock before printing your address book. Most office supply stores have the paper stock you need.

To print an address book, follow these steps:

1. Open the **File** menu and select **Print**. The Print dialog box appears.
2. Select the type of address book format that matches yours. ACT! provides a preview of the format.
3. Click the **Options** button to customize the address book.

There are a variety of options that can be put into effect. They are explained next. This illustration shows the Address Book Options dialog box.

Before printing an address book, take a moment to check the printing options first.

The default settings may be adequate. ACT! gives you the opportunity to select a maximum of three extra fields to print as part of each record. Simply pull down the list and select the field or fields to print. In the Print Settings section, if you are facile enough, you can choose to print on both sides of the paper by clicking the check box. Every time I try this, operator error seems to doom the process.

The Create Printout For section can be the most useful attribute in this dialog box. Referring to the problem updated, your first printing of the address book is likely to be all contacts. After that, you might want to create a lookup of all records by a specific edit date. So, if all contacts were printed on June 1 (the date is printed on the bottom of each address book page), you can use the Lookup By example (enter >06/01/99 in the Edit Date field) and print only those records that have changed. Then, add those pages at the end of your address book. It may be cumbersome, but otherwise you would have to print all contact records every time.

Another way to approach the issue is to create a group, lookup that group, and print the address book information for that group only. In this dialog box, you would click the radio button for Current Lookup.

Changing the Font

The default is to print a line between each contact record, making it easy for the eye to focus on one record at a time. A further refinement is to change the font and, as old age creeps up, enlarge the print from a default of 8 points—which is small. To change the font, click the **Font** button and select the size.

Printing Calendars

Due to the widespread use of paper planners, ACT! includes the templates that print to the forms that you can insert into Franklin, Day Runner, or Deluxe planners. ACT! can print your calendar in the format you prefer. From the **File** menu, select **Print**, and then select from the **Printout Type** pull-down list to choose a calendar. On the right portion of the dialog box, ACT! can display the form that matches your choice, giving you a visual reference as to whether or not it is the correct format. Select the correct form and then set any printing options. Print the calendar, insert it into your planner, and return to the Stone Age.

The Least You Need to Know

➤ ACT! makes it easy to create mailing labels or envelopes once you know where to look!

➤ Print labels and envelopes via the File menu, Print option.

➤ Print your ACT! calendar and addresses to a form that matches your paper planner.

"Let us be thankful for the fools. But for them the rest of us could not succeed."

Mark Twain

Chapter 14

Internet and Email

In This Chapter

➤ Communicating by email

➤ Internet links in ACT!

➤ Customizing your Internet links

"The reward of a thing well done, is to have done it."

Ralph Waldo Emerson

Setting Up Your Email Account

One of the most powerful features of ACT! is its cability to link with your email program, allowing you to send Internet messages to contacts instantly. If you don't already have an email program, ACT! provides one for you.

You might have configured ACT! to use an email program during setup. If not, the steps to do so are easy—but you should have the information from your Internet Service Provider at hand, because you will need it.

Open the **Edit** menu and select **Preferences**. In the Preferences dialog box, click the **E-mail** tab.

Next, click the **New Account** button. You can now make the entries as provided by your Internet service provider. ACT! opens a dialog box similar to the one shown here. What you see are the email clients that ACT! has located on your system. You can select more than one entry as an email client. Click **Next**.

ACT! presents a list of the email clients that it recognizes on your system.

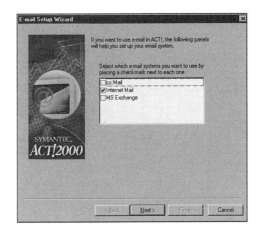

The next illustration shows a completed email account. Table 14.1 shows how to make the entries.

Table 14.1   Filling Out the E-mail Setup Wizard

Field	Description
Default Account (Username):	Enter the first part of your email address only. Mine is DWOLF@HOWTOSOFTWARE.COM, so my entry is simply DWOLF.
Outgoing SMTP Server:	This is provided by your ISP. Type it exactly as given to you.
Incoming POP3 Server:	This is provided by your ISP. Type it exactly as given to you.
Real Name:	Enter your proper name, like Douglas J. Wolf.
Organization:	If appropriate, make an entry—not required.
Reply to Address:	Enter your own email address.

The next check box involves passwords. Your choices are these: Have ACT! remember your password so that you are not required to type it every time you try and send or receive email. In an office, where someone else might gain access to your computer, you might want to require the password.

The next option requires a bit of thinking. Usually, an ISP deletes your email from its computer when you download it. However, you can select this check box so that the email remains on the ISP's computer. The reason for doing so is if you access your email from two locations—say, office and home—you might want to leave messages on the ISP's computer so that you can read the messages from either location, regardless of whether it has been downloaded already in another location. My suggestion is that you turn this option off.

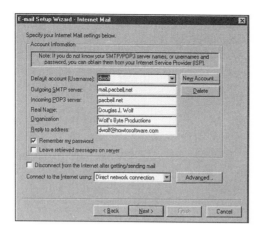

I've entered my email account information into the E-mail Setup Wizard.

If you connect to the Internet by modem, you might want to automatically disconnect from the phone line when all your messages have been sent and received, particularly if you use ACT! in a home office and have a single phone line for email and faxing.

Select the way you connect to the Internet. The default setting is via a direct network connection, which shows the bias of the programmers, but most ACT! users are still dialing via a modem. If you have a dialup already created, it will appear on the drop-down list.

The Advanced button is for testing your email connection. Clicking it allows you to indicate the authentication style used by your ISP (usually Passwords), and provides a button you can click to run a test. I suggest that you test the connection at this point. If it works, you're almost ready to begin sending and receiving all those email jokes you have heard so much about but could never get.

Click **OK** to close the test. Click **Next** and the setup dialog box for Windows Messaging appears. If you have this system on your network, you will have to get help from your system administrator to complete the setup. Click **Next** to access the final setup dialog box. If you have checked several email clients as ones that you will use, ACT! asks you to select one as the *primary* email client. For our purposes, Internet mail is selected, which means that ACT!'s email client is used.

Using Outlook 98 or Eudora as Your Email Client

You can choose to use either Outlook 98 or Eudora as your email client. What that means is that ACT! can read messages sent to the inbox and send messages to the out-box of either program. In short, you can check your email by using either Eudora or ACT! (or Outlook and ACT!). When you use these programs, any messages you create are sent via Outlook or Eudora. The advantage of using this option is that both are industrial-strength email programs that include HTML capability. A simple example is that if you receive an email, and it includes a URL (Uniform Resource Locator) such as www.howtosoftware.com, clicking the URL opens your Web browser and goes to that Web site.

Sending an Email

To send an email by using ACT!'s email program, open the **Write** menu and select **E-mail**. If the record has an email address, it is automatically added to the message. The email window opens. Enter the subject of the email, type the message you want to send, and click the **Send** button. ACT! sends the message directly, or if you have selected another program as the email carrier, the message is sent to the outbox of that client. If you use another email program for your messages, you will have to open it to send the message.

You do not have to send the email to the current contact—you can change the recipient by clicking the name of the current contact on the email form and pressing the **Delete** key. The insertion point moves to the field to the right of the To field. Enter the first couple of letters of the last name of the person to whom you want to send the message. ACT! searches its database for the record and if the person is in your database, inserts the name and the email address. The data entry is reactive—type the letter W, and the first contact record with a last name that begins with W appears. Type a second letter, O, and ACT! inserts the first last name it finds that begins with *WO*. You can scroll the list with the Up and Down arrow keys. When you find the name you want, press **Enter**, and the name moves into the large field beneath the To field.

Sending Email Messages via CC

To send the same message to more than one person, click the down arrow at the right of the **To** field. The CC abbreviation is an anachronism from the days of carbon paper—it means Carbon Copy. Everyone who gets the email can see the list of CC recipients.

To add a recipient:

1. Click the down arrow to open the list that provides the CC options.
2. Enter the beginning letters of the last name, or click the **Address Book** button and locate the recipient that way.
3. Press **Enter** if you used the Last Name method, or click **OK** to close the Address book dialog box.

If you select a person who does not have an email address, you can remove that person from the recipient list, or if you have the email address, add it on the spot, by clicking the **Edit Address** button. When you do, the E-mail Addresses dialog box appears, into which you add the email address by clicking the **New** button and entering the address.

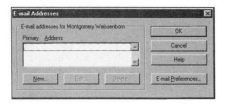

The E-mail Addresses dialog box appears for a recipient with no email address, allowing you to enter the address.

If you do not have an email address, you can keep the contact as part of the send. When ACT! actually tries to send the message or messages, it reminds you that this record does not have an email entry, at which point you can add the email address.

Sending Options, Priority Level, Get a Receipt!

There are some sending options. For one, you can designate the priority you think the message deserves. The receiver sees the priority level with the summary information when opening his email. The Create History option is selected by default, and that means that a history entry is added to the Notes/History tab after the message has been sent. If you want a Return Receipt, click that box. A Return Receipt is an automatic email message back from the recipient indicating that the message was received into the recipient's inbox—not necessarily that it has been *read*—an option Eudora offers.

The illustration shows the various sections of the email window.

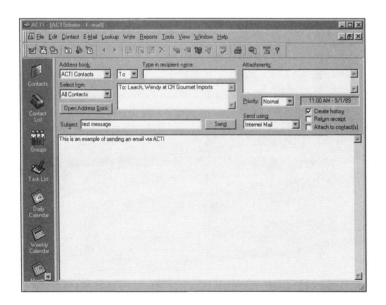

ACT!'s E-mail window provides a simple way to stay in touch via the Internet.

Sending to a Group

If you are the sales manager and want to send an email to all members of your team, you can use a Group send to do so. Before you can create a group send, you must have created the group first. See Chapter 15, "Working with Groups," for creating and working with groups.

To send to a group:

1. Open the **Write** menu and select **E-mail Message**. If you are in the email window, no email address is inserted. If you are in the contact record window when you start the message, delete the current contact by clicking the name and pressing the **Delete** key.
2. Click the **Open Address Book** button. The address book dialog box opens.
3. Click the drop-down list in the **Select From** field.
4. Select **Groups** from the list.
5. Select the group to which you want to send the email.
6. Click **Add**, and then **OK**. ACT! returns to the E-mail window so you can continue the message.

Attaching a Contact, Group, or File

If the person you are sending the message to is an ACT! user or Outlook 98 user, you can send a contact record as part of the email. You only can send Groups to other ACT! users, but you can send a file to anyone:

1. After creating the email, open the **E-mail** menu.
2. Select **Attach to Message**.
3. From the submenu, select the item you want to attach. You are not limited to a single attachment. If you select **Contact**, ACT! opens the Attach Contact(s) dialog box.

The Attach Contact(s) dialog box lets you choose which contact records to send with the email.

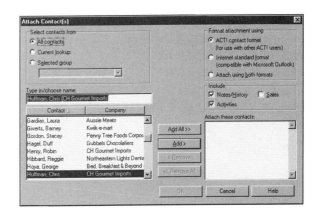

Narrow the list of contacts by selecting either **Current Lookup** or **Selected Group**. Click the name/company record you want to attach, and then click the **Add** button. You can then decide in what format to send the contact, and what else to include. Click **OK** to finish the attachment.

If you select **Selected Group**, ACT! opens the Attach Group dialog box, and you can select the group(s) you want to send.

Last, if you want to send a file, click that item. Depending upon the type of file you want to send, you might have to click the **Browse** button in order to locate the file. When you have located the file, click the **Attach** button. Remember, that an ACT! word processing file can only be opened by another ACT! user unless you have saved it as an RTF or ASCII file.

These group send options are described in Table 14.2.

Table 14.2   Group Send Options

Option	Description
Address Book	The address book can be pulled open and addresses from Outlook 98 or Eudora can be accessed.
Select From	This choice works in concert with the Open Address Book button. If you leave the entry in this field as All Contacts, when you open the address book, every record is included. Or, if you limit the entry to the Current Lookup, whatever was selected is included.
Open Address Book	Opens the selected address book. The ACT! address book can be searched by last name. Type the first letters of the person's last name. Even if the person does not have an email address, ACT! responds with the person closest to what you have typed. At that point, if the contact does not have an email address, you can add one.

Customizing Email Messages

Besides the message itself, you can customize a message by including text that has your "signature" on every email message—in reality, a standardized message indicating who you are and possibly how to reach you. Veteran email users often include their email address, Web page, and sometimes even phone, fax, or pager numbers as part of a signature, and sometimes even a quote. Some users get quite fancy with their signatures, enclosing the text in characters that resemble a frame or box.

To customize the email:

1. Open the **Edit** menu and select **Preferences**.
2. Click the **E-mail** tab in the Preferences dialog box.

3. In the **Signature** text field, type the signature you want on every outgoing email.

4. While you are in the Preferences dialog box, I recommend that you click **Colors and Fonts**, and make the email text larger.

5. Click **Apply**, and then **OK** to make the change effective. The next figure shows an email message with enlarged signature text.

Signature text is automatically added to an email message, and its text is enlarged for users now approaching middle age.

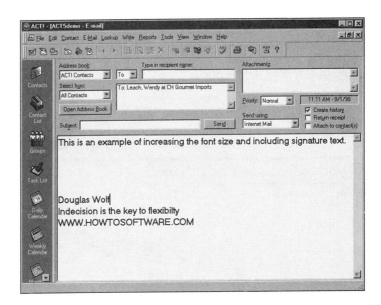

After you click the **Send** button, if you are on network connection, the email is sent immediately. If your modem has to dial and connect to your ISP, the Connect To dialog box appears, at which point you click the **Connect** button. If you decide not to connect, ACT! alerts you that the message was not sent, and that it is being sent to the email briefcase and can be sent when a connection is established.

Receiving Email Messages

To see email that has been sent to you, you either have to dial your ISP, or on a direct network connection, refresh your inbox. On a network, you can have ACT! automatically refresh the inbox at a preset interval.

To set the refresh rate:

1. Open the **Edit** menu and select **Preferences**.

2. Click the **E-mail** tab. On the left side, in the Inbox Settings section, click the **Notify Me** option and set a time interval.

3. Click **Apply** and **OK** to finish.

To open the email inbox, click the **View** menu and select **E-mail**. The E-mail window appears.

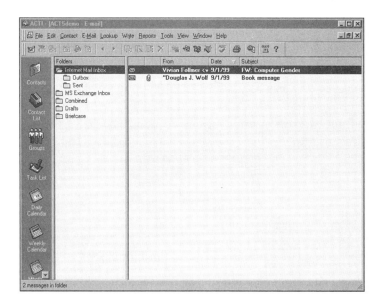

The ACT! E-mail window shows you the incoming mail folders and any folders you may have created at the left, and message headers on the right.

In this example there are two inboxes visible: Internet and MS Exchange. To refresh the inbox, right-click to open a pop-up menu. From the menu, select **Get/Send Mail**. Any mail that was awaiting being sent in your outbox is sent, and ACT! queries your ISP for any new mail. The messages show up in a list on the right. When you receive email, the entire message is not immediately visible; you must double-click the message header, or right-click and select **Read Message** from the pop-up menu.

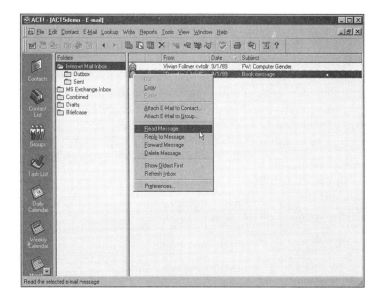

This pop-up menu appears after you right-click an email message header.

215

After reading the email message, you have several choices. You can print the message, delete the message, or move it to the folder that you have created for messages. I recommend that you create several folders, so that you can keep messages for different projects, or from different individuals, separate.

To create a folder for incoming email:

1. Right-click the **Internet Incoming** mailbox.
2. From the pop-up menu, select **Create Folder**. The Add Folder dialog box appears.
3. Type a name for the folder. In this example, the word Book appears in the field.

The Add Folder dialog box allows you to create new folders for incoming email, making it easy to locate messages at a later time.

After creating the folder, you can move email from the incoming mailbox to a folder:

1. Left-click and hold down the mouse button on the message you want to move.
2. Drag the message to the folder in which you want the email message stored.
3. Release the mouse button. ACT! alerts you with a warning dialog box that moving the message causes it to be deleted from the current location.
4. Click **Yes** to complete the move.

You can move multiple messages at one time. Click the first message, hold down the **Shift** key, and drag the messages so as to highlight them. Click and drag the messages to the destination folder. If the messages are not juxtaposed, hold down the **Control** key and click the messages you want to move.

When you receive email messages, they appear in your inbox. The E-mail window includes inbox icons for the email systems you have set up to use in ACT!, such as cc:Mail, Internet Mail, or Microsoft Exchange. Unless you use more than one of these email systems, your incoming email messages will always appear in the same inbox. If you use multiple email systems, you can view received email messages in the individual inboxes for each system, or you can view all received email messages for all systems in the Combined inbox. The Combined inbox appears only if you have set up multiple email systems.

You also can move messages from your inbox to the Briefcase, which lets you read your messages when you are offline.

Put Down the Briefcase

If you are using Eudora Pro or Internet Mail, you do not need to move messages to the Briefcase—you can read messages in your Eudora and Internet Mail inboxes when you are not logged on.

Do the Multiple Account Shuffle

If you are using Internet Mail and you have multiple email accounts, you can retrieve mail for one or more of the accounts. When you choose the **Get/Send Mail** command, a dialog box appears in which all your Internet accounts are listed. Select the accounts to check for new mail, or select the **Get Mail for All My Accounts** option to check all accounts at one time.

Attaching a Message to a Contact Record

You might prefer to attach a particular message to a contact in your ACT! database. That way, you can keep all the email traffic with a particular contact with that contact. To attach an email to a contact record, right-click the record and from the pop-up window, and select **Attach E-mail to Contact**. The Attach E-mail dialog box appears. Select the contact record by scrolling the list and clicking the correct name, or type the first couple of letters of the contact's last name. Click **Add**, and then **OK**. The message is added as an attachment to the selected contact record, but is *not* removed from the inbox.

Replying to an Email Message

After opening an email message, you can reply to the sender very easily. Right-click your mouse and, from the pop-up menu, select **Reply**. A dialog box appears, asking if you want to include the message body from the sender. It is a good idea to do so, because that way the thread of the messages is easy to follow. For example, if you send me a message asking for an answer to a specific question and I reply with the original text, I can be certain of what you asked and if the question was clear, and I can be certain that I supplied a congruent response. On the other hand, if you have been sending me jokes, I might not want to reply with the joke included.

Forwarding an Email Message

Forwarding an email is now the '90s version of "fax-the-joke" (and uses less paper, to boot). Before the plethora of email, faxing was the way to spread the best jokes—but the unintended consequence was that sometimes the wrong person read the fax. In the insane world of political correctness (and no sense of humor), this could cause a lawsuit and cost you your job. So, forwarding email jokes is safer—if you are certain that your company does not prohibit it and the recipient is agreeable. Still, any email you send is like a postcard and can be read by any of the many administrative personnel that maintain the servers that process the email.

To forward an email from your inbox or any folder, right-click the message and, from the pop-up menu, select **Forward Message**. The Address Book dialog box opens and you can select the recipients of the forward.

Forward Thinking

Email etiquette is not well established at this time, but one good idea is to get an OK from every recipient before forwarding jokes and the like. Not everyone likes being bombarded with nonessential messages.

To Create a Contact Record from a Received Email Message

A terrific feature of ACT! is the ease of which you can create a new contact record from an incoming email message. Although ACT! does not enter everything, it does add the email address for you:

1. Open an email message you received from a contact who is not in your database.

2. From the **E-mail** menu, choose **Create Contact from Sender**. The Add Contact dialog box appears with the contact's email address filled in.

3. Enter the contact's information and click **OK**.

4. The new contact is added to your database.

Moving in Email Messages

If you have more than one email message in the inbox or a folder, use the left and right arrow buttons on the toolbar to move to the previous or next message. To return to the list view and see all the message headers, click the **Inbox** button on the toolbar.

Using Internet Links

ACT! includes a series of links to Internet Web sites on the Internet Links menu, in the contact record window. When you open the menu and click a link, such as Bigfoot E-mail Services, ACT! locates your Web browser—probably Microsoft Internet Explorer *(resistance is futile—you will be absorbed)*—and opens the Dialer dialog box (unless you are on a direct network connection) so that you can connect directly to the Bigfoot Web site.

The links of note are the Symantec links, which take you directly to the Web pages that provide Technical support for ACT!. The Yahoo! links connect the Web pages as described. For example, you can look up a contact record, and then click the Yahoo! Driving Directions link. Your browser kicks in and when it gets to Yahoo!, you can create a map and detailed driving directions to the contact's address—without typing.

Customizing Internet Links

The real "oh wow" capability is being able to develop your own Internet or intranet links. This means that if you have favorite Web sites that you want to visit frequently, you can do so directly from ACT!. Or if your company has an intranet, you can go directly to it to find out the latest on downsizing! The very prospect is exciting!

Creating you own Internet link is accomplished by opening a text file in Windows WordPad (a simple word processor that comes with Windows) and creating the linking text, and then saving the text as file into the ACT\Netlinks folder. Here is an example:

1. Open Windows WordPad by clicking the Windows **Start** button and selecting **Programs**, then **Accessories**, and finally **WordPad**.
2. Type the name of the link, which will appear on the Internet Links menu, in brackets. So, for my Web site, type [Wolf's Byte].
3. Add the URL (Uniform Resource Locator). Type http://www.howtosoftware.com.

   The finished text should read as [Wolf's Byte]http://howtosoftware.com.
4. Open the **File** menu and select **Save As**.
5. Make sure you are saving to the ACT\NetLINKS folder.
6. The filename must have quotes around it and you must add a WEB extension. An extension is a holdover from the DOS days; it is a period followed by 3 characters. Type "WOLF.WEB".

7. Click the **Save** button.
8. Start ACT!.
9. Open the **Internet Links** menu and select the **Wolf's Byte** item.

With a little luck, the link worked, and you are propelled to the most informative, entertaining, and life-enhancing Web site of all. Thank you very much!

Using Live Update

I cannot emphasize too much that you should, on a monthly basis, open the **Help** menu and select the **Live Update** option. Believe it or not, every software company ships products that have errors. They can cause problems, and Symantec has developed the best way to get the problems fixed. Plus, new versions of ACT! are developed with enhancements—such as links to other programs, and they are free.

When you run Live Update, you are connected via your modem to a Symantec computer. The Symantec computer checks the file date of your version of ACT! and lets you know if there is an update available and its size. At that point, you can decide to update ACT!, or if you do not have time to stay online to get the file, you can return later for the file. ACT! does everything for you, the file is downloaded from the Symantec computer, and then applied to your program.

If you are on a network, your company probably has blocked this feature, so your MIS person or network administrator must run Live Update from the server, and then send it to your insignificant computer.

The Least You Need to Know

➤ Sending email in ACT! is as easy as selecting a command from a menu.

➤ ACT! can link to several popular email programs or use its own built-in software.

➤ ACT! comes with several useful Internet links, and you can add more if you like.

"Marketing is simply sales with a college education."

John Freund

Part 4

Hey, Why Didn't They Tell Me You Could Do That with ACT!?

The basics are yours. Now, take your use of ACT! to the heights. Using groups, designing your own look and feel to ACT!, forecasting your income, and giving the boss the reports he demands are all covered in Chapters 15 to 21.

Working with Groups

"Emancipation from error is the condition of real knowledge."

Henri Amiel

ACT! comes with one field in particular that, with judicious use, can be invaluable in helping you classify your data. In this chapter, you'll learn about the ID/Status field and how to put it to productive use.

Groups Versus ID/Status

One of the main fields in ACT! is the ID/Status field. By main, I mean that its use in your database should be considered judiciously. In Chapter 3, "Entering Records," I stressed the importance of the ID/Status and its relation to Groups. The key idea is that the ID/Status field can be used as the primary categorizing field. For example, if your firm is using ACT! as a sales tool, you might have four types of entries for ID/Status: Prospect, Suspect, Customer, and Inactive. With this system, you could look up all your customers, and send them a special direct mail, fax, or email on closeout pricing.

The use of Groups can involve subsets of the ID/Status. For example, you could create a group of customers who only purchase a particular product. Or, customers that only respond to closeout pricing offers. Or, you could create a group that includes an ID/Status of Prospect and previously was a Suspect. The possibilities are endless, because a contact record can be a member of as many groups as you want, and you can add an unlimited number of groups. In addition, you can create subgroups—which means that you can have a main group identified as widget customers and subgroups of those same widget customers, by geographic territory.

After a group is created, you can access it by clicking the **Groups** icon at the left of the contact record window. An important idea of groups is that the contact records do not have to have any relationship before being assigned to the group.

Creating a New Group

The ACT5demo database has several groups already. You can use the demonstration database, or your own, to follow the steps to make a group.

1. Click the **Groups** icon. The groups window opens.

You've opened the Groups window in the ACT5demo database.

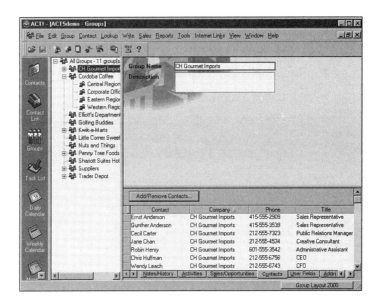

2. Open the **Group** menu.

3. Select **New Group**.

4. Enter a name for the group.

5. Enter a description for the group. This is important. As the number of groups increases, the description helps to eliminate the problem of people creating duplicate groups.

6. Open the **Group** menu again.

7. Select **Group Membership**.
8. Select **Add/Remove Contacts**. The Add/Remove Contacts dialog box appears.

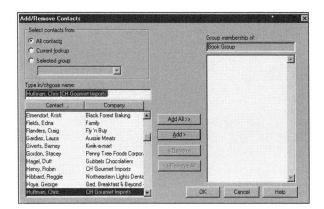

You then open the Add/Remove Contacts dialog box for the new group.

9. Select the radio button for **All Contacts**, **Current Lookup**, or **Selected Group**.
10. Click the name or company that you want to include in the group, and then click the **Add** button.
11. After selecting all the contacts that are to be members of the group, click **OK**.

ACT! creates the group, and the group members are shown on the Contacts tab.

Recalling a Group from the Contact Window

To see how the group is recalled, close the group window, or change to the contact record windows by clicking the **Contacts** icon at the left. At the bottom of the window, there are two buttons: one for selecting groups and the second for selecting layouts. In the illustration, the mouse pointer is pointing to the Group button, and the list of groups is opened.

The default is No Group. Click the **Group** button and ACT! displays a list of all groups in the database. If you have many groups, you might have to scroll the list. Click the name of the group that you want to recall.

After selecting the group, the name of the group appears on the group button—as a way of alerting you that you are working within a group.

The mouse pointer is pointing to the Groups button, and the list of groups appears.

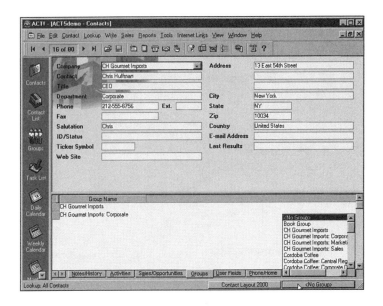

Grouping and Its Effect on Lookups

When you are working in a group, you can always create a new lookup that considers all contact records for the lookup. But, if you want to use the Add to the Lookup option, you cannot. You can use the Narrow option while in a group, but ACT! is only going to use the Group members in its search. So, if you have a group active, and you want to lookup contact records in that group that have an ID/Status of Customer, you can do that by opening the **Lookup** menu, selecting **ID/Status**, entering customer, and clicking the radio button for **Narrow**.

Adding New Members to a Group Using a Lookup

You do not have to add members to a group upon its creation. You can simply go as far as creating the group by giving it a name and stop. Suppose that you have a large database and you want to use groups. I recommend that you decide on the groups you want and create them. Next, you can create a lookup that finds most (or all) of the members of the group. At that point, you can open the groups window, select the group to which you want to add the contact records, and select **Current Lookup** as the records from which to choose the new members.

But, what if the group you want to create has nothing in common, making it difficult to create a lookup? In Chapter 6, "Working in the List View," you were introduced to the concept of working in a List view of the contact records. So, create the lookup by opening the **List** view, opening the **Lookup** menu, selecting **All Contacts**, and changing to **Tag** mode. Now, you can scroll the entire database and click the records that are to be members of the new group. After tagging the records, click the **Lookup Tagged** button, open the groups window, and then select the **Group** menu and the **Group Membership** option. From the dialog box, you can select the radio button for **Current Lookup** and add the tagged records to the group.

Adding an Existing Contact Record to a Group

New with the release of ACT! 2000 is an automated way to add a member to a group. Let's look at the manual way first:

1. Look up the contact record that you want to add to a group.

2. Click the **Groups** tab (between the Sales/Opportunities and the User Fields tabs) at the bottom of the contact record window—*not* the Groups button. Check the results against the illustration to make sure the correct tab is selected.

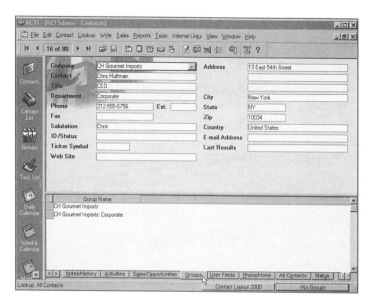

Your contact record looks like this with the Groups tab selected.

3. Right-click in the tab space to open the pop-up menu.

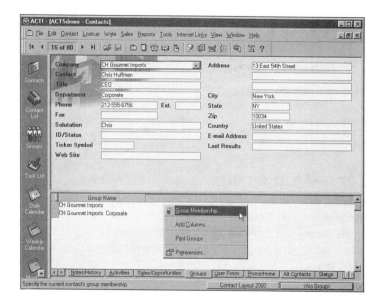

Right-click to open this pop-up menu in the Groups tab.

4. Select **Group Membership**. The Group Membership dialog box appears.

This Group Membership dialog box appears when you select Group Membership from the pop-up dialog box.

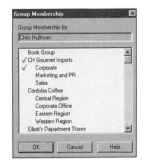

This dialog box is a reverse of the Group Membership dialog box that you see when you arc adding members as described earlier. Only a single contact record is available, but all the existing groups are listed.

5. Scroll the list and when the group name appears, click the group. A check mark appears in front of the group name, indicating that the record has been added to that group. Click as many groups as appropriate.

6. Click **OK**. The group name appears in the Groups tab.

Adding a New Contact Record to a Group

If you know that you are going to enter a new contact record, and you know that the contact record belongs in a certain group, you can add the record to the group at the same time. Select the group to which you want to add the contact record, by using the **Groups** button. Then, click the **New Contact** button and create the record. Because you selected the group before making the entry, ACT! assumes that the record belongs to that group. This can work the wrong way too, so make sure that the group button either reads No Group or has the group name you intend.

Removing a Contact from a Group

In the same way you added a contact to a group, you can remove a record by clicking the **Groups** tab, right-clicking to open the same Group Membership dialog box, and then clicking on a group name. The check mark is removed, removing the contact from that group.

Associating Activities with a Group

When you schedule an activity, one of the fields in the Schedule Activity dialog box is Associate with Group. By pulling down the list, you can select the group. What this does is add the activity to the group via its Activities tab. But, it does not schedule an activity with all members of that group. By associating an activity with a group, group reports reflect that activity.

Grouping and Synchronization

Another aspect of grouping is its use in synchronization. Generally, a company has a large database in its office and sales representatives with laptops in the field. If the company database has 20,000 records, it is not practical to synchronize all 20,000 records with each salesperson, especially when it is highly unlikely that a single salesperson is going to work with all 20,000 contact records. So, ACT! uses groups to split the database into smaller pieces. What most companies do is create a lookup by state (or states) or zip code (or codes) and then create the group. The group is then synched via email or shared folder to the salesperson. As the salesperson makes changes, ACT! tracks the dates of the changes, creating a log. When the salesperson executes the synchronization process, only the changed records are sent to the company database. Likewise, the company database tracks changes and sends the changed records, in that group, to the salesperson. Chapter 25, "Synchronizing with Remote Users," covers the record tracking process in more detail.

Creating Subgroups of Groups

Refining the concept of grouping records even further, you can create subgroups of an existing group. In the ACT5demo database, there are several excellent examples of how this can be put to use. One of the groups is named Cordoba Coffee. When you open the groups window, at the left is a list of the existing groups. A minus (-) or plus (+) sign preceding the group name indicates subgroups under the parent group. To see the subgroup, click the minus sign and the list is expanded. You can see an example of an expanded list here.

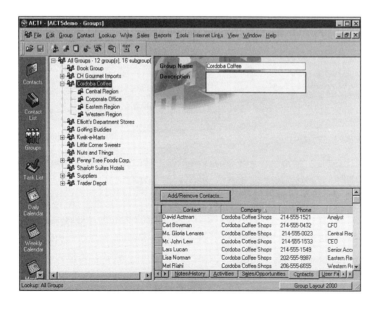

You've selected and expanded the Cordoba Coffee group to show its subgroups.

229

To create a subgroup:

1. Right-click the parent group. The popup menu appears.

This pop-up menu appears after you right-click the parent group name.

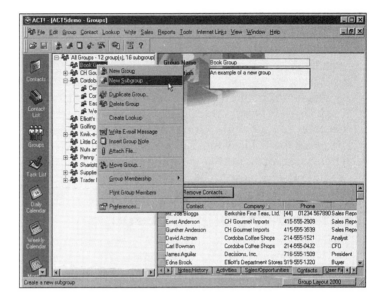

2. Select **New Subgroup**.
3. The Group Name field has the word Untitled in it.
4. Enter the name for the subgroup.
5. Add a description if the name does not make it obvious.
6. Open the **Group** menu and select **Group Membership**.
7. Add the members to the group.
8. Click **OK**.

Group Layouts

To fire your imagination in using groups, several layouts are included. In Chapter 16, "Customizing Your Layout," layouts are discussed in detail. For the moment, take a look at the Account Layout shown here.

To see the layout, click the button at the bottom of the window labeled **Group Layout 2000**. A list appears. Select **Account Layout** from the list.

As you can see, this layout reveals a great many more fields. The new fields provide a place to enter information that is more relevant to a group of contact records than it would be to a single contact. The idea is that you might have tens of individuals in your database that all work for the same company and even in the same location.

Ergo, you can group those individuals, and then have a place to enter information that applies to all in a general way.

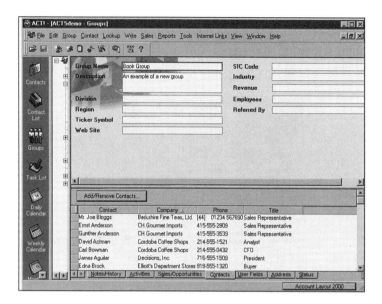

You can invoke this Account Layout alternative to the default layout.

Adding New Group Fields

Adding new fields to a group layout is nearly identical to adding fields to the contact record layouts. For the details, see Chapter 17, "Creating New Fields."

Creating Group Membership Rules

This aspect of groups is particularly important to companies that synchronize databases. Consider a company with a home office database and 20 sales representatives with laptops who receive updates for their group of records via email synchronization. If the home office is generating new contact records as leads and inputting those leads into ACT!, very strong input discipline must be exercised by the home office so that every new lead is correctly assigned to the appropriate group. Tim Kelly in Le Center Minnesota, covers Minnesota, North and South Dakota, Iowa, and Wisconsin. The home office generates new sales leads via direct mail and prospects calling its toll free number. Once a week, Tim synchronizes his database and receives the new leads, while sending his activities to the home office database. Many companies are good at generating new leads, but not very good at getting them to the sales force in a timely and effective manner. In this case, when the lead is added to ACT!, the home office person doing so has to know which salesperson covers which territory and make sure that the lead is identified as being part of his group. You can see the problem. ACT! 2000 automates the process of adding new contact records to the correct group, so the only thing the home office has to do is execute the process.

1. The manner in which contacts are going to be grouped, by state or zip code or by an entry in an ACT! field, must be determined.
2. Click the **Groups** icon to open the groups window.
3. Select the group to which you want to add a membership rule.
4. Open the **Group** menu and select **Group Membership**.
5. Select **Define Rules**. The Group Membership Rules Wizard dialog box appears.

The Group Membership Rules Wizard is your key to defining rules.

As you can see, creation of the membership rule begins by identifying how the contact record is added to a group: because of an entry in a particular field, or as a result of a query. Remember that a query is an advanced form of a lookup and can be saved for reuse. (Chapter 5, "Advanced Record Lookups," covers queries quite well in my opinion.) In the scenario outlined previously, Joe Salesman has several states in his territory. So, looking at a field value might be the easiest rule to create.

6. For this example, select **Field Values** and click **Next**.
7. The Rule 1 dialog box appears. Select the field that you want ACT! to check to follow the rule. In this example, the State field is selected.

Select the State field as the field to evaluate in following the rule.

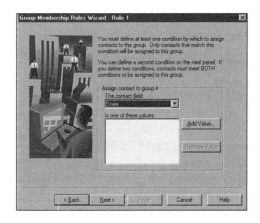

8. Click the **Add Value** button. ACT! opens the list of entries from the field selected. In this case, a list of the states appears.

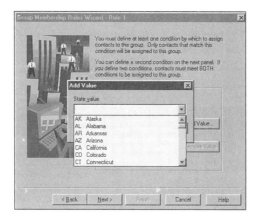

In the Add Value dialog box, you've selected the State field and opened the list of states.

9. Click the first value that matches your rule.

10. Click **OK**. The value is added.

11. Repeat the process until all values are selected. The value *does not* have to be in the list in order to be entered. So, if you are building a new database and have not added any records or field list drop-downs, you can still proceed.

12. Click **Next**.

13. Add a second condition as you did the first. (It is optional.) So, if you wanted the contact record to be in a certain state *and* have an ID/Status of New Prospect, you can add that second condition.

Remember, if you add a second condition, the contact record must match *both* conditions, not one or the other. Be careful!

14. Click **Next**. The last Group Membership Rules Wizard dialog box is shown here.

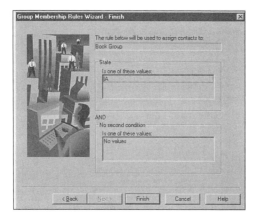

The final Group Membership Rules Wizard dialog box displays the rule you have craftily designed.

15. Click **Finish**. ACT! records the new rule, and then prompts you with a dialog box asking if you want to execute the new rule right away. If you have more rules to add, or have more pressing business in ACT!, click **No**. Otherwise, run the new rule to see if it accurately identifies the contact records.

The following illustration shows a dialog box that resulted from running the sample rule (by states) and changing the state entry in the Chris Huffman record in the demonstration database to IA.

Here are the results of executing the new rule for state values.

If the contact record was already a member of the group, it is not added again. If no records are identified as per your rule, ACT! displays that in the dialog box. You can also click the **Save** button and the results of running the rule will be saved as a text file, thereby giving you a log of which records were added to the group. ACT! gives you this option every time you run the rules.

Viewing and Deleting Existing Rules

Before creating new rules, or if you want to delete an existing rule, you can easily see the current rules in place:

1. Click the **Groups** icon.

2. Open the **Group** menu.

3. Select **Group Membership** and, from the submenu, choose **View Rules**.

Here's the Group Membership Rules dialog box from the demonstration database.

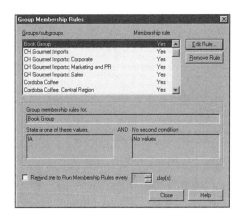

From this dialog box you can change an existing rule by clicking the rule, and then clicking the **Edit Rule** button. Or, remove an existing rule.

The Least You Need to Know

➤ Use groups to create permanent lookups, or subsets of the ID/Status field.

➤ To have ACT! automatically add records to Groups, create rules that define which records belong in the group.

"Nothing is as easy as to deceive one's self; for what we wish, that we readily believe."

Demosthenes

235

Chapter 16

Customizing Your Layout

In This Chapter

➤ Customizing the user fields

➤ Switching layouts

➤ Sharing layouts

"Philosophy teaches us to bear with equanimity the misfortunes of others."

Oscar Wilde

Because ACT! is a general purpose contact management tool with a nod toward sales, it has a number of user-definable fields that you can customize for your enterprise. In this chapter, I outline the tools that ACT! provides for this task.

Working with Layouts

The first thing to understand about ACT! and its layout capabilities is this: An ACT! database can have 1,000 fields, but if you're using a layout that is designed to display only 20 fields, those are the only fields you will ever see. So, the layout acts as a mask over the database fields—only the fields you choose to display are seen.

To understand this potential, it is necessary that you look at the different layouts that come with ACT!.

1. Open the **ACT5demo** database.

2. At the bottom-right corner of the ACT! record window, next to the Groups button, is the Layout button. When you click the **Layout** button, you'll see an opened layout list next to the mouse pointer, as in the following figure.

The Layout button, clicked open in the lower-right corner, lists the available layouts.

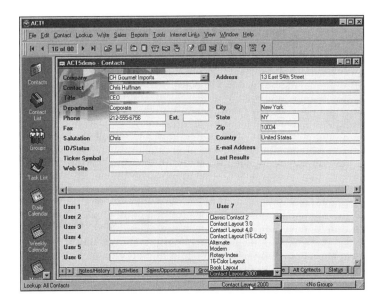

3. The default layout is named Contact Layout 2000. But you have many more layouts to choose from! Click the layout named **Modern**. The interface changes appearance dramatically, as you can see in the following figure.

The Modern Layout changes the look of the database.

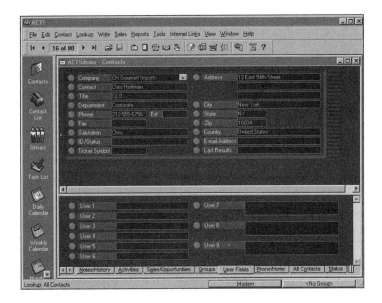

238

4. Open the **Layout** list again, and select **Rotary Index**. This figure shows the result.

This layout is a dramatic departure from the previous two layouts. Its design imitates an actual rotary index file card. More dramatic is the change in which tabs appear at the bottom of the window. Gone are the User Fields, Phone/Home, Alt Contacts, and Status tabs. To repeat, the data in the database is not affected and the fields are still there—they are just not visible in this layout.

5. Click the **Layout** tab again to select the **Contact Layout 2000** layout.

Changing Layouts Doesn't Change the Data

It is important to recognize that none of the data in any of the fields is affected by this change of layout, only the manner in which the data is displayed and which fields are seen.

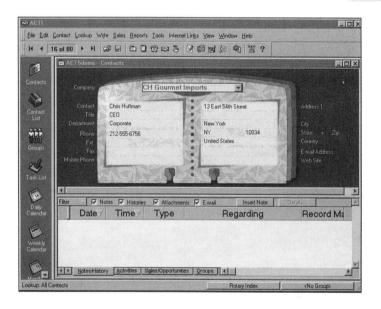

The Rotary Index layout provides fewer tabs at the bottom of the window.

Because ACT! has the capability to display different information depending on the layout you choose, you can use the same database across different aspects of your business. That is, the sales department can look at one layout, and the service department another, while in the same database.

Customizing the User Fields

ACT! is a general-purpose contact manager; therefore, it's designed to be customized for your business. The customization can be extensive or minimal. It's up to you to decide how much tweaking you want to do. In this chapter, the focus is on changing the display of existing fields. In Chapter 17, "Creating New Fields," I'll cover how you add new fields.

First, get a piece a paper and make a plan outlining which fields you think you want to modify, and how the data is going to be retrieved. Next, determine what type of data is going into each field: dates, characters, numeric only, and so on. Finally, forecast how long each entry could possibly be.

Renaming a Layout File

The easiest modification is to rename one or more of the existing user fields. In many cases, this is all you will need to do. Suppose that in your plan, you decide that you need to have two fields that are not currently in your ACT! database. One is for entering a birth date, and the second for a Social Security number. Before you make the changes, I recommend that you save the default layout as a new file.

1. Open the database and select the layout that most nearly matches your desired layout. If you are making only minor changes, such as renaming the user fields, the default Contact Layout 2000 is fine.

2. Open the **Tools** menu.

3. Select the **Design Layouts** option. The window changes radically, as you can see in the following figure.

This window appears after you select the Design Layouts option from the Tools menu.

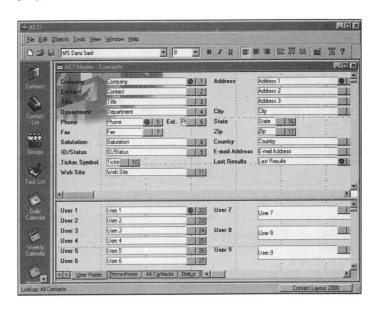

4. Open the **File** menu.

5. Select **Save As**. The Save As dialog box appears, as shown in the following figure.

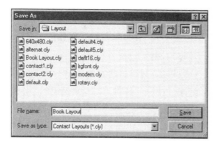

The Save As dialog box is used for renaming and saving layouts, making it easy to add a custom layout name.

Note that the Layout folder is opened and all the files have CLY as their extension, such as `default4.cly`. Some of the filenames are recognizable, too—the Rotary Index layout is saved as `rotary.cly`.

6. Enter a filename for this new layout. In this example, type `Book Layout`.

7. Click **Save**.

8. Click the **Close** button on the toolbar. (It's the third button from the right.)

The Design Layout window closes and the Layout button reflects the new name. At this point it is identical to the ACT! 2000 default layout. So, in case the worst happens, you can always reapply that layout to your database.

Renaming User Fields

Renaming existing fields might be enough to modify your ACT! database so that it fits the need of your business. Before you make changes, make a backup copy of the database (as described in Chapter 22, "Maintaining and Backing Up ACT! Data") in case you inadvertently shorten an existing field, thereby losing data.

1. Open the database for which you want to change the layout.

2. Open the **Edit** menu and select **Define Fields**. The Define Fields dialog box appears.

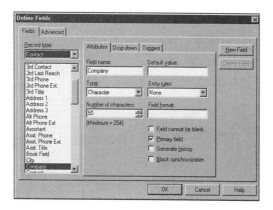

The Define Fields dialog box lets you rename existing fields, change field attributes, delete existing fields, or add new fields to your database.

3. Scroll the list until you see the field named User 1, and click **User 1** so that the name appears in the Field Name field. Note that it is, at present, a character field, and up to 50 characters can be inserted into the field.

4. Delete the name **User 1** and type `Birthdate`.

5. Move to the type field and pull down the list. Select **Date**.

   ACT! immediately alerts you that making this change, from a character field to a date field, might result in loss of data. Because the format of the field was characters and the length was 50, ACT! is warning you that any entries longer than what a date field allows will be lost. In this example, it is not a problem, as the User 1 field was empty in all the records. In your database, before you change any field, be sure that valuable data is not going to be destroyed.

6. If you are certain that you are not destroying any data, click **Yes** to continue.

7. Click the **User 2** field.

8. Delete the field name **User 2**, and type `Social Security #`.

9. Because this field has a defined entry pattern—three numbers, a dash, two numbers, a dash, and four numbers—click the Field format field and type

   `###-##-####`

   The # sign stands for a number. So the person making an entry into this field must enter numbers in this format: 555-55-5555.

10. With the two fields modified, click **OK**.

ACT! thinks about the changes for a minute, and then you see a dialog box that announces that ACT! is updating the database. Presently, you see the changes, as shown in the following figure.

You've added new field labels and formats to the database.

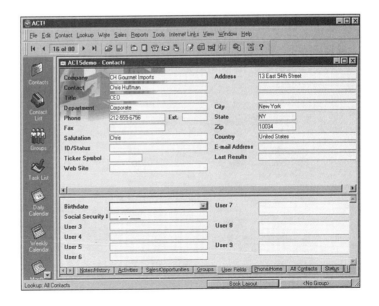

If you made the modifications with this exercise, you can test the fields:

1. Click the **Birthdate** field. A drop-down arrow should appear at the far right, as in the next figure.

2. Click the drop-down arrow, revealing the calendar.

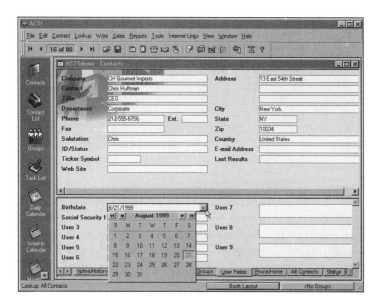

The Birthdate field appears complete with a calendar drop-down.

3. Click the **Social Security #** field and try to type any letter. ACT! ignores any entry that is not a number. Type a series of numbers to test the format.

Even though the field definition for the Social Security # field was not changed from 50 characters, adding the field format restricted the number of entries ACT! would allow.

A very important point you must understand is that there are many options in the Define Fields dialog box. The following list explains the options:

➤ **Record Type** The first option is the type of layout, Contact or Group. To change a field in the Group window, pull down the list and select **Group**.

➤ **Attributes Tab**

   ➤ **Field Name** The Field Name field is used to change the name that appears in the layout, but also changes the field name within ACT!.

   ➤ **Type** The Type field determines what type of data can be entered into the field. The choices are Character, which is any type of entry; Currency, which formats number entries into 19.5 places (19 plus 2 decimals); Date, which formats entries as MM/DD/YY and adds the calendar drop-down to the field; Initial Capitals, which automatically formats text entries with a capital letter on each word; Lowercase, which formats the text as lowercase; Uppercase, which makes all text uppercase; Numeric, which allows only numbers to be entered; Phone, which allows numbers only in the XXX-XXX-XXXX format; Time, which allows M:SS entries and creates a Time drop-down to the field; and the URL format, which makes the field an active Web page address field allowing you to enter a www.xxx.com entry. When you click a field formatted as URL, it starts your browser and tries to open the Web site.

Some of the Type options might not be available for all fields. The Company field cannot be changed into a Date field. All the user fields and any new fields you create can be any type of field.

Changing Field Names

If you create a mail merge template with a field name inserted, and subsequently change the name of the same field in the Define Fields dialog box, the mail merge template will not work properly because ACT! will no longer find the field in the database. You have to reopen the document or report template and reinsert the new field name.

➤ **Number of Characters**   The key purpose of this field is saving space, although in the era of 20-gigabyte hard drives (soon to be terabytes!), this is not as important as it used to be. But, your database runs more efficiently if the field sizes are only as long as they need to be.

➤ **Default Value**   This attribute allows you to have ACT! enter a specific value every time you create a new record. This attribute does not affect existing records. You can still enter a different value if the one ACT! inserts is not appropriate.

➤ **Entry Rules**   If you want a field to be protected, that is not modifiable by the user, select this option. Otherwise, you can insist that any entry into the field must come from the drop-down list that you supply.

➤ **Field Format**   The Social Security # field shows an example of which types of characters can stand for others. The # sign is for numeric characters, @ for alphabetic, and % for alphanumeric.

➤ **Field Cannot Be Blank**   If you have people creating new contact records who might be inexperienced, or just lazy salespeople, you can specify that a field must have an entry before they can go on to the next record. My advice is to use this power judiciously, not making more than one or two required fields.

➤ **Primary Field**   One of the options for creating a new contact record is the Duplicate-Contact menu. Duplicate-Contact opens a dialog box that asks whether the entries from the Primary fields or All fields should be duplicated from the current record. Making a field a Primary field means that it is included upon creating a duplicate record.

➤ **Generate History**   Turn this attribute on if you want any changes made to the field to be recorded on the Notes/History tab. For example, if you created a field that recorded a customer's annual sales, and every year you updated the field, it would useful to be able to track the year-to-year changes.

➤ **Block Synchronization**   When you synchronize data, ACT! sends changes in a record to the other database based on a time stamp. You might decide that a field in your database does not need to be updated when synchronizing and so turn this option on.

➤ **Drop-Down Tab**   Click this to create a drop-down list for the current field. If you are adding new fields or modifying an existing field, you can add the entries you want for the field. To add a new item to the list, click **New** and type the item. Add a description if necessary. Some companies use the description field to amplify the entry in the list—the list entry could be a part number and the description would identify the part.

➤ **Import Button**   Used to import a file that has been created in a different ACT! database via the Export button. So, to import a list, you must first create an export file from a different ACT! database, from this same dialog box. ACT! formats the export file so that it imports properly.

➤ **Allow Editing**   Enables anyone using ACT! to add or delete items on the drop-down list. Even if this option is off, anyone can type an entry in the field; they just cannot add it to the drop-down list.

➤ **Automatically Add New Items**   This option is new in this version. When on, an entry into the field that is not already on the drop-down list is added for you. Use this attribute for a field such as City. After a new city is entered into the field, the next time a record is being added with that city, ACT! uses type-ahead to insert the city name for you.

➤ **Show Descriptions**   Enables anyone who opens the drop-down list to see the concomitant description.

➤ **Use Drop-Down List From**   This, too, is a new feature of ACT!. When you are modifying an existing field or adding a new field, and know that a separate field in the database already has the list of drop-downs you want, you can duplicate that existing list easily, by selecting this attribute, and selecting the field you want to duplicate.

➤ **Triggers Tab**   The Triggers tab is an advanced attribute in ACT!. A field can be formatted so that when a user clicks the field, or makes an entry and then

245

exits a field, a totally different program is activated. If you are ambitious enough, you can link ACT! to an accounting program or spreadsheet. There is even a software development kit that you can get from Symantec to create your own programs that work with ACT!. See Chapter 26, "ACT! Add-on Products," for information on how to get your SDK.

After making the changes you want to a field or set of fields, click **OK**. If there are but a few records in the database, ACT! installs the changes quickly. With a large database, this is a slow process because ACT! must modify each record, one at a time. A warning—be patient with this process. It might appear that ACT! has stopped responding to the system but, it is working. This is a good time to check out your favorite Web sites.

Tips and Cautions on Layout Design

When you're designing a new layout, keep in mind these suggestions:

➤ Consider that the resolution of your computer monitor might be higher than those of other users, so position fields so that they can been seen by all logon users.

➤ If you need more fields than the user fields provide (15 in all), rather than renaming fields that you are not planning to use, create new fields as described in Chapter 17.

➤ The top half of the record window should contain the key fields that you want anyone who accesses the record to see.

➤ I recommend that you not drastically modify the fields that are on the Lookup menu.

➤ Plan before making the changes—saving time and frustration.

Creating a Lookup from the Renamed Fields

By modifying User 1 and User 2, changing them to Birthdate and Social Security # fields (or, whatever you have named the fields), you can perform lookups based on those fields:

1. Open the **Lookup** menu.
2. Select **Other Fields**, and the Lookup dialog box appears.
3. In the **Lookup** field, pull down the list and select the field you want to use. In this example, you select **Birthdate**.
4. Enter the birth date you want to find, exactly as entered into the field, or enter a partial date. For all the birth dates in June, you can enter 06.
5. Click **OK**.

Moving/Deleting Fields in the Contact Layout

Changing the position of fields in a layout does not modify any of the data in those fields, even if you modify the display length of the field! (This is not the same as *field length*, which is determined in the Define Fields dialog box.) Moving a field is simply clicking and dragging. Before you begin editing a layout, you might want to save the layout, by using the File/Save As method to preserve the current layout.

To see how, open the demo database, or create a database on which you can experiment.

1. Open the **Tools** menu.

2. Select **Design Layouts**. The window changes to resemble the one in this figure.

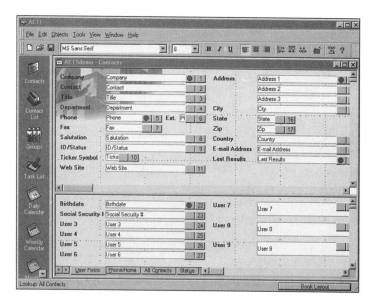

The Design Layout window lets you create your own custom design schemes.

A field in a layout consists of two main parts, the field display and the field label. The name of the field appears in the field. Each field has two gray boxes at the far right, which are used to set the tab entry order and the Enter key entry order—more on this in Chapter 17.

3. Click the **Ticker Symbol** field so that handles appear on the field.

4. Click the **Ticker Symbol** field again, this time holding down the mouse button, and drag the field underneath the Last Results field.

5. Release the mouse button to drop the field in its new position. The result appears as shown in the following figure.

You've moved the Ticker Symbol field to a new position.

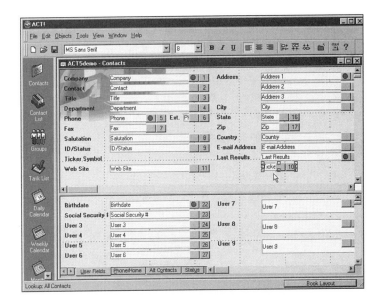

Note that the field label did not automatically follow the moved field.

6. Click and hold the mouse button on the field label you want to move, in this example, **Ticker Symbol**.

7. Drag the field label to its new position and release the mouse button.

After moving the field, you must save the change to the layout. Open the **File** menu and select **Save**—or **Save As** if you want to create a new layout file.

Deleting a Field from the Layout

Remember, removing a field from a layout does not affect the underlying field or any data that might have been entered into that field. One field that you might not need on the top half of the contact record is the Country field—especially if your business is strictly domestic.

1. Click the field you want to remove from the layout.

2. Right-click to open the pop-up menu shown in the following figure.

3. To remove the field and place it on the Clipboard, so that you can paste it elsewhere in the layout, select **Cut**. To remove the field, select **Clear**. If you cut several fields, only the last field cut remains on the Windows Clipboard.

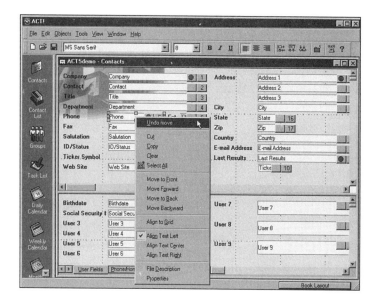

This pop-up menu appears when you right-click a field. In this example, the first menu item is Undo Move, because, just prior, you moved the Ticker Symbol field to a new location.

Remove Fields and Labels Together

To remove a field and its label at the same time, click the field, press the **Shift** key, and then click the label. Then, right-click to access the pop-up menu, and choose the proper menu command to cut or clear the field.

Moving a Cut Field to a Different Location in the Layout

Use the cut field method to move a field from the top portion of the contact record to one of the tabs, or vice versa. After cutting a field, move the mouse pointer to the area of the layout where you want the field to appear. Right-click and select **Paste**. The field might not appear exactly where you want it to, so you might have to adjust its position.

Resizing Fields

The amount or length of data you can enter into a field is determined in the Define Fields dialog box. For example, if you modify a field and give it a two-character field length, no matter how large you make the field display in the layout, no more than two characters can be entered into the field. Conversely, you can allow less space for the field display than the actual field length. So, the field display might be short, but you can enter data that is longer than what can be seen. When you click the field, you can scroll the entry so that you can see it all.

To resize a field:

1. Click the field so that the field handles appear.

2. Click and hold on a handle, and drag the outline of the field to the length/height desired.

3. Release the mouse button.

Changing Field Properties

The properties of each field can be modified in a number of ways. The font, fill color, frame width, and fill pattern can be changed in order to highlight the field.

To change the property of a field, you must be in Design Layouts.

1. Right-click the field.

2. From the pop-up menu, select **Properties**. The Object Properties dialog box appears, as shown in the following figure.

This Object Properties dialog box appears when you right-click an object in Design Layouts.

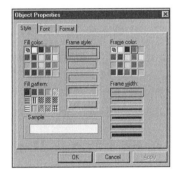

Style Tab

As you make choices in the Style tab, the results are displayed in the Sample field, giving you a preview of the effect. The following is a list of your choices:

➤ **Fill Color** The fill color is the color that appears in the field. Use this property to highlight the field.

➤ **Fill Pattern** While making an entry into a field, you can select the pattern that appears as you type. The pattern is seen only as you are making the entry—this property makes it easier to see which field you were working on when your significant other called to make a lunch date.

➤ **Frame Style**   Use this property to set off a field from the others in the layout.

➤ **Frame Color**   Use this property to further enhance a particular field or fields.

➤ **Frame Width**   Draw a thicker border around a field by selecting a wider frame width.

Click the **Apply** button to save the modifications.

Font Tab

When you change the font, from 8 points to 14, and click the Apply button, the size of the field is adjusted onscreen so you can see the effect before saving the change. The following figure shows the ID/Status field with the font changed to 14 points and the fill pattern and frame changed.

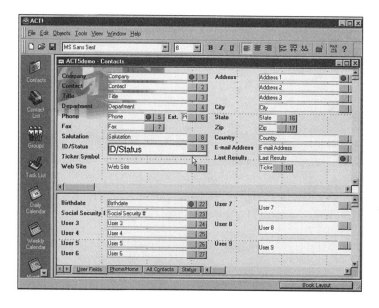

You've modified the ID/Status field with a new fill pattern, wider frame width, and larger font.

Format Tab

The Format tab provides information and has no attributes you can change. The information is the field name and type, character, date, and so on.

After making adjustments to the field, you still have to save the layout for the changes to become permanent.

Changing the Background

The top half of the window and any of the information tabs can have a background that is a specific color or pattern. Use this attribute to distinguish one tab from another.

251

To change the background on a tab or the top of the contact record window:

1. In Design Layouts, right-click the mouse at a place where no fields or field labels are selected. In other words, right-click so that only the background is selected. When you do, the pop-up menu that appears has fewer choices than the other pop-up menu that you see when an object is selected, as shown in the next figure.

The Background pop-up menu appears when you right-click the form's background.

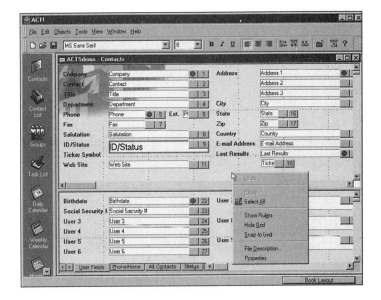

2. The pop-up menu appears. Select **Properties** from this menu. The Background Properties dialog box appears, as shown in the following figure.

The Background Properties dialog box appears when you select Properties from the menu you just saw.

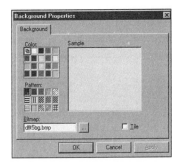

3. The attributes you can select are the color and pattern of the background; you can also insert a background bitmap. Symantec includes a bitmap named dflt5bg.bmp, which you see in the upper-left corner of the contact record window. You can replace the bitmap with one of your own choosing. Click the **Browse** button at the right of the Bitmap field and locate the bitmap you want.

You can display it as a single image or a tiled image. This illustration shows a handsome new bitmap added to the background.

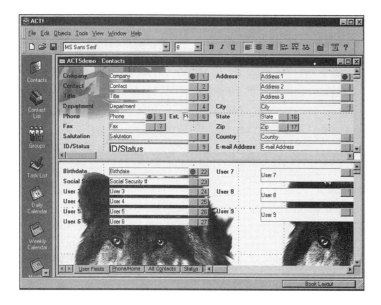

You've added a new background bitmap to the ACT! layout.

Sharing the Layout on a Network

If you are sharing a database on a network, and want everyone to see the same layout for that database, you have to make certain that everyone's copy of ACT! is pointed to the same layout file. On a network, I recommend that you create a folder in the same location as the folder that contains the database. Then follow these steps:

1. After creating a shared folder on the network, open the **Tools** menu and save the file to that folder.

2. Go to each of the computers of the people who are logging in to the ACT! database. Open the **Edit** menu and select **Preferences**. In the Preferences dialog box, the General tab is visible.

3. Pull down the list under **File Type**, in the Default Locations section.

4. Select **Layout**.

5. Browse to the folder that contains the shared layout.

6. Click **Apply**, and then **OK**.

7. Click the layout button at the bottom of the contact window and select the layout that you want the user to see.

253

Customizing the Toolbars and Other Aspects of the Interface

Customizing layouts is one aspect of changing the look and functionality of ACT!. Another related aspect is the interface of ACT!. The interface is the look of the program itself. Many of the aspects of the interface that you can customize are dependent upon the screen resolution you have selected in Windows. The higher the resolution, the more real estate that is visible on your screen. The size of the monitor is a factor, too.

Changing the toolbar affects only your version of ACT!, not anyone else's on a network.

Modifying the Toolbars

At the top of the contact record window and to its left is a pair of toolbars. To modify either, right-click the toolbar to open a pop-up menu, as shown in the following figure.

This pop-up menu is for modifying the left-side toolbar.

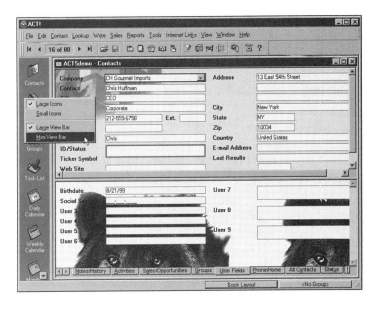

The defaults for this toolbar are Large Icons and Large View Bar. The Mini View Bar option moves the icons to the lower-right corner of the window, à la ACT! version 4.0. Try the various options to see what appeals to your work style. Whatever you choose, when you exit ACT!, the settings are saved and appear the next time you open ACT!.

The toolbar at the top of the screen can be modified in several ways, too. First, if you do not want a toolbar at all, right-click the toolbar at the far left to open the pop-up menu. Click the **Standard** toolbar so that the check mark is removed, which removes the toolbar. Retrieve the toolbar by right-clicking the mouse in the menu bar at the top of the window. The pop-up menu appears and you can select the Standard toolbar again.

You can also grab the top toolbar and drag it to a different position in the window. After moving the toolbar, you can resize the toolbar to a more square shape by clicking and dragging a corner.

To return the toolbar to the top of the window, drag it to its original position and drop.

Adding an Icon to the Top Toolbar

If you find that you are using a particular ACT! process frequently, you might be able to add the process to the toolbar.

To add an icon to the toolbar:

1. Open the **Tools** menu.

2. Select the **Customize Contacts Window** option to see the dialog box shown in the next figure.

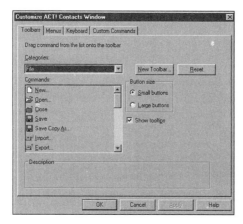

The Customize ACT! Contacts Window dialog box lets you add a frequently used process to the toolbar.

The list you see pertains, loosely, to File functions. Scroll the list in the **Commands** field. Some of the commands are already on the toolbar, so there is no point in adding a second icon. If the command you want is not listed, go to the **Categories** field and pull down the list to see the other categories, under which there are different commands.

One icon that I always add to my toolbar is the Run Macro icon. To add it to your toolbar, open the **Categories** list and select **Tools**. Scroll the list until **Run Macro** appears. Click the icon and drag it to the toolbar where you want it positioned. It *must* be in or to the left of the existing icon buttons—you cannot drag it to the right of the Help button. Release the mouse button and the new icon appears on your toolbar.

There is no easy way to distribute changes to the toolbars to other users on a network; you must change each user's computer individually.

The Least You Need to Know

➤ How to change the names of user fields

➤ How to change the definition of a field

➤ How to change the name of a layout

➤ How to move and delete fields in a layout

"Consistency is the last refuge of the unimaginative."

Oscar Wilde

Chapter 17

Creating New Fields

In This Chapter

➤ Creating a new field

➤ Advanced field attributes

➤ Adding a new field to a layout

➤ Creating a new tab

"You can fool too many of the people, too much of the time."

James Thurber

Creating a New Field

In the previous chapter, you modified several existing user fields in ACT! by changing the field names and their attributes. In ACT!, there are 15 user fields; if you need more, you have two choices. One is to change some of the other fields, such as the 2nd Contact field, to what you want. Or, you can create new fields. I have found it more effective to add new fields because they are easier to track. If there are unwanted existing fields in ACT!, you can delete the field, or preferably remove it from the layout, as I explained in Chapter 16, "Customizing Your Layout."

Before you create any new fields, consider their purpose. The type of data—will it be used in reports? Will the data be used for lookups? After you decide the purpose, the rest is easy. One caveat: If you have an existing database with thousands of records,

Once Is Enough

A field can be displayed only once in a database.

the process of adding fields is slow. Plan on doing this when you will not need to access the database for hours. Or, if you are adding many fields, it might be better to design the database, and then synchronize the existing database to the new structure, as explained in Chapter 25, "Synchronizing with Remote Users."

Too, keep in mind to which *layout* you want to add the new field (or fields).

To add a new field:

1. Open the database to which you want to add a new field. Also, select a layout to which you want to add the field by choosing the **Layout** button at the bottom of the screen and selecting the desired layout from the pop-up list.

2. Open the **Edit** menu and select **Define Fields**. The Define Fields dialog box opens the following figure.

You add new fields to your database in the Define Fields dialog box.

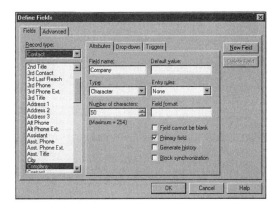

3. Click the **New Field** button.

4. ACT! creates a generic field name. Change the name to what is appropriate. In this example, I have named the field *Book Field*.

5. Add any attributes to the field, such as data type, length, a default value, and any drop-downs that you want.

6. Click **OK**. ACT! responds with a message that it is updating the database.

If you want to add multiple fields, do so before clicking **OK** to exit the Define Fields dialog box.

Adding the New Field to the Layout

So, where is the new field? Well, you can't see it at this point, because the layout doesn't include your new field.

1. Open the **Tools** menu.

2. Select **Design Layouts**. If the Tool Palette is not visible, retrieve it.

3. Open the **View** menu.

4. Select **Show Tool Palette**. The Tool Palette appears, as shown in the illustration.

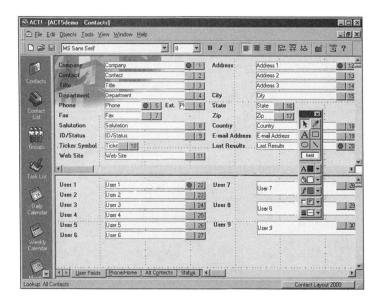

The Design Layouts window appears like this with the Tool Palette visible.

5. Click the **Field** button in the Tool Palette.

   When you select the Field button, and move the mouse pointer into the design window, the pointer becomes a crosshair shape instead of an arrow. Use the crosshairs to draw a rectangle for the location of the new field.

6. Click the mouse button and draw a rectangle, releasing the mouse button when you have created the rectangle. When you release the button, the Fields dialog box appears, as in the following figure.

7. Click the field you want to add to the layout. You have the option of including the field label.

8. Click **Add**.

   The field is added to the layout. The next illustration shows the sample field, Book Field, added to the layout.

New field added to the layout.

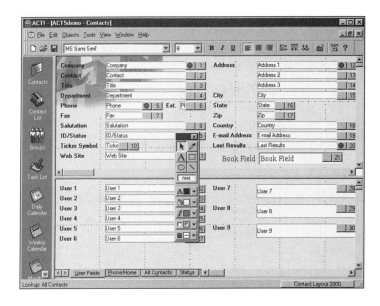

The Fields dialog box lists the available fields for adding to the layout.

9. Finish the process by closing the Fields dialog box, and then save the layout by opening the **View** menu and selecting **Records**. A dialog box appears asking if you want to save changes to the current layout. Click **Yes**.

The new field appears on the layout. If you switch to a different layout, the field is not visible.

Deleting a Field

You can easily delete a field in the Define Fields dialog box. Before you do so, be certain that the field does not contain any information that might be critical at some later date. My advice is to simply remove the field from the layout. The data still exists if you should ever need it. In addition, make a backup copy of the database in case you delete the wrong field.

To delete a field:

1. Open the **Edit** menu and select **Define Fields**.
2. Scroll the list of fields and click the one you want to delete.
3. Click the **Delete Field** button.

ACT! checks with you before it executes the deletion.

Creating a New Indexed Field

Most databases use a feature called indexing to accelerate the process of locating records. ACT! does also and several of the fields on the Lookup menu, Company through ID/Status, are indexed fields. You can add an index to a field if you expect to be using the field for frequent lookups. Again, a caution: If you have thousands of contact records, this process takes time to complete.

To add an index to a new field:

1. Open the **Edit** menu and select **Define Fields**.
2. Click the **Advanced** tab.

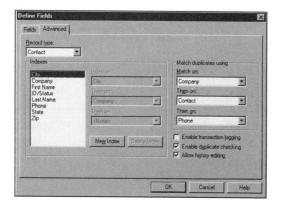

You've selected the Advanced tab in the Define Fields dialog box.

3. Click the **New Index** button.
4. Click the drop-down list in the **Index On** field and scroll the list to locate the field.
5. Click the field name and then click **OK**.

Adding a New Tab

Adding a new field or multiple fields is now at your command. Taking this new skill a bit further, you can add several fields to the database, and then put them all on a new tab that you also create. This is a efficacious way to group a series of related fields in the same physical location in ACT!.

To add a new tab:

1. Open the **Tools** menu and select **Design Layouts**.
2. Open the **Edit** menu.
3. Select **Tabs**.

The Define Tab Layouts dialog box lists the default tabs.

4. Click the **Add** button. The Add Tab Layout dialog box appears.

You can add tab layouts in this dialog box.

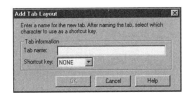

5. Enter a name for the tab. In this example, enter the word Book.
6. Click **OK**. The newly named tab is added to the list of tab layouts.

   Before closing this dialog box, you can adjust the display position of the tab by clicking the tab name and then the **Move Up** or **Move Down** buttons. You might delete a tab or rename a tab at this point, too.
7. Click **OK** to close the Define Tabs dialog box.

Now, click your newly created tab and add the fields that you want to that tab. There is no limit to the number of tabs you can add, but, from a practical standpoint, it is a good idea not to have so many tabs that the users are required to scroll the window to see them all.

Field-Arranging Tools

When you add a single field to the database, it is easy to align the field to existing fields. But, you might want to add a series of fields and, in that case, aligning them so that their left edges are straight can be a challenge. The Objects menu in Design Layouts has several choices to assist you in this task.

To see the options, click a field so that it is selected (the handles appear), and then open the **Objects** menu. The options are as follow:

➤ **Move to Front**   In ACT! you can layer objects such as bitmaps underneath the fields. This command moves any object so that it is on top of any others, making it visible.

➤ **Move Forward**   If you stack several objects, use this command to move the selected object up one level in the stack.

➤ **Move to Back**   If you paste a bitmap on the layout, it may cover up other objects. Selecting this option moves the object to the bottom layer.

➤ **Move Backward**   This option moves the selected item one level down in any stacked objects.

➤ **Align**   This option is active only if you have selected several objects before opening the Objects menu. The Align dialog box is shown in the illustration following this table.

➤ **Align to Grid**   There is a set of squares that form a grid upon which the objects in the layout can be aligned. Select the objects and select this option, and ACT! does its best to align the objects to the underlying grid. The grid size can be modified by opening the **View** menu and selecting **Ruler Settings**. In the Ruler Settings dialog box, select **Units of Measure**, and then reduce or increase the divisions shown, which then adjusts the grid size.

➤ **Make Same Height/Width**   This option makes it easy to makes all selected objects the same size.

➤ **Add Label**   When you insert a field, you have the option of including a field label or not. On a field that you neglected to add a label, select the field, and then select this option to add the label.

The Align dialog box contains options that allow for the correct alignment of multiple objects in a layout.

The options seen here are used when you have selected multiple objects and are trying to get them to line up, based on the various options. My advice is to open a layout where you can try the various aligning functions. If the alignment selected does not produce the result you expected, open the **Edit** menu and select the **Undo** option and the most recent action is reversed.

To select multiple objects, click the first object, and then press the **Shift** key and click the second object. Continuing to hold **Shift**, you can select as many objects as you want.

Changing the Field Entry Order

When you enter a new contact record, you can use the Tab key to move from field to field as you enter the information. But, if you have added new fields or rearranged the fields, the order in which the Tab key moves you from field to field might not be what you want or expect. Also, ACT! includes a way to set the order that the Enter key moves among the fields. In Chapter 10,"Setting Your Preferences," one of the preferences that you learned to set was using either the Enter key or the Tab key to move from field to field.

When you are looking at the Design Layouts window, each field has two gray boxes at the far right. If the Enter key is set to stop at a field, the first gray box has a red dot in it. The second gray box lists the order number for the Tab key stop. If you set your preferences so that the Enter key moves the insertion point from field to field, the gray box at the far right relates to the entry order for that key.

To reorder the way the Tab and Enter keys take you through the fields:

1. In Design Layouts, open the **Edit** menu.

2. Select the **Field Entry Order** option; a submenu opens.

   Your options are to Hide, Clear, or Reset the order. I recommend that you select Clear, which removes all numbers.

*Edit menu, Field Entry
Order submenu.*

3. Select **Clear**.

4. Starting with the first field—that is, the field where you want the insertion point to go first—click the far right gray box so that the number 1 appears.

5. Go to the next field and click so that the number 2 appears.

6. Repeat the process until all the fields that you want the insertion point to move to have a number on them. You are not required to add a number to every field. After the insertion reaches the last number field, it returns to the number 1 field.

7. If you want to set the order for the Enter key, click the gray box that is the second from the right so that a red dot appears.

8. Click the **Close** button and save the changes.

The Least You Need to Know

➤ You create a new field in the database and layout in which you want the field to appear.

➤ Adding a new field to a layout makes the field visible.

➤ Creating a new tab lets you pack even more information into a contact record.

"What we call progress is the exchange of one nuisance for another nuisance."

Havelock Ellis

265

Chapter 18

Forecasting Sales

In This Chapter

➤ Adding a new sales opportunity

➤ Setting the sales stages

➤ Creating sales reports

"The basis of optimism is sheer terror."

Oscar Wilde

Tracking Sales Opportunities

Although ACT! is touted as a general-purpose contact manager, the vast majority of its users are engaged in the sales process—natural optimists all, terrified by having to forecast their sales. Ergo, in ACT! 2000, several new capabilities have been introduced to track, forecast, and report on sales opportunities—thereby mitigating the feeling of terror. A new tab has been added to track the sales opportunities, and a new menu named Sales appears.

The sales process has become much more sophisticated and the means to measure progress of the sales force has evolved to a general standard that ACT! reflects. Most companies now use a sales funnel to graphically represent the stage of a salesperson's opportunities. ACT! provides an easy-to-modify, colorful sales funnel chart. ACT! also includes a graphing function that allows you to create a variety of graphs to represent sales.

Adding a New Sales Opportunity to a Contact Record

A sales opportunity is just what it says it is: the probability of a sale being made to an existing customer or to a new customer. The first step in creating a sales opportunity record is to lookup the contact record to which you want to add a sales opportunity. After locating the contact record:

1. Open the **Sales** menu.

2. Select the **New Sales Opportunity** option. The Sales Opportunity dialog box, shown in the following figure, opens.

The Sales Opportunity dialog box opens, one of the ways of adding a new sales opportunity to a record.

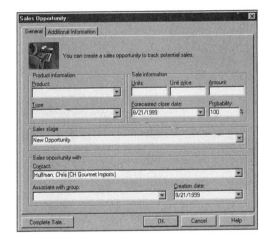

The various options for filling the Sales Opportunity dialog box are

➤ **Product**   This field has an editable pull-down to list the products/services that your company offers. When you enter a new product/service, ACT! automatically adds the product to the list.

➤ **Units**   Enter the number of units that you anticipate the customer might buy.

➤ **Unit Price**   Enter the cost per unit.

➤ **Amount**   ACT! calculates the total based on the entries in the Units and Unit Price fields. But, you can override the field entry if necessary to reflect a discount or special deal.

➤ **Type**   The type of sale field allows you to add details that might or might not be company specific. For example, if you are offering a special price for orders over a certain dollar amount, you can enter that information in this field. When you enter a new type, ACT! automatically adds the type to the list.

➤ **Forecasted Close Date**   Enter the date you expect the customer to either take delivery of the product, or when you expect they will pay.

➤ **Probability**   Every salesman is an optimist. But, putting 100% in this field for every sale diminishes the utility of this tool. Enter a realistic estimate.

➤ **Sales Stage**   This field's drop-downs should be closely scrutinized by you as the owner of your company or by the sales manager. The scrutiny is required so that all salespeople understand how to accurately categorize the state of the current opportunity. In addition, you want everyone using the same list so that the sales funnel works properly. The list that ACT! provides might be adequate for your firm and fit well. Otherwise, you can create the list you want. The means to modify the list are discussed later in this chapter.

➤ **Sales Opportunity With**   The default entry is the current contact. However, you can select a different contact record by opening the drop-down list and typing the last name of the contact, or by clicking the Company column and typing the company name.

➤ **Associate with Group**   Select the group to which you want to associate the sales opportunity.

➤ **Creation Date**   Enter the creation date, if it is different from the current date.

➤ **Complete Sale**   When your ship comes in, you can use this dialog box to record the final disposition of the opportunity.

After recording the information, the new sales opportunity appears on, not unexpectedly, the Sales/Opportunities tab. This tab is shown in the next figure with opportunities listed and the Filter section open.

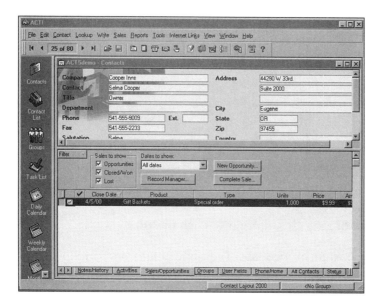

The Sales/Opportunities tab is selected in the contact record, with the Filter section expanded to display the options.

On the Sales/Opportunities tab, you have several filters that can be selected. For example, you can set a filter to see only pending opportunities, and then select which Record Manager's opportunities you want to see. The opportunities themselves are completely editable by clicking on the data you want to change. For example, to change the Sales Stage, click the current sales stage and select a new stage from the list. Sort the list by clicking the column header, in the same way as for other columnar lists in ACT!. Print the information on the tab by opening the **File** menu and selecting **Print Sales/Opportunities**.

Viewing a Sales Graph

The Sales graphing capability creates a visual representation of the sales opportunities that are in the company pipeline. This is terrific tool for managers trying desperately to calculate the income stream for the company. Obviously, the numbers generated are not set in stone and are only as good as the people entering the forecasts, but over time good managers can glean an intuitive sense of the accuracy of the data. The ACT5demo database has a series of Sales Opportunities already entered, which can be used to generate the sales graph and the sales funnel. To see how the graph looks, you can open that database and follow these steps:

1. Open the **Sales** menu.
2. Select **Sales Graph**. The Graph Options dialog box appears, as in the following figure.

The Graph Options dialog box is used to refine the data used as the basis for the graph.

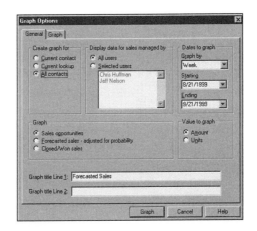

3. After adjusting the settings in this dialog box, click **Graph** to see the results.

The settings in this dialog box are on two tabs. The General tab has the following:

➤ **Create Graph For**   Create a lookup before opening the Sales Graph option if you want to graph data from specific contact records. Use the radio buttons to select the set of contact records to be used in the graph.

➤ **Display Data for Sales Managed By**   In a single-user database, this setting is irrelevant, but on a multi-user database, you can select which salespeople's contacts are going to be included in the funnel. If you combine this with the lookup capabilities in ACT!, you can fine-tune a graph in a number of ways.

➤ **Dates to Graph**   To see the examples from the ACT5demo database, you will have to enter a date range that corresponds to the sales opportunities in the database. In Graph By, your choices are Day, Week, Month, Quarter, and Year. Then enter the date range.

➤ **Graph**   Three options are presented for graphing the sales opportunities. Sales Opportunities shows all opportunities. The Forecasted Sales—Adjusted for Probability option creates a graph that reflects the total adjusted by the percentage. So, if the total sales opportunities is $50,000, factoring in a percentage reduces the total graphed (unless all opportunities had a 100% probability assigned). The Closed/Won Sales option graphs those opportunities that were concluded successfully, based on your other settings.

➤ **Value to Graph**   Choose whether you want the graph to display the number of Units or the dollar Amount. You can combine this option with the Forecasted Sales setting to assist the manufacturing division in forecasting production runs.

➤ **Graph Titles**   Enter one or two titles that reflect what is being graphed. For example, if you are graphing units, add that to the title.

The Graph tab enables you to customize the graph. Select from a bar or line graph, whether it is three-dimensional or two-dimensional, or between a full size graph or one that fits in a dialog box. The scaling options are used to determine what range of data is included in the graph; do so by selecting Define and entering minimum and maximum values. Horizontal or vertical gridlines can be added to the graph to aid tracking values. Last, you can select the colors you want for the graph, which is the line or bar itself, the text to appear as titles, and finally the background color which appears behind the graph.

After making adjustments, click **Graph** to see the results. The next figure shows a graph that includes gridlines.

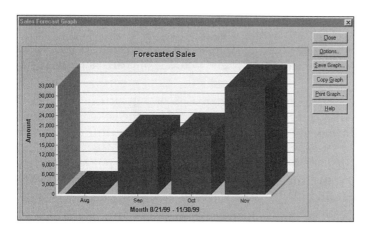

A Sales Graph with adjustments that included adding gridlines.

Viewing a Sales Funnel

If you are not experienced with the concept of sales funnels, there are plenty of good books on the subject to bone up with. The basic concept is that, from the initial contact to the close of a sale, a percentage of the possible sales opportunities are lost. So, the starting point at the opening of the funnel is wide and the other end is smaller. To see the results of creating sales funnels, open the **ACT5demo** database, which has a plethora of sales opportunities already.

1. After opening the ACT5demo database, click the **Sales** menu.

2. Select **Sales Funnel**. The Sales Funnel Options dialog box appears, as in the next figure.

The Sales Funnel Options dialog box.

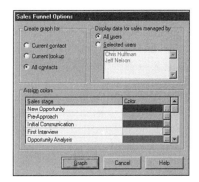

The options for creating a sales funnel are as follows:

➤ **Create Graph For**   Before opening this dialog box, you can create a lookup for the purpose of viewing the sales funnel for specific contact records.

➤ **Display Data for Sales Managed By**   In a single-user database, this setting is irrelevant, but on a multi-user database, you can select which salespeople's contacts are going to be included in the funnel. Combine this with the lookup capabilities in ACT! and you can fine-tune a funnel in a number of ways.

➤ **Assign Colors**   To modify the colors of each of the sale's stages, click the small gray box, with three tiny dots, to the right of the color. The Color dialog box opens and you can select the color you want. If the standard colors are not cool enough, click the **Define Custom Colors** button and, in the resulting dialog box, adjust the color to the exact hue and then click the **Add to Custom Colors** button. The Custom Colors option is not available for application to the sales stage.

To change the color asso-ciated with a sale's stage, open the Color dialog box and select the stage and a new color.

The funnel itself is a series of stacked slices getting smaller. Each slice corre-sponds to a step in the sales process.

3. After setting your options, click **Graph**. An example sales funnel graph appears in the next figure.

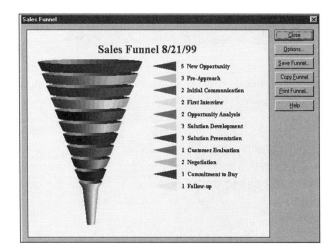

A sales funnel can include a numeric legend to add clarity to the underlying numbers.

The funnel graph shows the number of sales opportunities by stage in the legend to the right of the funnel.

Modifying the Sales Stages

The Sales Stages that ACT! provides might be a perfect fit for your business, but I doubt it. Assuming that you know the stages of your own sales process, redefining is easy. To make changes:

1. Open the **Sales** menu.
2. Select the **Modify Sales Stages** option. The Edit Sales Stages dialog box appears.

The Edit Sales Stages dialog box.

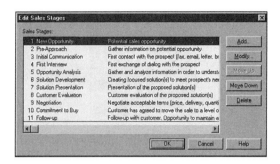

The technique to modify one or more of the stages is straightforward. Select the stage you want to change and click the **Modify** button to open the Modify Sales Stage dialog box, as in the following figure.

The Modify Sales Stage dialog box makes it easy to change one or all of the default sales stages in ACT!.

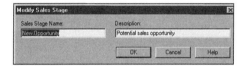

3. Type a new sales stage name and description. The number that you see preceding the sales stages in the next figure are generated by ACT!.

4. Click **OK**.

The other buttons in the Edit Sales Stages dialog box allow you to position the sales stage where you want it. Or, you can delete sales stages that you do not need. The sales stages are not attached to the layout but to the database.

Completing a Sale

A completed sale is a happy sale and when the time comes to record the fact, you must do so to make the sales opportunity reports accurate (and, perhaps, to get paid your commission). To complete a sale, lookup the contact and select the **Sales/Opportunities** tab. Click the sales opportunity from the list, and then click the **Complete Sale** button. Enter the information requested. The Complete Sale dialog box appears in the following figure.

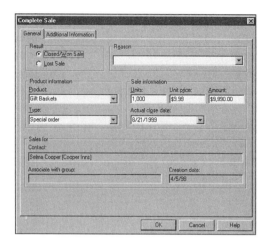

The Complete Sale dialog box allows you to record what happened to the sales opportunity, good or bad.

Sales Reports

ACT! offers a plethora of reports that are derived from the information you have entered as sales opportunities, won/lost, and complete sales. To see the reports, open the **Reports** menu and select **Reports**. Select a sales report, and then set your options. One option, on the General tab, is where the output is sent. I suggest that you send the output to Preview—which prints the reports to a window that you can zoom to see the detail. Each of the reports are outlined as follows:

➤ **Sales Totals by Status** Generates a report that shows the total number of units and dollar amount in the report header. In the detail section of the report, each opportunity has the company, contact name, and phone number, plus the expected close date, the product, type number of units, and the price per unit, total amount of the opportunity the assigned percentage probability, and the record manager.

➤ **Sales Totals with Probability** Generates a report that has the total forecasted units and dollars in the header. Each opportunity is listed with the contact, company, phone number, sales stage, expected close date, product number of units, dollar amount, and probability. This report prints in landscape mode.

➤ **Sales List** Generates a report that has the contact, company, and phone number, followed by the status of the opportunity, the close date, product, type, units, price, amount, probability, and the record manager.

➤ **Sales Funnel Report** This report generates contacts by sales stages, with the name of the contact, company, phone, close date, product, number of units, unit price, total sale and probability of closing. In addition, you can choose to see the report by the closed/won sales and/or lost sales. You can also sort the report in many ways, making this an extremely useful report.

➤ **Sales by Record Manager**   Generates a report that lists the record manager in the report header. Each opportunity has the status, close date, product, type, units, price, amount, percentage, and the contact.

➤ **Sales by Contact**   Generates a report that lists the name, company, and phone number, followed by the status, close date, product, type, units, price, amount, probability, and the record manager.

➤ **Sales Graph**   Generates the graph shown in the preceding figure of the Sales Forecast Graph.

➤ **Sales Funnel**   Generates the graph shown in the preceding figure of the Sales Funnel.

To create a sales report, follow these steps:

1. Open the **Reports** menu.
2. Select the **Sales Reports** option.
3. Select the type of report you want from the submenu.
4. Set the options for the report in the Run Report dialog box, and the **Sales/Opportunities** tab, which is shown in the following figure.

In the Run Report dialog box, the Sales/ Opportunities tab is selected, displaying further options for refining the report.

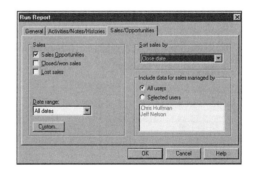

5. Click the **General** tab and pull down the list for **Send Out To** and select **Preview** to see the report on screen.
6. Click **OK**.

The report might take some time to print (or to appear on screen), as this process takes time. At the lower-left corner of the report window, a message appears indicating that the report is running. The next figure shows the Sales Funnel Report previewed.

A preview of the Sales Funnel Report is displayed onscreen.

The Reason Field Is Key

The key field to modify in the Complete Sale dialog box is the list that appears in the Reason field. Any good sales manager wants to track *why* sales are won or lost—not just the ratio of wins to losses. By entering a reason, marketing and sales strategies can be adjusted to focus on the most successful techniques.

Modifying a Report

Sales reports can be modified if you want to add or change the data presented. Chapter 19, "Working with Reports," is devoted to reports and the means to change existing reports or to create new reports.

Accessing Dale Carnegie Techniques from the Web

ACT! 2000's deliberate orientation toward salespeople is extended with this link. The Dale Carnegie Corporation specializes in training folks for sales, leadership, time management, and other crucial life skills. If your life is perfect as it is, you have no need to check this Web site. If, on the other hand, stress is an issue or you need specific skills for presentations, this is good to browse. The opening page, shown in the following figure, presents a series of self-assessment tests for various areas of your life. They are fun to take, with the understanding that they do lead you toward one of their courses—Relationship Process.

The Relationship Process is not really a process in ACT!; rather, selecting this option triggers the appearance of an Adobe Acrobat document that describes the Dale Carnegie training course on managing the relationship process.

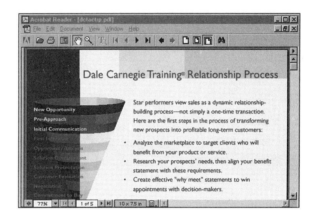

The Least You Need to Know

➤ Accurate sales forecasting is achievable with the Sales Opportunity dialog box.

➤ Add your sales model to ACT! by modifying the sales stages.

➤ Report on the sales activity either won or lost using the sales reports.

"An optimist is a man who has never had much experience."

Don Marquis

Chapter 19

Working with Reports

In This Chapter

➤ Looking at the standard ACT! reports

➤ Customizing a report

➤ Adding a customized report to the Reports menu

"Moderation is a fatal thing. Nothing succeeds like excess."

Oscar Wilde

The most difficult job of a salesperson is not selling, but creating reports on what has been done. No salesperson I know likes doing "call reports" but without them, it is nearly impossible to know where you are headed. ACT! has several standard reports that cover the needs of both the salesperson and the sales manager, especially the new reports that are generated via the Sales/Opportunities tab.

Standard ACT! Reports

Running any type of organization requires reports, and ACT! has what might be considered an excess amount of predefined reports. The reports run the gamut of targeted information from a contact record to the whole enchilada: every piece of data that is in the contact record. The best way to decide which report you want to run is to preview the report and see whether it contains the information you need. At the end of this chapter, I have provided a brief summary of what information is included in each type of report and for what purpose it is best suited.

To preview a report, you print the report to the computer screen, instead of a printer:

1. Open the **Reports** menu.
2. Select the report you would like to preview.
3. The Run Report dialog box appears, with the General tab selected, as shown in the next figure.

The Run Report dialog box appears with the General tab exposed.

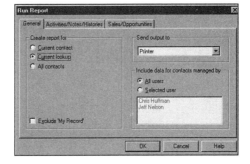

4. Change the **Send Output To** from Printer to **Preview** by pulling down the list in the field.
5. Select the radio button that coincides with the scope of contact records you want included, and then select the users.
6. Click **OK**.

The report is shown onscreen. This illustration shows a preview of the Contact Report. To see the report in detail, click the **Zoom** button to enlarge the report image.

You can zoom in on your preview of the Contact Report.

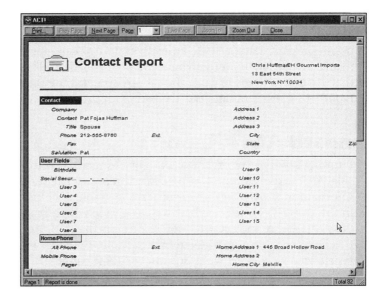

Run Report Options

Depending upon the report, you are presented with a series of options to fine-tune the results. After you select a report, the Run Report dialog box appears. The General tab has only three sets of options. The first set of options determines the scope of the records that are to be included in the report. As you become more skilled with creating lookups, you are able to target the report results, thereby gleaning better data from the database. So, click a radio button that meets the report needs.

The second option is where to send the report output. The available destinations, shown in the next figure, are described in the following list of General tab options:

➤ **Printer** Sends the report to the Windows print manager.

➤ **Preview** Sends the report to the screen in a window.

➤ **Fax** Sends the report to WinFax Pro, from which you can send to a fax recipient.

➤ **E-mail** Creates the report, and then opens the E-mail window; the report is attached as a file. At that point, you enter the details of the email message.

➤ **File-ACT! Report** Creates the report, and then opens the Save As dialog box so that you can name the report and save it. Later, you can open the report if you want. The report is saved with a RPT extension. You can save the report as a text file or in rich text format.

➤ **File-Editable Text** Creates the report, opens the Save As dialog box, and assumes that you want to save the report in RTF (rich text format). After saving the report, ACT! opens a prompt asking if you want to open the report in the default word processor.

➤ **Select Users** In a multi-user database, a contact record can be identified by the person who actually works with the contact record. (Check the Status tab for the Manager field.) So, when you create the report, you might want it seen by a specific manager(s).

➤ **Exclude My Record** Generally, you do not want the My Record included in the report.

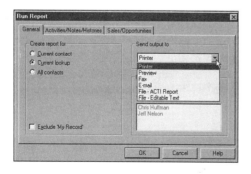

You have a variety of report output destinations available.

Email Reports

Any report your create in ACT! can easily be sent to, and read by, other ACT! users via email.

Activities/Notes/Histories Tab

The options in the Activities/Notes/Histories tab from the Run Report offer further refinement of the report. Note that not all reports have the options shown in the next figure. Select the items that you want included from the Notes/History section. If you include attachments, the attachment itself does not print, only the line item describing the attachment. This is true for the email, too.

The Run Report dialog box's Activities/Notes/Histories tab lets you include a variety of items in your report.

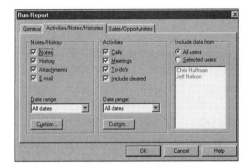

The Date Range drop-down has many preset ranges. If they are not sufficient, you can select **Custom**, and ACT! opens a calendar. Click and hold the mouse button on the first date you want to include and then drag the other days, or press the **Shift** key and use the arrow keys to highlight. It is tricky to move from month to month. I recommend that you use the Shift key and the arrow keys. When you have to move to a different month, use the **Page Down** or **Page Up** keys.

The Activities settings are the same as the Notes/History settings—select the type that you want to include and a date range for those items. You can have one date range for the Notes/History items and another for Activities.

The Include Data From setting allows another refinement. This is different from the Manager setting on the General tab. In this case, you can select Notes/Histories and Activities by the person who added them to the contact record. So, if you have a company in which both salespeople and customer-support people access the same contact records, you might want reports that isolate information by the person who added the information to the report.

Sales/Opportunities

The Sales/Opportunities tab is only active when one of the sales reports has been selected. For more detail on the individual sales reports, refer to Chapter 18,

"Forecasting Sales." One setting that you should look at is the Sorting options. Because the sales opportunities have unique datatypes, ACT! provides them as sort options. Pull down the list to select the order as the main sort order.

Customizing a Report

When you take on this task, it is usually because one of the predesigned reports does not exactly meet your needs. So, the logical starting point is to use one of the existing reports that is close to what you need. Or, you can create a brand new report by opening the **File** menu and selecting **Report Template**.

If you read the chapter on customizing layouts, the path is similar. When you are customizing a report, you cannot do anything else in ACT!. So, if you need to make a phone call via ACT!, you must close the editing session to do so.

1. Open the **Reports** menu.

2. Select the **Edit Report Template** option. The Open dialog box, shown in the next figure, appears.

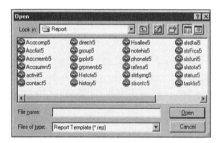

The report filenames listed in the Open dialog box are fairly inscrutable.

3. Select the report that is closest to what you want. (Unfortunately, the filenames that ACT! provides are not very helpful in identifying what they do. So, you might have to open a couple to get the one you want.)

4. Click **Open**. The report template opens as in the following figure.

5. Before making any changes, save the report with a different filename so that the original report is not lost.

6. Open the **File** menu.

7. Select **Save As**. The Save As dialog box appears.

8. Type a new name. In this example, I typed BOOKREPORT.

9. Click **Save**.

10. Open the newly renamed report. Open the **File** menu and select **Book Report**. The new report name appears at the top of the report window.

The Contact Report template is divided into sections that show the individual fields from the database.

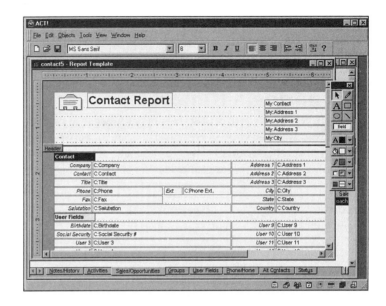

All ACT! reports are divided by the sections described here:

➤ **Header**   The report header prints at the top of each page in the report and usually has the name of the report, and the My Record information.

➤ **Primary Contact/Group**   This section of the report has the details from the contact or group record. Every report has either a primary Group or Contact section, but not both. However, a Contact might have a Group subsection, or a Group might have a Contact subsection.

➤ **Summary**   This section of the report contains totals derived from formulas in the section, such as totals, counts, maximum, and so on.

➤ **Footer**   This section of the report usually contains information such the print date of the report.

One of the problems that you might run into if you use an existing report is that some of the elements—for example, the section name—cannot be removed. You might have to start with a brand new template, as described later in this chapter.

Adding/Deleting Fields from a Report

Any of the fields in the report can be removed very easily. Click the field you do not want, so that the Windows handles appear. Right-click to open the pop-up menu and select **Cut**, as shown in the following figure.

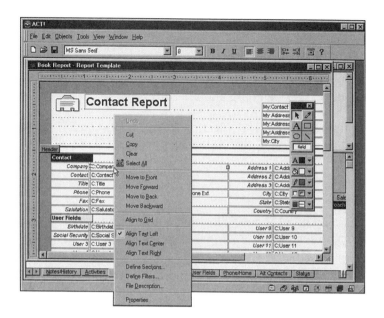

Access the pop-up editing menu in the report window.

To add a field, follow these steps:

1. Open the tool palette and select the field tool. (If the tool palette is not visible, click the **View** menu and select **Show Tool Palette**.)

2. Click the **Field** button in the tool palette. When you do, the mouse pointer is modified to crosshairs. With the crosshairs you draw the field outline.

3. Click and hold the mouse button on the crosshairs at the beginning point where you want to start the field.

4. Drag the mouse to the right (or to the left) to draw a rectangle.

5. Release the mouse button. When you do, the Field List dialog box appears as shown.

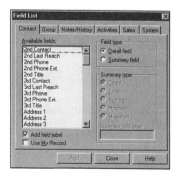

The Field List dialog box shows the information you can add to your report.

This dialog box offers many options for entering fields. The options are outlined in the section following.

6. Click the name of the field you want to add to the report. The Add Label attribute is on by default.

7. Click the **Add** button. The field name is inserted into the report. You can add several fields at the same time by selecting another field and clicking **Add**.

8. Save the report by opening the **File** menu and selecting **Save**.

Test the report by opening the **File** menu and selecting **Run**. The Run Report options dialog box appears. I suggest that you send the output to Preview, so that you can look at the results on your monitor.

Field List Dialog Box

The Field List dialog box, as shown in the preceding illustration, has many options. To better understand how the different options work, take a moment to read about the Contact tab options:

➤ **Available Fields**   ACT! lists the fields it has found in the database in alphabetical order. Unlike layouts, a report can have the same field used more than once. Generally, the information is pulled from the contact records, but you can pull information from the My Record by clicking the box.

➤ **Field Type**   Most of the time, you want a report to show the detail from the field in the contact record. The other choice is a summary field, which can be used when you have a field that has numeric information, except for the Count summary, which totals the number of entries in the field. So, if you use the Count summary, and the range of the records in the report is 30 records, and 20 of those records have entries in the field, then the summary field would display the number 20. It is a good idea to add a field label to a summary field.

Group Tab

The Group tab options are identical to the Contact tab options. Select the field you want to add to the report.

Notes/History, Activities, and Sales Tabs

These fields are very similar when added to reports. Select the field, and then determine whether you want a detail or summary field.

System Tab

System fields are generated by ACT! or Windows. You can access them by clicking the Field List dialog box's System tab, shown in the next figure. As an example, the Date field information is gleaned from the Windows system clock. So, if the date shows up incorrectly, then you have to reset the clock. The Activities, Notes/History, and Sales fields are derived from the settings you enter in the Run Report dialog box. Add a field label, too, because you will likely forget what the value represents.

The Field List dialog box's System tab gives you access to fields automatically generated by ACT! or Windows.

Running a Newly Created Report

To run a newly created report or one you modified, you have to open the **Reports** menu and select **Other Report**, because this is where reports are stored.

1. Open the **Reports** menu.
2. Select **Other Report**. The Open dialog box appears.
3. Click the report you want to run.
4. Click **Open**.
5. The Run Report dialog box opens and you can select the options to fine-tune the report.
6. Click **OK**.

Starting from Scratch

If none of the existing reports that come with ACT! are remotely close to what you envision, or have too much formatting that cannot be removed, you can start with a blank report and add exactly what you need.

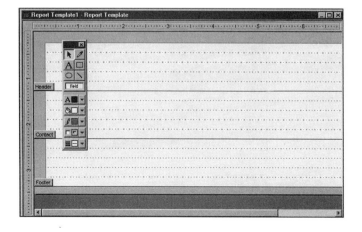

An unadorned new report template is ready for editing.

1. Open the **File** menu from the contact record window.
2. Select **New**.
3. From the dialog box, select **ACT! Report Template** and click **OK**. The blank report template appears.

At this point, you have to decide if the primary section is going to be a contact or group. By default, the template assumes that the report is going to have contact as the primary section.

Adding/Deleting Sections

To add a new section, or to delete an existing section, right-click in the report. Click the **Define Sections** option. The Define Sections dialog box appears, as shown in the following figure.

The Define Sections dialog box shows three section options.

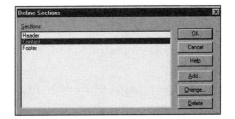

If you want Group as the primary section, click the **Contact** section name and click **Delete**. To add Group as the primary section, click the **Add** button, and the Add Section dialog box appears.

The Add Section dialog box lets you add a group as the primary section.

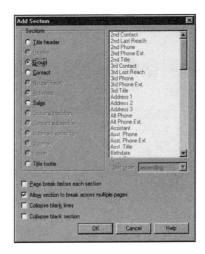

Select the section you want to add. Not all the section choices are active depending upon where you want to add them. If you want to create summary information—that is, fields that display the results of a formula—you must add a Summary section in which to display the field. I describe each of the sections briefly in the following list of Add Section dialog box options.

➤ **Title Header**   A Title Header is a section that prints once at the very beginning of the report. The normal Header section appears on all other pages of the report.

➤ **Notes/History**, **Activities**, and **Sales**   Each contains information from that tab in the contact record. Although you can add fields from any of the tabs in other sections, adding these as sections makes it easier for the reader of the report to distinguish the information.

➤ **Group/Contact Subsection**   This section appears in the dialog box because Contact is the primary section of the report. If Group was the primary section, then Contact subsection would be active.

➤ **Summary Sorted By**   Add this section and, not only can you add calculated fields, you can also sort by the field you select.

➤ **Summary**   Add this section to show the results of ACT! calculated fields.

➤ **Footer**   Add this section if you have deleted the report footer from the report and want to add it back.

➤ **Title Footer**   This section prints once on the first page of the report. The remaining pages have the normal footer.

➤ **Page Break Before Each Section**   After a section prints, you can have the report print the next section on an entirely different page.

➤ **Allow Section to Break Across Multiple Pages**   A section of the report can be very long and might consume several pages. For example, if the section is Notes/History, it might be very long. So, you can have the section print from page to page without being interrupted by a header or footer.

➤ **Collapse Blank Lines**   Some of the records might not have information and, with this option set to on, you save paper.

➤ **Collapse Blank Section**   If the fields you insert into a section have no information, selecting this option makes the report print the section name but no space is left blank.

Adding Fields

You already know how to add fields to the report. Click the **Field** button in the tool palette and select the fields from the dialog box.

Adding a Text Object

To add text to the report header, open the tool palette, and then

1. Click the **Text** tool. It looks like a large letter **A** on the tool palette.

2. Draw a rectangle in the header by clicking and dragging. Release the mouse button and you can begin typing.

3. In this example, I typed BOOK TITLE, as shown in the following figure.

The new text, BOOK TITLE, appears in the header.

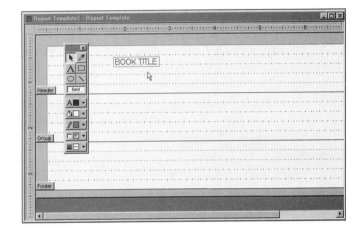

To add color to the text header background, click the tool palette and select the pointer tool. Next, click the text you just added. With it selected, you can add color to the background. The **Background Coloring** tool is the fourth one from the bottom of the tool palette. Click it and the color palette appears. Last, click the color you want for the background. The other tools can be used to add objects such as an ellipse or lines to the report or to add enhancements to fields.

Resizing a Section

If you need more room for fields in a section, you can easily add more space. The method is not obvious, however—no menu choice exists to aid you.

1. Click and hold the mouse button on the name of the section you want to enlarge or diminish.

2. Drag the name up to diminish, or down to enlarge.

ACT! allows you to change the size of the section within limits. In the predesigned reports, you have less sizing leeway.

Adding a Logo to the Report

To add a logo, you must have it saved in a bitmap (BMP) format. Open the report template in ACT!. Open the Windows Paint program by clicking the Windows **Start** button, and then selecting **Programs**, **Accessories**, and **Paint**. In Paint, open the logo file. Use the **Edit** menu in Paint to select the logo image, and then use the **Edit** menu again to select **Copy**. The logo image is now saved in memory on the Windows Clipboard. Return to the ACT! report template, and right-click the mouse to open the pop-up menu and select **Paste**. The logo image can be moved and resized as needed. Save the report and try printing. If the design is not enchanting, simply repeat the editing steps and modify the design.

Adding Filters to a Report

This is a very desirable feature to add to your report. The reason is that it makes it easy for a person not very familiar with ACT! to run the report with the data you expect.

1. Open the report template to which you want to add a filter.
2. Right-click the report template, and the pop-up menu appears.
3. Select **Define Filters**.
4. The only tab that is active is the General tab. You can select the range of contacts, the destination for the output, and the user's data that is to be included.
5. Save the report template.

When you run the report, the settings become the defaults for the report. But, the Run Report dialog box still appears, at which point you can make choices other than the defaults.

Adding a Custom Report to the Reports Menu

After you spend the time and effort to design a report, make it easy to run.

1. Open the **Reports** menu.
2. Select the **Modify Menu** option. The Modify Menu dialog box appears, as shown in the following figure.

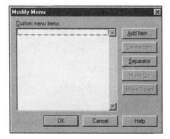

You can add a report to a menu via the Modify Menu dialog box.

3. Click the **Add Item** button. The Add Custom Menu Item dialog box appears, as shown in the following figure.

The Add Custom Menu Item dialog box lets you add your report to the menu of your choice.

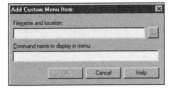

4. Click the small gray box with three dots at the far right of the Filename and Location field. This opens the Open dialog box, from which you can select your custom report.

5. Click the report name and click **Open**. Enter a name (I entered BOOK REPORT) that you want displayed on the Reports menu.

6. Click **OK**, and then click **OK** again.

The next figure shows the new report added to the Reports menu. Note that the Envelope report is already listed from Chapter 13, "Printing Labels, Envelopes, Address Books, and Calendars."

The new report is added to the Reports menu and is ready for action.

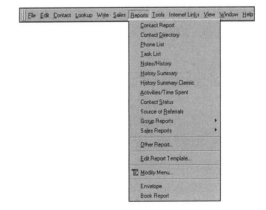

Summaries of the Standard Reports

Each of the predesigned reports has evolved over time because of feedback from ACT! users. The following is a synopsis of each and the intent of the report:

➤ **Contact Report**   This report prints everything that is in the contact record—every field and all the information on the various tabs.

➤ **Contact Directory**   This report prints the company, contact, and address information, including the four phone fields.

➤ **Phone List**   This report has the company, contact, phone, phone extension, and mobile phone number.

➤ **Task List**   This report prints the contact name, and his concomitant type of activity, its status (Open or Cleared), date, time, regarding, and the person for whom the activity is scheduled.

➤ **Notes/History**   This report prints the company and contact name, and the notes and histories.

➤ **History Summary**   This reports prints the company and contact name with a total of the number of field changes, meetings held, calls, to-dos, and synchronizations sent.

➤ **History Summary Classic**   This report disappeared for a time in ACT! and the hue and cry from ACT! users brought it back. The report prints the total number of attempted calls, completed calls, meetings held, and letters sent.

➤ **Activities/Time Spent**   This report prints the activities that have been cleared and are still open. Each contact is listed with the status, type of activity, date and time, duration, and regarding.

➤ **Contact Status**   This report includes the name and company, the phone number, the last reached, the last results, the ID/Status, a section on activities, and the last meeting.

➤ **Source of Referrals**   This report is terrific for judging the results of marketing programs. The reports lists the source of referrals and the total from that source, followed by the name and company, title, and phone number of the referred contact. Any contact that does not have a Referred By entry, prints at the beginning of the report.

The following are the reports on the Group Reports submenu:

➤ **Group Membership**   Prints a report that lists the name of the group and its total number of members, followed by the name, company, phone, and title of the members. Also, each of the subgroups and its contacts are listed.

➤ **Groups Summary**   This report prints a report similar to a contact report with the group name and address information and all the user fields, plus some system fields such as the record creator, the create date, and the edit date. Also the subgroups are included with the activities, notes, and history.

➤ **Groups Comprehensive**   This report prints everything that is in the group record, by group name.

➤ **Groups List**   Prints the name of each group, its description, name of the subgroups, and the number of subgroups.

For details on the Sales reports submenu, see Chapter 18.

The standard reports cover 95% of what most ACT! users need. But, you can enhance any report or create a new report if needed. ACT!'s report writer is limited in functionality, so if you need more extensive reporting, check Chapter 26, "Act! Add-on Products," for information on Seagate Crystal Reports, which is a software program for specifically creating reports.

The Least You Need to Know

➤ The standard reports that come with ACT! cover 95% of what most companies need. Test them to see which is closest to your reporting needs.

➤ You can modify any existing report and rename it, or create a new report from scratch.

➤ After modifying or creating a report, add it to the Reports menu if you use it frequently.

"Everybody who is incapable of learning has taken to teaching."

Oscar Wilde (who else?)

Chapter 20

Using SideACT!

"In the mountains of truth you never climb in vain."

Nietzsche

What Is SideACT!?

One of the criticisms of ACT! that has been consistent since the initial DOS version in 1989 was the lack of an easy way to record a task that was not necessarily related to a contact in the database. In other words, you basically had two courses of action if you wanted to be reminded to pick up your dry cleaning. One was to enter the dry cleaner as a contact record (a *profile*, back in the DOS days), and then, if on a network, make the record private so that the boss did not see it while reviewing your weekly activity report. Or, you could add the errand as a to-do attached to the My Record. Either way was cumbersome, especially the latter, because your History would become cluttered with effluvia.

So, in version 4.0, SideACT! was introduced and continues in ACT! 2000. This is a separate program that allows you to willy-nilly enter tasks within (and this is the sexy part) or *without* ACT!. This concept posed a considerable challenge to the software designers, because almost since its inception, ACT! has had an official *Task List* (refer to Chapter 8, "Tackling Activities") that combines the activities of all the records in the database. The challenge is two-fold—how to get around the semantic (no pun intended) problem of adding what is in reality a second form of a task list, and how to connect the new task list to ACT! They also added a SideACT! icon to the ACT! toolbar, so that you could pop into SideACT! easily from within ACT!.

When you install ACT! 2000, an icon appears on your desktop and an entry is made to the Startup folder, that will start SideACT! regardless of whether ACT! itself is running. To begin using this new attribute, you simply double-click the desktop icon or choose **SideAct!** from its **Start** menu folder. When you do, the SideACT! window appears.

The SideACT! opening window appears when you launch the program.

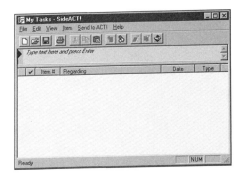

At the top of the window is the title *My Tasks*. Although most users will likely use only one SideACT! file at a time, SideACT! allows you to create many unique files consisting of one or many tasks, although you can only have one open at a time. But, it is great to have the facility to create different files in case you have several projects going for which you want to keep separate lists.

Entering a Task

With SideACT! open, the insertion point is automatically positioned so that you can begin typing the task you want to record. So, type a task as I have done in this illustration. (Because this book's obviously done, you might use a different task such as Buy cat food.)

Enter an initial task into SideACT!.

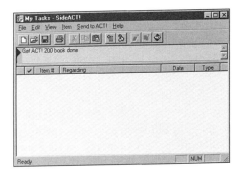

After typing the task, you add it to the SideACT! list by pressing **Enter** or clicking the **Add** button. The task is now listed in the bottom portion of the window, as in the next figure.

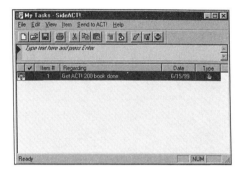

Your task is added to the SideACT! list.

That was easy enough! Now, the advantage of being able to build a list of tasks without having to open ACT!, is most apparent if you're like me. You have ideas popping into your head constantly and tend to scribble notes on pieces of paper, which have a nasty habit of disappearing about the time you need them. These tasks and ideas are not necessarily connected to any particular person. Or, if you tend to work in a different application most of the time and would rather have all system memory available, then you close ACT! rather than having it on the desktop.

When you are finished adding a task, you can minimize the SideACT! window, close the SideACT! application, or start ACT! 2000 and decide if you want to move or copy the task or tasks to ACT! itself. By the way, all tasks entered into SideACT! are assumed to be to-do's—unless you change the default setting to another type of activity or change an individual task item after adding it to the list. If you simply close SideACT!, all items are retained, you do not have to take any steps to save the list. This is true even for an entry in the text entry area above the list. Having added a series of tasks, let's move to the next step of connecting the tasks to ACT!.

Completing a SideACT! Task

To mark a task in SideACT! as being completed, right-click the mouse on the item and from the pop-up menu, select **Mark as Completed**. SideACT! draws a line through the item. This menu also allows you to delete, cut, or copy a task.

Getting SideACT! Tasks into ACT!

The tasks in SideACT! can be moved or copied to ACT!. Moving a task removes it from the list in SideACT!, while copying duplicates the task to your ACT! database. You can move the task items as a whole, or select individual items. In the following figure, the first item in the list is selected.

297

To move or copy a task from SideACT! to ACT! 2000:

1. Right-click anywhere on the item to open the pop-up menu.

2. Select **Send to ACT!**.

3. Select either **Move** or **Copy**. When you do, a dialog box appears, quizzing you for the destination for the item.

This dialog box checks with you for the correct destination for a SideACT! item.

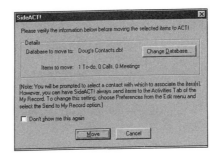

4. If the database that ACT! suggests for the destination is correct, click **Move** (or **Copy**). If not, click the **Change Database** button to select the destination database.

5. After clicking Move or Copy, the destination database is opened and the Associate with Contact dialog box appears. ACT! assumes that you want to associate the item with the My Record.

In the Associate with Contact dialog box, the My Record is selected by default.

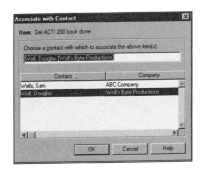

At this point, scroll the window listing the contact names and their respective companies to locate a different target record, or type the initial letters of the last name of the contact and ACT! lists the matching name in the field. Click **OK** to accept. After being moved or copied to the database the item appears in two places: on the Activities tab in the contact record and in the Task List—the same as any other activity.

Setting Preferences for SideACT!

To set the preferences, you open **SideACT!** and open the **Edit** menu and select **Preferences** from the menu. The dialog box offers the options to make any new item a Call, Meeting, or To-do. You can sort the list so that any new item is added either to the top or bottom of the list or so that any items you mark as completed are moved to the bottom of the list or left in place. You can set the default to send all items directly to the My Record. In addition, you can shut off the transfer confirmation window that appears when moving or copying items and you can have ACT! display the SideACT! icon in the Windows taskbar at the bottom right of your computer screen.

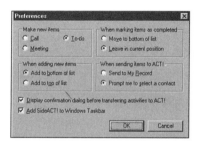

You can set your own Preferences for SideACT! in this dialog box.

Creating and Opening a Second SideACT! File

One of the uses of SideACT! is for personal goal setting. If you have educated yourself on goal setting, you know that goal setting should include financial, spiritual, physical, and emotional goals. SideACT! is an excellent place to store those goals as they are readily accessible. But, they are private, so you might not want your goal list to be on your desktop at all times. Plus, you might have several projects for which you would like to create lists—not as a detailed project manager but as guideposts or check items.

To create a second SideACT! list:

1. Open the **File** menu.
2. Select **New**.

    A new SideACT! window appears with the word *Untitled* in the upper-left corner.

3. Open the **File** menu and select **Save**.
4. The Save As dialog box appears. Type a name for the new SideACT! list.

To switch between lists, use the **File** menu and select **Open**. In the resulting dialog box, click the list you want to see.

Printing the SideACT! List of Tasks

The workday is over and as you prepare to head for home, you can print your list of chores. For example, you might have entered into SideACT! your grocery list. Or, you might have entered the stores to visit: supermarket, dry cleaners, and cigar shop. In either case, print the list so you can stuff it in your pocket on the way out the door. Simply click the **Printer** button and the list is hard copy.

The Least You Need to Know

➤ SideACT! is a small program that lets you enter tasks without associating them with an ACT! contact.

➤ To add an activity to SideACT!, click the desktop icon or click the SideACT! icon in the ACT! toolbar, and start typing. Finish the new entry by pressing Enter.

➤ You can move or copy SideACT! tasks to ACT!.

"Whatever you cannot understand, you cannot possess."

Goethe

Chapter 21

Importing/ Exporting Data

In This Chapter

➤ Getting data into ACT!

➤ Getting data out of ACT!

➤ Checking for duplicates

The dream of seamless data portabilty—that is, moving data from one application to another easily—has been a dream for many years, and not only in the PC world. Even today, one need look no further than the obstacles for sharing Macintosh and PC data files. This chapter is devoted to the movement of data into ACT! and out again. This is a trial-and-error process and I show you how to avoid the nastier problems that you can encounter.

Older Versions of ACT!

Before looking at importing data from other programs, a quick note is necessary on getting data from older versions of ACT!. When you install ACT!, it is supposed to check for a prior version of ACT! and check for databases created by that version. If found, ACT! prompts you to convert the database to the current version. It is possible that you have an ACT! database on your hard drive created by an older version, but that the old ACT! program is not on your computer and so ACT! does not identify the old database. The conversion of an old database can done by you:

1. Close any database you have open.
2. Open the **File** menu.
3. Select **Open**. The Open dialog box appears.
4. Click the pull-down arrow in the **Files of Type** field.
5. Select the matching ACT! database type. You will probably have to browse to the folder that contains the older ACT! database.
6. Click the old database, and then click **OK**.

ACT! alerts you that the database was created by an older version of ACT! and that it will be converted. You also have the option of making a backup copy of the older database, which is always a good idea.

Importing Data from Other Programs

ACT! can import data from several file types. That means that if you have information in a different program, it can be converted into ACT!. The most common file type in use in creating databases is *dBASE*. Now, dBASE itself comes in several flavors, and not every flavor can be imported into ACT!, but the vast majority can. The second file type is called *Text-delimited*, (ASCII is a synonym) and in some cases where a database cannot be imported as a dBASE file, the program that created the database might be able to export its data into a delimited text file, thereby allowing ACT! to import it. You will not know until you try to import the other database what the results will be. That is why I recommend that you create a database that is a temporary holding place for the data. You can look at it and see if it is correct, or delete the imported records and try again.

The steps to import data are

1. Create a new, blank database in ACT!.
2. Open the **File** menu and select **Data Exchange**.
3. Select **Import**. The Import Wizard dialog box appears.

The Import Wizard dialog box appears after opening the File menu and selecting Data Exchange and Import.

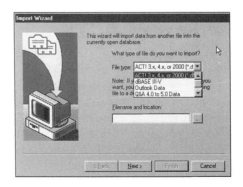

The next step is to determine what file type you are trying to import. Open the pull-down list for file types.

4. Select the file type of the database you are trying to import. Check the source program's documentation for help. In most cases, select the dBASE or Text-delimited item.

5. In the **Filename and Location** field, type the name of the file, or click the **Browse** button (the gray box with three dots) to locate the file. dBASE files have an extension such as ADB, DB, DBF, or something very similar. Delimited text files have a TXT, CSV, or ASC extension. After you have located the file, click it, and then click **Open**.

6. Click **Next** to move to the next dialog box.

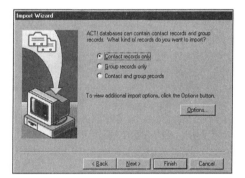

The next Import Wizard dialog box asks for direction on which records to import.

ACT! does not know if the database you are trying to import has only contact or group records. If it is not an ACT! database, it will not have group records, and so you can select the Contact Records Only option.

The Options button is important if you are *merging* a database into an existing database. For example, if you are merging an ACT! database into an existing ACT! database and you suspect that there are records in both that are alike—maybe not identical, but essentially the same records—you need to click the Options button and review the settings. See the section later in this chapter on handling merge options.

7. Click **Next**. The Import Wizard CONTACT MAP dialog box appears. (Unless you are importing from a database other than ACT!. In that case, you will get a dialog box with map files for some other contact managers, such as GoldMine. Click the radio button in front of **Use Predefined Map** and select the program from which you are importing.)

The Import Wizard Contact Map dialog box is used to match field for field from the database you are importing to the ACT! database.

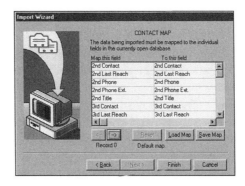

This is where you physically map the data in the source database (the one you are importing) to the ACT! destination database.

On the left, under the heading Map This Field are the field names ACT! has read from the source database. On the right, under the heading To This Field is the field into which ACT! thinks the data from the source database belongs.

ACT! reads the file information header from the source database and tries to match the fields in the source with its own fields. In other words, the source database has at the beginning of the database the name of the fields. So, in the source database, there might be a field called COMPANY, which has all the company names in it. So, ACT! matches the source database COMPANY field with its company field. If ACT! cannot match a field from the source with any of its fields, it leaves a blank for you to map.

8. Click the right arrow button above **Record 0**, so that it reads Record 1. When you do, the field names on the left are replaced with information from the first record in the source database, making it much easier for you to see if the data is going where it belongs. Scroll down the map to check all the fields. If the data is across from the correct field, you can finish the import.

   If you think you might need the map at another time, save it by clicking the **Save Map** button. Plus, if the import was off just a little, you can reload the map and tweak it, saving you the time of having to remap every field.

9. Click the **Finish** button.

If you have many records—say, in the thousands—now is the time for that latte break, as this will take time.

After ACT! has finished and the data is in the correct fields, you have to perform maintenance in order for ACT! to be able to work with the records.

1. Open the **File** menu and select **Administration**.

2. Select **Maintenance**. The Database Maintenance dialog box appears.

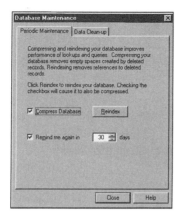

The Database Maintenance dialog box lets you reindex your imported records.

3. Click the **Reindex** button. This, too, can take some time, so back for some spumoni with your latte.

When ACT! is finished, your database is ready to go. If you look at the newly imported records and see that there are major problems, you have two choices: Move the data in one ACT! field to the correct field, or trash the database and start over.

To delete a database, you must be the administrator of the database. You cannot delete the database at which you are looking.

1. Open a different database.
2. Open the **File** menu and select **Administration**.
3. From the submenu, select **Delete Database**. The Delete Database dialog box opens.
4. Click the database to be deleted and click the **Delete** button. ACT! checks to make certain you are the administrator before allowing the deletion.

Copying Data from Field to Field

This subject is useful at more times than just importing, but this is where it seemed to fit best. In the scenario where you have imported the data and reindexed the database, and find that some data that should have gone into one field has arrived in another, you can copy the data to the correct field or swap the data in one field with data in another. Nifty.

To copy data in one field in ACT! to another:

1. Click the **Edit** menu.
2. Select **Replace**. ACT! displays a blank record.
3. Open the **Replace** menu and select **Copy a Field**. The Copy Field Contents dialog box appears. Click the drop-down arrow under the **Copy Contents Of** text box to see a list of fields.

305

The Copy Field Contents dialog box contains a drop-down field list.

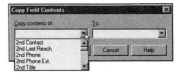

4. Scroll the field list under **Copy Contents Of** (or type the first letter of the field name) to identify the field in which the data is wrong.

5. In the **To** field, pull down the list and select the destination for the data.

6. Click **OK**.

ACT! warns you that the action modifies all contacts in the lookup. Click **OK** to finish. If the data was copied from or to a Lookup, Company, First Name, or Last Name field, perform a reindex, as described previously.

You must have seen the other option, that being to swap contents of one field with another. Use that option when the data in field A should be in field B and the field B data should be in field A.

Making a Field Blank

One other option is to erase the data in a field. A note here: This method does not work with *all* fields in ACT; for example, it does not work with the Salutation field or Web Address field. Open the **Edit** menu and select **Replace**. Click the field that you want to make blank. Press the spacebar, which ACT! interprets as a valid entry. Click the **Apply** button on the toolbar. All the data in that field is erased and replaced with a blank character.

Copy, Swap, or Blank Specific Records After a Mistake

Suppose that you have imported records into your working database instead of a blank database. You goofed. ACT! allows you to modify records in a lookup, but the question is: How do you lookup only the newly imported records?

1. Open the **Lookup** menu.

2. Select the **By Example** option.

3. Click the **Status** tab.

4. In the **Merge Date** field, enter the date that matches the import date.

5. Click the **Run** button on the toolbar.

ACT! finds all the records that have been imported per your date entry. Now, you can use the **Contact** menu to delete the current lookup, or use the **Edit** menu to copy, swap, or blank the affected field(s).

Mapping Fields That Do Not Match

The easy scenario seldom happens, so let's look at the other mapping steps you might have to take to get the data into your database. The ACT! side of the map allows you to select the destination field from a drop-down list to match the source field. In the following figure, the field list is open.

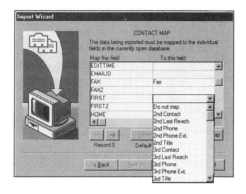

You've opened the field list in the Import Wizard's mapping dialog box.

You can scroll with the mouse to select the correct field, or you can type the first letter of the field name. So for ID/Status, type the letter ɪ, and the field appears. Click the field to add it to the map.

For some imports, you might have a source database that uses two separate fields for First Name and Last Name. Because ACT! uses the single field, Contact, for both names, Symantec provides a way to create the map by including mapping fields, First Name and Last Name. Use these fields, and ACT! puts the incoming names into the Contact field correctly.

There might be fields in the source database that do not exist in your ACT! database. You have two choices. You can cancel the import process, and then add new fields to the ACT! database, as described in Chapter 17, "Creating New Fields." Then, return to the import process, and map the fields. Or, you can map the fields from the source database to one or more of the User fields. If you choose the second path, take a moment to make a paper map, noting which source field was mapped to which user field.

Finally, if there are fields that you do not want to include in the import, the first option on the drop-down list is Do Not Map.

Merge Options

Following my recommendation, you should have created an empty database into which you imported records. The newly created ACT! database, if the import has worked correctly, can then be imported into your working database. It is possible that records in your working database match the records you are importing—that is they might be identical based on the Company, Contact, and Phone fields, which are the fields ACT! uses to determine if the records might be duplicates. (You can change the fields ACT! uses for this purpose, as described in the following section.) The following figure shows the Merge Options dialog box that you can open when running the Import Wizard. Keep in mind that the *source* database is the one you are importing into the currently open database, which is called the *destination* database.

Use the Merge Options dialog box for importing records.

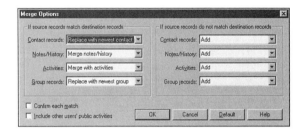

If the source and destination records match:

➤ **Contact Records**   Your options are to replace with the newest contact, replace with source contact, or do not change. If you choose to replace with the newest contact, ACT! looks at the edit dates of both records, source and destination, and keeps only the newest record. If you choose to replace with the source contact, the record in your database is overwritten by the incoming record.

➤ **Notes/History**   If source and destination records match, you can merge the notes and history, which combines the notes/history of both records. Or, you can replace the notes in the destination record with the source record notes/history. Or, you can choose to not make a change.

➤ **Activities**   If the source and destination records match, you can merge the activities, which combines the activities of both records. Or, you can replace the activities in the destination record with the source activities. Or, you can choose to not make a change.

➤ **Group Records**   If the source group matches the destination group, you can replace with the newest group, replace with the source group, or make no change.

If source records do not match destination records:

➤ **Contact Records**   You can choose to add the record or not. It is possible that you might want to perform a merge that only affects matching records in both databases and you do not want to add records that do not match.

➤ **Notes/History**   If you add records that do not match destination records, you can decide whether or not to include the notes/history.

➤ **Activities** If you add records that do not match destination records, you can decide whether or not to include the activities.

➤ **Groups Records** If groups do not match, you can choose to add the group or not.

The two check boxes appear at the bottom of this dialog box. The **Confirm Each Match** option causes ACT! to stop the merge when it thinks it locates a matching record in the destination database. A dialog box appears at that point asking you if you want to merge the records (based on your settings), add the record as a new record, or skip the record, which means the record is not imported or merged. If you know there are many matching records and you are confident in your merge settings, leave this off. Otherwise, you must sit in front of the computer and confirm every match—a time-consuming practice. The **Include Other Users' Public Activities** option is off by default. I recommend that it be set to on; you can always delete activities later.

Checking for Duplicates

Most of the time the fields ACT! uses by default to check for duplicates (and matches during import routines) is acceptable. But, you might have modified your ACT! database in such a way, or are using fields in such a way, that you want to use a different field or fields to check for duplicates. An example of the latter case is the ID/Status field. Many companies use this field for the customer account number, which you do not want to be duplicated. Because ACT! does not allow you to create an entry rule for a field so that only a unique number is entered, it is possible to enter the same number in two or more records. In that case, you would want ACT! to check the ID/Status field for duplication. To change the field or fields that ACT! checks, take the following steps:

1. Open the **Edit** menu.
2. Select the **Define Fields** option. The Define Fields dialog box appears.
3. Select the **Advanced** tab at the top of the dialog box.

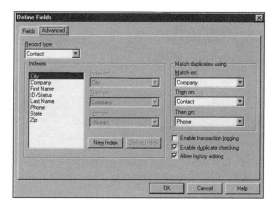

The Define Fields dialog box appears with the Advanced tab selected.

ACT! uses three fields to check for matching records, and for a match to be made, any of three fields can match. In other words, if a record has the company as Megatex, the contact as John Braun, and the phone number as 555-555-5555, and a second record has the company as Megatex, ACT! interprets that has a match. At that point, you intervene and determine if it is a duplicate and should be merged with an existing record, added as a new record, or skipped, which means that it is not imported.

4. Change the fields you want ACT! to check for duplicates by opening the drop-down list and clicking the field name. Be sure that **Enable Duplicate Checking** is checked.

5. Close the dialog box by clicking **OK**.

6. Open the **Tools** menu.

7. Select the **Scan for Duplicates** option.

If ACT! finds any suspected duplicates, the record counter will read 1 of X. At that point you can move from record to record to compare the records. I prefer to change to the list view so that I can easily put the fields side by side to see which record is correct, and then delete the incorrect record.

Exporting Records from ACT!

You can export records from ACT! in two formats: as text-delimited or as ACT! 2.01 for DOS. In the process of exporting, you can export only certain records. Let's take a look, using ACT!'s Export Wizard.

First, if you need to, create a lookup of the records that you want to export.

1. Open the **File** menu and select **Data Exchange**.

2. Select **Export**.

The Export Wizard dialog box lets you control how you export your contact records.

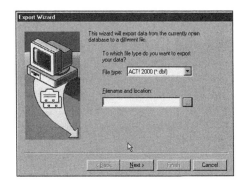

3. Select which type of export you want. If you are exporting to an ACT! database, it must already exist. If you are exporting to a text-delimited file, ACT! creates it for you.

4. In the **Filename and Location** field, browse to locate the destination database. Or, for a new text-delimited file, browse to the folder, type a name for the file, and click **Save**.

5. Click **Next**. Choose to export the contact records or the group records.

   For a text-delimited export, click the **Options** button and choose the type of delimiter. You might have to ask the person who plans to import the records which delimiter is preferred. Also, ask if they want the field names to be exported with the records. Normally, the answer is yes.

   For exporting to an ACT! database, you can export contact records with or without groups. Click the **Options** button and the Merge dialog box opens. Read the section on merging records to determine the settings you need.

6. Click **Next**. You now can choose to export the current record, lookup, or all records.

7. Click **Next**. If you are exporting to an ACT! database, you must map the fields as explained earlier in this chapter. For text-delimited exports, the dialog box shows only one list of fields.

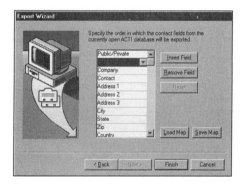

The text-delimited options of the Export Wizard dialog box let you provide your contact information to users of earlier programs.

As you can see, you can arrange the order in which the fields are exported (starting from the top, which is the first field exported) or decide whether or not the field data is exported at all. To exclude a field from the export, open the pull-down list and scroll to the very top of the list, which is a blank entry, and click. The field is eliminated from the list, giving you control over what information is sent to the delimited text file.

The Least You Need to Know

➤ Getting data into ACT! is not necessarily an easy process, depending upon the source file structure. If it is an ACT!-to-ACT! import, the process is easier (provided the fields are the same in both databases).

➤ Getting data out of ACT! is very straightforward. You can export all the data from every field, or simply export the fields you want in the order you want.

➤ ACT! performs a duplicate check as determined by the fields you select. You can run a manual check for duplicates from the Tools menu.

"There are two good things in life—freedom of thought and freedom of action."

W. Somerset Maugham

Part 5

Now That It Works, Don't Break It

Keeping the machine running smoothly and extending ACT!'s reach is the theme of Chapters 22 to 26. Maintenance is very important, as anyone who has lost his database can tell you. As important is having your data with you when you need it and making sure that the data is accurate and up to date. ACT! also can be used with several other software products that are explored here.

Chapter 22

Maintaining and Backing Up ACT! Data

In This Chapter

➤ How to maintain your database

➤ Creating automatic reminders

➤ Distributing your database

➤ Repairing you database

"All is flux, nothing is stationary."

Heraclitus

It is an unfortunate fact of life that nature is always in the process of creating and destroying at the same time. It would be great if computers never crashed, if backup tapes never broke, or if databases did not become corrupted because the second most important asset a business has is its information. (Its people are first.) Information comes in many forms, and your ACT! information is likely your present and future customers. If you think of the cost of acquiring those customers, you can see the value of investing time and energy in maintaining your ACT! database.

Backing Up Your Database

The most important aspect of keeping this prized asset intact is making backup copies regularly. Many customers wonder how often a backup should be made. The long answer is determined by how old your database could be and not cost you more in lost business than the cost of making the backup. The short answer is to back up your database at least once per day. It is even better to back up once at the beginning of the day and again at the end of the day. The end-of-day backup assures you that if a computer crashes at startup (the most likely time), you have lost nothing. The end-of-day backup should be taken off site in case of computer theft or a disaster in the building.

Network Backups

Many companies now have systems that back up data every evening. That might be sufficient, but if the server crashes, how long could you go without your ACT! data? It can take hours to repair a server, and then replace the lost data files. Also, some network backup systems do not do full backups—only incremental backups, which are not sufficient for ACT!. Only a full backup of all the database files will work.

Backup Styles

A full backup backs up everything. For an incremental backup, the backup software looks at the file date and, if the date is later than the last backup, copies the file to the backup media. ACT! files are date sensitive, so if one of the files is backed up out of order, the backup is no longer any good.

The ACT! database consists of a series of files, not one large file. So, it is important that you use ACT!'s backup program to make the backup.

To make a backup of your database:

1. Open the database you want to back up.
2. Open the **File** menu.
3. Select the **Backup** item.

The Backup dialog box lets you copy an existing ACT! database.

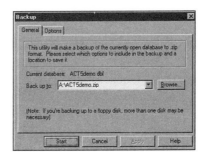

The backup program in ACT! creates a compressed copy of the database and any other files you designate (more on this in the next step). A very large database can be stored on 3.5-inch disks, because the compression program can create a series of disks that contain one large file. If you are on a network, you can send the compressed file to a different drive, as directed by your network administrator, by using the Browse button.

4. Click the **Options** tab in the Backup dialog box to determine whether you want to include more file types. The following illustration shows the other files that you can make part of the backup file.

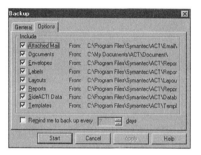

The Backup dialog box's Options tab lists the other file types you can include in your backup.

5. Click the file types you want to include in the backup. The file locations are derived from the settings ACT! finds in the Preferences dialog box's General tab. (Select **Preferences** from the **Edit** menu and click the **General** tab to see ACT!'s file types.)

6. Set the time reminder for backing up your database. I'd recommend that you do this twice a day, but that isn't an option, so set the reminder at every day.

7. Click **Start**. If you are backing up to 3.5-inch disks, and the database has several thousand records, you can't go to the coffee shop for that mocha, because you must stand by and insert new disks as needed. ACT! overwrites any data on the disk, so be certain that the disk is not a backup of your accounting data or anything else important.

That's the process! After several minutes, the backup is completed and you are good to go on your way.

Restoring a Saved Database

In the unhappy event where your system has crashed and you need that backup to bring your ACT! data back, you'll find the restore process just as easy as backing up:

1. Open the **File** menu.

2. Select **Restore**. The Restore dialog box opens. Assuming that you have backed up the database to the A drive, click the **Browse** button and select that floppy

disk drive. If you have backed up to a different drive (such as a network drive), select it instead.

The Restore dialog box lets you recover a database that you have backed up.

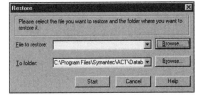

3. In the **To Folder** field, accept the path that ACT! has selected or use the **Browse** button to select the folder.

4. Click **Start**. ACT! displays a dialog box alerting you that the currently open database will be closed and the restored database opened.

5. Click **OK**.

ACT! begins reading the data from the disk or location where you have stored the backup. If all goes well, the database will be restored.

A Further Bit of Advice

If you use 3.5-inch disks to back up your database, make at least two sets of disks with every backup. That way, if a floppy disk dies, you have another set. It might take longer, but a 20-disk backup is no good if even one disk gets lost, damaged, or corrupted.

Reindexing Your Database

The ACT! database includes a series of indexes that it uses to locate contact records, notes, histories, and so on. These can become corrupted in several ways, such as ACT! writing data to a questionable portion of the hard drive, shutting off the computer with an ACT! database open, the operating system not behaving, or by the position of the moon. (This last situation is know as lunar luck or moonstruck.) The corruption becomes apparent when ACT! shuts down when you are doing a lookup or trying to add a note, or when the record counter reads *125 of 14* (a larger number cannot precede a smaller one).

Patience Pays

On a network, you must be patient. Sometimes it appears that ACT! is not running, when in fact it is trying to complete an assignment. Users often try the Ctrl-Alt-Del key combination, and the Windows Task List displays ACT! as *not responding* when in fact it *is* running. Give it more time and it generally responds.

Reindexing should be done a minimum of once per week. ACT! 2000 makes it easy to remember to do this by presenting a dialog box when you start that lists reminders. When you run the reindex program, ACT! resets the files that point to the data in the database.

To reindex your database, do the following:

1. Open the **File** menu and select **Administration**.
2. From the Administration submenu, select **Database Maintenance**. A dialog box appears.

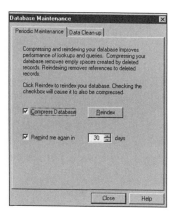

The Database Maintenance dialog box appears when you begin to reindex your database.

There are two main options here. You can Compress and Reindex, or simply Reindex. Use the Compress option when you have deleted records from the database.

3. Click **Reindex**. If you are on a network, ACT! checks to see if any other users are currently logged into the database. If they are, you, as the supreme administrator,

can close them out at a certain time. They get a message on their computer screens that alerts them that they are going to be kicked out of ACT!, giving them an opportunity to finish what they are doing.

Depending on the size of your database and the speed of your computer, the reindexing operation is usually very fast.

Other Maintenance Options

In the Database Maintenance dialog box, you have a few other options that need to be considered. The Data Clean-up tab in the Database Maintenance dialog box presents a host of options.

The Data Clean-up tab shown in the Database Maintenance dialog box lets you perform a variety of maintenance chores.

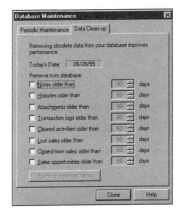

The current date, shown in the Today's Date box, comes from your computer's system clock. Make sure it's correct. If it is wrong, you have to reset it via Windows.

Each of the items listed can be selectively removed from your database. For example, you might never want to delete notes from your records, but attachments might be useless after 12 months. The key here is to have a backup of the database, and then purge the items that you think are no longer necessary. One of the benefits of deleting older information is that ACT! runs faster if less data is part of each record.

After setting the dates for each, click the **Remove Selected Items** button. ACT! then removes the items and reindexes and compresses the database.

Resetting Your Windows Clock

If the date or time in your computer's system clock is wrong, you can easily change it:

1. Click **Start**.

2. Select **Settings**.

3. Select **Control Panel**.

4. In the Control Panel, double-click the **Date/Time** icon.

5. Click the portion of the time that is incorrect, and then use the up or down arrows to the right of the field to adjust the time.

6. Click **OK**.

Setting Reminders for Maintenance

It's all very well to intend to perform maintenance chores on a regular basis, but it can help if ACT! reminds you about these vital tasks. The File menu's Set Reminders option is your key to having ACT! prompt you at regular intervals. The resulting dialog box offers the following maintenance options and some other ACT! actions:

➤ **Backup**   Select this option to have ACT! remind you daily to back up. If you are connected to the network and are not the administrator, leave this option off.

➤ **Database Maintenance**   Select this option if you are the administrator and open ACT! every day so that you see the reminder. This procedure should be done weekly.

➤ **Update ACT! and Outlook Calendars**   If you are sharing calendar information with Outlook 98 users, you can have ACT! automatically update the Outlook users.

➤ **Run Group Membership Rules**   When you create groups in ACT!, (refer to Chapter 15, "Working with Groups") one of their prominent uses is for synchronizing the database with remote users. But, in the past, when a new contact record was added to the main database, someone had to add that contact record to the correct group so that it was sent to the remote user via synchronization. ACT! 2000 eliminates the possibility of a new contact record not being added to the correct group by allowing you to create rules whereby ACT! automatically recognizes that a new contact record belongs in a certain group. Still, on occasion, someone has to run the rules-checking procedure, and you can have ACT remind you.

➤ **Synchronize** ACT! has an automatic synchronization schedule in which you can program the time and dates to synchronize. But, you might not need a rigid schedule and only want to be reminded occasionally. This setting allows you to do that.

➤ **Roll Over Activities to Today's Calendar** Activities that are not cleared can be rolled over automatically using the Edit menu and Preferences/Scheduling dialog box. If you have not set the activities to automatically roll over, ACT! can search for uncleared activities and roll them over with this option.

After making the setting you desire, click **OK**. The next time you start ACT!, it checks to see if any reminders are pending.

Creating a Copy of the Database

There might be instances where you want an exact copy of the database, but not in the compressed format that is created by the backup program.

To make an exact copy of the currently opened database, take these steps:

1. Open the **File** menu.
2. Select **Save Copy As**. The Save Copy As dialog box appears.

The Save Copy As dialog box lets you create a copy of your database complete with records or a blank copy.

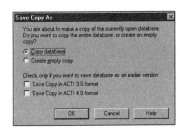

If you want a complete copy, select the **Copy Database** option. ACT! opens the Save As dialog box, in which you can browse to another drive or folder to save the copy and add a new name.

Fixing Databases

You might not be aware of it, but your ACT! installation includes a diagnostic program that can help iron out some system difficulties. This program is not supported by Symantec for implementation by end users. But, if you are desperate because your database keeps crashing, give it a try. Besides the index fix outlined here, there is a plethora of tools in this program for fixing ACT! problems.

1. Make a backup copy of the database.
2. Open **Windows Explorer** and browse to the folder where ACT! is installed.
3. Look for the **ACTDIAG** application file. When you find it, double-click the name.
4. The ACT! 2000 Data Diagnostic Tool dialog box appears.

The ACT! 2000 Data Diagnostic Tool appears in the form of this dialog box.

5. Click the **Remove Indexes** icon. The Open dialog box appears.
6. Select the database that is broken.
7. Click the **Open** button. A warning dialog box appears. Click **Yes** to complete the process.
8. Open ACT!. You might get a message that the database is in need of repair. Click **Yes** to finish the repair.

This process should solve your database problem. If not, read the next section as another way to resolve the dilemma.

Synchronizing One Database to Another

This resolution depends on your being able to get into the damaged database. If the database is on a server, copy the damaged database to a workstation, and then execute this process on your local drive. Assuming that you have already run the diagnostic, as outlined previously, try the following:

1. Create a new, blank database and close it. Use a bogus name for the My Record, such as *File Repair*.
2. Open the **File** menu in the damaged database.
3. Select **Synchronize**. The Synchronize dialog box appears.

4. Select **Send Updates**, and click off **Receive Updates**.

5. Select **Database to Database**.

6. Click the **Setup** button. The Synchronize Wizard starts.

7. In the Filename and Location field, click the **Browse** button to locate and select the new blank database.

8. Click **Next**.

9. Select all the options in the Types of Data dialog box.

10. Click **Next**.

11. Select the **All Groups and All Contacts** option.

12. Click **Next**.

13. Select **Send and Receive Private Data**.

14. Click **Next**.

15. Select the **Send and Receive Database Field Definitions** option. Under Field Definitions, select **Field Definitions from My Database**.

16. Click **Next**.

17. Select **Send All Records**.

18. Click **Finish**. The wizard closes and you are returned to the Synchronize dialog box.

19. Click **Synchronize**.

ACT! sends all the data in the damaged database to the new blank copy, and in the process, filters and fixes information it deems damaged. Again, be patient with this process. A 6,000-record database can take several hours to synchronize, depending upon the amount of information in each record. If you try to check with Windows via the Ctrl-Alt-Delete Task Manager, it appears as if ACT! has stopped responding. It has not.

After the synchronization is finished, open the new database and see if the processes that caused problems before still do. On a multi-user database, be sure to add yourself as a new user and assign the My Record from the database; however, *do not create a new My Record*. Assign yourself Administrative rights, and delete the bogus record, moving all contacts associated with the bogus record to your record. Now, add the other login users, and assign the My Records from the database.

Have one login user at a time open the database on his or her computer and see if a particular machine is causing a problem.

Symantec Database Repair

If all else fails, you can send the damaged database to the folks at Symantec and they can repair it. They do not guarantee that all the records or all the information will be saved. But, they are impressive and have pulled many chestnuts out of the fire. To access this service, go to the Symantec Web site at `www.symantec.com`. Select ACT! as the product in which you are interested and click to the technical support page. Or, if you can open another ACT! database, open the **Internet Links** menu and select **Symantec**, and then **Technical Support**. Once there, you will find the link to the page that has the cost and the method to send the database to Symantec.

If you must go this route, it means that you will be without the services of ACT! for at least a week. To mitigate the trauma, you can try several strategies. First, if you can get into the database, use it as a lookup-only tool. Do not add new records, schedule activities, write letters, or attempt anything beyond finding information. Revert to paper and record everything that you normally would enter into ACT!, adding it later to the repaired database.

The Least You Need to Know

➤ You should back up your database at least once a day.

➤ At least once a week, reindex your database and purge any information that is out of date.

"Great intellects are skeptical."

Nietzsche

Chapter 23

Network Tricks and Traps

In This Chapter

➤ How ACT! works on a network

➤ Settings you should include

➤ Tips for better performance

"Anyone can do any amount of work, provided it isn't the work he's supposed to be doing at the moment."

Charles Baudelaire

The proper way to run ACT! on a network is for the database to be stored on a file server with all the users logging into that database. That way, as records are updated, everyone can see changes and the information resource of the company is effectively leveraged.

A Shared File Application

ACT! is a shared-file application. That means the database resides on a network file server—a computer that is designated and designed to be the place where the network software resides. Most networks are controlled by Windows NT or Novell NetWare software. Fortunately, ACT! doesn't care which software runs your network.

Peerless Functioning

It is possible to run ACT! on a peer-to-peer network, but I find that if there are more than four users or 5,000 records, the performance is too slow.

ACT! is network-ready out of the box—that is you do not have to buy a network version of ACT!. Not surprisingly, Symantec insists that you own a copy of ACT! for every workstation that is accessing the ACT! database on the network. You can install ACT! so that a workstation is running the program from the server, but the performance is slow and usually not acceptable.

For my clients, I recommend that they have as a minimum system configuration:

➤ Windows NT Workstation on the computer that is the network file server

➤ At least 128 megabytes of RAM on the server

➤ Four connections to the network file server, 100BASE-T

➤ Ethernet switches instead of hubs

➤ 48 megabytes of RAM on each workstation, especially if you want to use Microsoft Word instead of ACT!'s word processor (Word is a notorious memory hog)

➤ Physically map the drives to the server instead of using UNC

On the network file server, at least two shared folders should be created. Create one for the shared ACT! database files and another for shared layouts.

Installing the Program for Multiple Users

You are not required to install ACT! on the server, but I recommend it as an easy way to do any required maintenance.

If you do install a copy to the server, ACT! automatically creates folders for the database and for layouts. You can use these folders as the shared folders.

When you create the first database, the person who creates the My Record is the default administrator—that cannot be changed. This fact presents no serious problems in that any login user can be given administrator privileges.

Installation Expert Help

Remember, if you get in over your head, or want a network install to be painless, Symantec has an online list of folks like yours truly, ACT! Certified Consultants, who can come to your office and do this for you. They will expect cash in exchange for this service! Check www.symantec.com and go to the ACT! page. You also should have a list of consultants in the paraphernalia that came with ACT!.

Adding Login Users

After creating the database, follow these steps from any workstation:

1. Open the **File** menu.
2. Select the **Administration** option. The submenu appears if you have Administrator privileges.
3. Select **Define Users**. The Define Users dialog box appears.

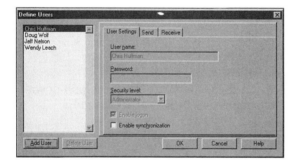

The Define Users dialog box lets you add network users to your ACT! system.

4. Click the **Add User** button.
5. Fill in the username. It should match the name of the person as he or she is going to enter it into the My Record.
6. The password entry is optional.
7. Set the security level. There are three levels:
   ➤ Administrator, which allows the user to do anything to the database
   ➤ Standard, which allows the user to edit records and delete records but not add fields or change layouts
   ➤ Browse, which allows the user to use ACT! only for reference—no editing is allowed
8. Click **OK**. ACT! then prompts you for more information on the new user.

329

Because your new users have no My Record entries, the Assign My Records dialog box appears.

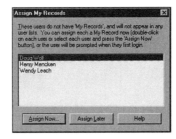

You have two options at this point:

➤ If the user already has a record in the database, click **Assign Now** and use the **Select** button to locate that person's record and click it to use the information. Or, if you are certain the person does not have a record, type the requisite information into the dialog box.

➤ If that person is not in the database, click **Assign Later**. When the new user tries to access the database, ACT! will ask him or her to complete his or her My Record.

Editing User Preferences

After adding a new user, you must stroll to his or her machine and set his or her preferences so that his or her copy of ACT! points to the correct place on the network for the shared folders.

1. Open the new user's copy of ACT!.
2. From the **Edit** menu, select **Preferences**.
3. In the Preferences dialog box, on the General tab, click the pull-down arrow to select the file type. For the database, select the database file type.
4. Click the **Browse** button.
5. Navigate to the folder that has or will contain the matching file type. For example, if the file type is database and you have created a folder on the network server named ACTDATABASE, navigate to that folder.
6. Click **OK**.

After doing so, when the user opens the **File** menu and selects **Open**, ACT! begins looking in this folder for database files. Repeat the steps for each type of file that you want shared by all ACT! users on the network.

ACT! is programmed to open the last accessed database every time you start. So, if you opened the SALES database on your C drive, and then shut down ACT!, the next time you start ACT! it opens the SALES database. In order for the users to have ACT! open the shared database, the next step is to open the **File** menu, and then select

Open. Because you have changed which folder ACT! is to look in when opening a database, the shared database should be available. Select the shared database and open it. Next, exit ACT!. Now, reopen ACT! and the shared database is opened automatically.

Deleting Login Users

The procedure for deleting a login user involves deciding if you are going to also delete the contact records that were managed by the user. Usually, you do not delete the contact records. So, when ACT! asks you if you want to reassign them to another user, select the person to whom the records will belong. It is best to have another user created before starting the deletion process. If you simply want to stop someone from accessing the database, you do not *have* to delete them as a user, simply shut off their login privileges.

If you decide to delete a user and reassign the contact records, be aware that this process is very slow. ACT! has to go through every record, every note, and so on, and reassign them one at a time. If you have several thousand records to be reassigned, do this at the end of the day, and run the process from the server, not a workstation. Make a backup of the database, first.

Let the Administrator Hold the Records

If you are deleting a user, and you aren't certain who should get his or her records, you can assign them to the Adminstrator for safe keeping.

Windows NT Networks

There are a couple of server settings that you can adjust in ACT! to maximize its performance:

➤ If your network has no true client-server applications, open the **Performance** tab on the server in the **System** Control Panel and set the slider bar to **None**.

➤ Set the **Paging** file **Size** to **150**.

➤ The Shared folders must allow the user to have read, write, and delete privileges.

➤ Make sure Opportunistic Locking is off. The ACTDIAG program will do that for you. Check Chapter 22, "Maintaining and Backing Up ACT! Data," for information on running ACTDIAG.

Novell NetWare

ACT! 2000 functions under Novell networks, but with a few restrictions. Long filenames for ACT! databases will not work. They must be eight characters or less. The Shared folders must have read, write, create, erase, modify, file scan, and access control.

The Least You Need to Know

➤ To run ACT! on a network, you need a license for everyone accessing the database.

➤ The file server must have at least one folder that is accessible by everyone on the network and it is the location of the shared database.

"I do not like work even when someone else does it."

Mark Twain

Chapter 24

Connecting to Hand-Held Devices

In This Chapter

➤ Windows CE connection

➤ Palm Computing connection

➤ Sending numbers to a portable phone

"A man is rich in proportion to the number of things he can let alone."

Thoreau

The rage of the late 90s is data portability. That is, the ability to take your life with you electronically wherever you travel. ACT! has direct connections to the major portable devices and in this chapter, we take a look at the steps to connect and some third-party software that improves the transfer of data.

Download the CE Version of ACT! Free

You can download the CE version of ACT! directly from Symantec and it's free! Use your browser to go to www.symantec.com, select **Products**, and then choose **ACT!**. From there, you can select the ACT! for CE option.

Windows CE

Windows CE devices (CE is Compact Edition of Windows) are alleged to be the PDAs (Personal Digital Assistants) of today. Unfortunately, the market has, for the moment, taken a cool view of these products because of the lack of horsepower to drive them. However, Symantec does have a version of ACT! that runs on a CE device—ACT! CE. The chief benefit of using the CE version is that you have ACT! talking to ACT! from the desktop to the hand-held device. So, in order to exchange data between a desktop and a CE device, you must download ACT! CE.

To connect to the CE, do the following:

1. Open the **File** menu and select **Link with Handheld Device**. The Link dialog box opens. The settings you see are the defaults.

The Link dialog box lets you connect to the ACT! CE device.

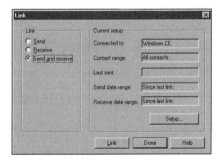

2. Click the **Setup** button.

The Link Setup Wizard appears to help you configure your attachment to your hand-held computer.

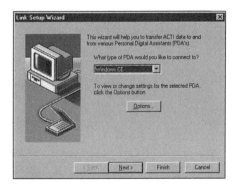

If this is the initial setup, click the **Options** button. At this point, you can delete all the data in your CE device, so as to guarantee a fresh start.

3. Click the **Next** button. This dialog box allows you to customize the settings for your connection. The key idea to understand is that the CE has limited memory. So, you can limit the amount and type of data that is sent to it. Select the settings you want and click **Next**.

4. Set the date ranges with which you want to work. Normally, you are going to send and receive data from the last link.

5. Click **Finish**. You return to the Link dialog box from which you can click the **Link** button.

Synchronize Your CE and Desktop

Anywhere you go, with your CE device and ACT!, you can add a new contact, schedule an activity, or add a note and upon returning to your desktop computer, synchronize those changes with ACT!.

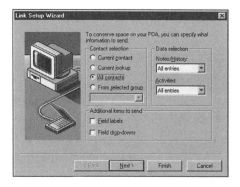

You have a variety of filtering options for sending data to the handheld PC.

Because the data transfer process is handled by a serial link, you must be patient. Upon starting the initial link, if you have many contact records, you can take a stroll to the water cooler and get the latest office gossip.

On Symantec's Web site there is a listing of the CE devices that have been tested and found compatible with ACT!. It is updated on a regular basis, so check it before purchasing any CE device you plan to run with ACT!.

Palm a.k.a. (Pilot)

The Palm series of PDAs has been widely popular and for good reason. They are easy to use and many developers have written programs for them. Symantec does not have an ACT! version that runs on the Palm. Instead, it has linking software that sends and receives data from the Palm. The tricky part is that when the data is sent to the Palm, it is split into several parts. All the address and phone information is copied to the Palm address book. Meetings and Calls are copied to the Palm calendar. The Palm has a separate program for to-dos, so that is where they go.

Pilotless

You might think of your Palm hand-held computer as a PalmPilot, but that is no longer the official name. The 3COM people were sued and can no longer use the Pilot as part of the name for their PDA.

Any activity you add in the Palm is sent to the My Record, so that when you synchronize to your desktop database, you will have to move those activities to their respective contact records. In addition, the Symantec linking software does not recognize groups and does not send Notes to the Palm.

CompanionLink for Palm

If you rely on your Palm hand-held computer for keeping your contacts organized, you have more choices than ACT!'s default software. For example, some good third-party software produced by CompanionLink and described in Chapter 26, "ACT! Add-on Products," does much more than the Symantec linking software. It will send Notes, transfer any of the user fields you designate, and recognize groups. So, if your database is like mine and has multiple types of contact records, you can put the contact records that you want in your Palm and those are the only records sent.

Intellisynch to Your Phone!

A second company that provides the same type of enhanced third-party synching to both the Palm and CE devices is Puma Technologies. To get more information on its products, browse to www.pumatech.com or dial (800) 774-7862.

Intellisynch also has software that can transport the phone numbers in ACT! to your cellular phone! Similar to the Palm, your phone rests in a cradle that is connected by wire to your computer. Depending upon the phone memory, you can have up to 250 names and numbers transferred. At this writing, two companies are manufacturing phones with this capability: Ericksson and Nokia.

The Least You Need to Know

➤ Connecting ACT! to a hand-held device is easy—if you have the correct software.

➤ You can connect to your hand-held computer using software by Symantec or third parties.

➤ Third-party software even exists that will transfer ACT! phone numbers to your cell phone.

"There is nothing more frightening than ignorance in action."

Goethe

Chapter 25

Synchronizing with Remote Users

> **In This Chapter**
>
> ➤ How synchronization works
>
> ➤ Different synchronization methods
>
> ➤ Preparing for the initial synchronization
>
> ➤ Problem solving

"The pure and simple truth is rarely pure and simple."

Oscar Wilde

Keeping everyone on the proverbial "same sheet of music" is the genesis of synchronization. The problem it attempts to solve is the communication between the home office and the field salesperson, both of whom interact with the customer. In this chapter, I explain how it works and the procedure for creating synchronization users.

What Is Synchronization?

Synchronization is the process whereby two contact records are kept up to date in two different databases. For example, your company has a master ACT! database with all your customers and you have three salespeople who cover three distinct territories, each having a portion of the master database on a laptop. Suppose that a customer calls the main office and asks for service on a product. The office person who takes the call looks up the customer and then adds a note regarding the request. The salesperson,

Third-Party Software Can Differ

Synchronization is an entirely different process from using products such as Laplink or Symantec's PC Anywhere, in which the older files are simply copied over by the newer ones.

who has the same contact record, adds a new sales opportunity to the contact record. At this point, we have a contact record that is no longer synchronous. That is, it is the same record but the information in both is not identical. The process of synchronization updates both records so that both the main office and the field salesperson have the same information.

When you execute a synchronization, ACT! creates a computer file that contains the changed records and the information the receiving database needs in order to apply the changes. The file can be sent via modems, sent to a computer folder, or sent as an attachment to an email, which is the most common method.

Unique Identifications

When an ACT! database is created, a unique identification number is generated and assigned to the database. Also, when a new contact record is created, it gets a unique identification number. So, when synchronizing, ACT! first checks that the databases are not identical—that is, the updated information cannot be applied to itself. Many new synch users are frustrated because they make an exact copy of the main database and copy it to a laptop, and then wonder why it will not accept synchronizations. After the Unique ID test, ACT! matches the unique record IDs to determine where updated information is to be recorded.

The update process is determined by the entries in the *Transaction Log*, which is not turned on until synchronization is enabled. The log tracks the unique ID of each contact record and the date on which changes were made to the individual fields of the contact record. So, after the first synchronization, the only contact records that are included in the synch are the ones that have changed since the prior synchronization.

Different Types of Synchronization

Because the synchronization process creates a computer file, it can be sent from one to database to another in one of four ways, as the following list describes:

➤ **Shared Folder**   This method is used primarily when you have several users on a network but they do not share a main ACT! database. The synchronization files are sent by ACT! to a folder. The receiver's ACT! then looks in the folder for synch files and applies them to the currently open database.

➤ **Database to Database**   This method is used when you want to synch from one database to another on the same computer or on the same network. This method does not work with more than two databases.

➤ **Email**   This is the most commonly used method to synch a master database with several remote databases. The office has a master database and several field salespeople have a portion of the master database on their laptops. The synch file is attached to an email. When the remote user opens his email, he sees the message with an attachment, which can then be applied to the currently open ACT! database.

Synchronization Anxiety

If setting up synchronization sounds overwhelming, call an ACT! Certified Consultant. They can help you do this right the first time, thereby saving much time and grief.

➤ **Modem to Modem**   This method has ACT! sending the synch file over a phone line directly to the remote ACT! database. The synchronization file is not applied to the remote, but is copied to the Drafts folder in ACT!'s email. It is then applied after the connection is closed.

Getting Ready for the First Synchronization

Assuming that you are the person handed this hot potato, the first thing to do is decide how the synchronization is going to be set up for each user. You can have a mixed system—some users using email while others use a shared folder.

Start with the master database. Even if it is new, purging the transaction log insures a happy result:

1. Open the **File** menu and select **Administration**.
2. Select **Database Maintenance**.
3. Click the **Data Clean-up** tab.
4. Click the check box in front of the **Transaction Logs Older Than** item.
5. Enter 0 (zero) as the number of days.
6. Click the **Remove Selected Items** button. ACT! checks with you on the remove. Click **Yes**.

The log is reset and the database is reindexed and closed. Open the database with **File** and **Open**.

You've selected the Database Maintenance Data Clean-up tab, revealing the Remove obsolete data options.

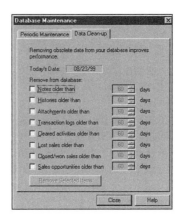

Creating the Remote Databases

In all cases, the remote databases must be copies—not duplicates—of the master database. Before starting the process, make sure that you have entered all the remote users into the master database. Also, create the Groups that are to be synched to each remote user. They do not have to be populated—that is, you do not have to add the contact records at this point, but create the Group records as described in Chapter 15, "Working with Groups."

1. Open the **File** menu and select **Save Copy**.

The Save Copy As dialog box allows you to make a copy of the currently opened database.

2. Select **Create Empty Copy** and click **OK**.

3. The Save As dialog box appears. I counsel my clients to name the remote database by territory or region instead of by salesperson. That way, if the salesperson leaves, the name can remain the same. Also, because this new remote database is destined for another computer, save it to a floppy disk or to an empty folder where you can easily copy all the files.

4. Click **Save** and the My Record dialog box appears. The remote user has a contact record in the master database; click the **Select** button and locate that record. Click **OK**.

ACT! creates the remote database.

Installing the Synchronization Settings for the Remote User

In my experience, the best practice is to prepare the synchronization process for the remote user, before giving him the database. That way, you can be certain that the settings were correct before the remote database left your hands.

1. Open the newly created remote database.

2. Open the **File** menu and select **Synchronization Setup**.

3. The initial dialog box for the Synchronization Wizard does not require input from you. Click **Next**.

4. In this scenario, the remote user will be synchronizing with another user. So, click the **With Other Users** radio button. Click **Next**.

5. Set all five of the options in the What Data? dialog box to On by checking the boxes. Click **Next**.

6. The next dialog box is named With Whom?. The remote user is only going to synchronize with you, the administrator. So, click the **New User** button.

The New User dialog box appears atop the With Whom Synchronization Wizard dialog box.

7. Enter your name as it is entered in the My Record of the master database. Click **Next**.

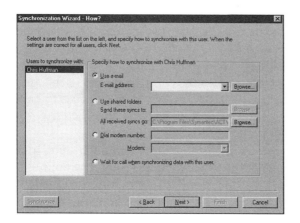

The Synchronization Wizard's How? dialog box is for selecting the connection method for synchronization files.

At this point, you have a multitude of connection choices. In this scenario, the email method is used. The shared folder and modem methods are discussed in separate sections of this chapter.

8. Enter your email address. (Remember, you are entering the settings for the *remote* user!) Click **Next**.

9. The Receive What Data? dialog box opens. It is not likely that you will need to send Private Data to the remote user. But, you might want to send Field Definitions to the remote user. That way, if you add a new field, change field sizes, or alter field types, the changes are sent and applied to the remote user's database.

Send the Layout, Too!

If you add a new field and synch it to the remote users, they cannot see the field until you send the layout file, which is not part of the synchronization process. You must send the layout file separately to the remote users as an email file attachment and have them copy it to the ACT\LAYOUT folder.

The next option is whether or not to use a collection group. The remote user is going to be sending all contacts and groups to the master database, so there is no reason to have a collection group. Click **Next**.

10. The Send What Data? dialog box appears. The remote user sends all contacts and all groups, so select those two radio buttons. The send range is going to be Only Changed. The reason is that on the first synchronization, you are going to send this user all the records in his group. He in turn will have nothing to send as he could not have made any changes.

The private data setting is determined by the company policy. Generally, the remote users do not send private data. But, if the company needs to have the exact schedule of the remote user—including doctor visits—then this button should be selected. Click **Next**.

11. The final dialog box is for creating an automatic synching schedule. In order for this to work, ACT! must be running at the scheduled time. The options for this are covered in a separate section. Click **No**, then **Next**, and then **Finish**.

12. The Synchronize dialog box appears. You cannot synchronize at this point, so click **Cancel**.

Now, you have to copy the remote database to the remote user's computer. Hand him the floppy disk on which his database is saved and he can copy all the files to his

ACT\DATABASE folder. Or, create an email with all the files attached and he can copy the files from the email attachment to the ACT\DATABASE folder.

Repeat the process as described previously, for every remote user.

Creating the Master Database Synchronization Settings

The remote user's settings are different from the master database. The key differences are what data is being sent and received. Open the master database and follow these steps:

1. Open the **File** menu and select **Synchronization Setup**. Click **Next** in the initial dialog box.

2. Select all the check boxes in the What Data? dialog box, and click **Next**.

3. The With Whom? dialog box appears. Click the **Contacts** tab. To enter remote users into the master database, click the name of the remote user and click the **Add** button, until all remote users are selected. Click **Next**.

4. The How? dialog box appears. On the left is the list of remote users. Click a remote user's name. At this point, you can enter the connection method for that remote user. Click the appropriate connection method. In this example, click **E-mail**. Then, enter the email address for the recipient. After entering the connection method for each remote user, click **Next**.

Devil in a Blue Address

The email system you employ determines the correct email address. If everyone connects via Internet mail, you simply enter their email address. If you are using a more esoteric system such as cc:Mail, you will need assistance from your system administrator to make sure you have the correct email address.

5. The Receive What Data? dialog box is now open. All the remote users are listed at the left. Select a remote user and enter his settings. Again, there is a decision to be made in regard to receiving private data from the field. Next, the default setting is not to receive field definitions from remote users, which is my recommendation. It is not likely that you want the remote users to add fields or field definitions to the master database.

AOL Is Not A-OK

You cannot use America Online email to send and receive synchronizations.

The Collection Group setting is important for this reason. If the remote user creates a new record, it is sent on the next synchronization to the master database. But at that point it might not be identified as a contact record that belongs to a particular remote user. So, to make certain new records are sent back and forth to the correct user, click the **Collection Group** button.

6. From the drop-down list, select the group that pertains to the remote user selected. ACT! creates a group name for you by using the name of the contact—such as the Doug Wolf group. Click **Next**.

7. In the Send What Data? dialog box, select a remote user and then click the radio button for **Contacts in These Groups**.

8. Click the group for that remote user. The All Records (This Time Only) radio button should be selected. This will switch to the Only Changed Data setting automatically after the initial synch is sent.

9. Under the Other Data section, the important setting is the Field Definitions setting. If it is on, changes you make to the drop-downs, new fields, or field attributes are sent to the remote user. Remember, if you create a new field, it is sent to the remote user but he will not *see* the new field in his layout until you send an updated layout file.

   You can also elect to send private data, which means that the remote user can better judge the schedules of other users—even though he cannot see with whom the activity is scheduled.

10. Click **Next**, and the When? dialog box appears. This dialog box is for creating a schedule of synching to each of the remote users. Remember that ACT! always checks for incoming synch files first, before doing a send (unless you have Receive Updates shut off), applies the changes it receives, and then sends changes. Click **Yes** and then **Next** to open the scheduling dialog box.

   Click the days you want the process to run, and then click the times. Automatic synchronization is optional, so you can skip this part of the setup entirely.

11. Click **Next** and then **Finish** to complete the setup. The Synchronize dialog box appears as in the following figure.

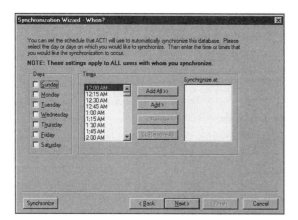

The Synchronization Wizard's When? dialog box lets you schedule synchronization to occur at regular intervals.

You can use this Synchronize dialog box to manually execute a synchronization.

At this point, if the remote users have their databases, you are ready to send them your initial synchronization. When you execute the synchronization, the remote user must open his email—in ACT!. The message should alert him that a synchronization file is attached to the email and ask him if he wants to apply it to the currently open database. Assuming that the correct database is open, he can click **Yes** and away we go—sort of. Because it is an initial synchronization, ACT! wants to confirm that the *sender* is correct. The user then should confirm the link to you as the sender. A few more OKs and the changes are added to the database. To check what has been received, the remote user can go to his My Record and check the Notes/History tab. It should read "Initial synchronization received from XXXX, 500 contacts, 300 notes" and so on.

At the master database, you too will receive an email with a synchronization file attached from each remote user. You must go through the same linking process. After you apply a synchronization received via email, the file is automatically deleted by ACT!.

Synchronization Logs

Not only does the process of synchronization create a history entry on the My Record, but ACT! can also generate a detailed report of each synchronization. This report shows which contact-record/group-record aspect of that record was altered and how. First, ACT! has to be set to create the report:

1. Open the **Edit** menu and select **Preferences**.
2. Click the **Synchronization** tab.
3. At the bottom left, there is an option with a check box which reads, oddly enough, **Generate Synchronization Report**.
4. Click the check box and click **OK**.

After the initial synchronization, changes made to the contact records and group records are duly recorded in an ordinary text file. To read the text file, you can open it with Word or Windows Notepad. The file has the extension LOG, so you might have to adjust the settings in your word processor.

There are two types of synchronization reports. There is the master log, which is appended at its beginning with every synchronization, and then the individual logs for each individual synchronization. By opening either, you might be able to determine what is happening.

Shared Folder Synchronization

This method is used when all users are attached to a local area network, but because of the security desired, they are not logon users. Before creating the copies of the main database, create the groups that will be used by each of the shared folder users. To set this up, follow this procedure:

1. Open the master database.
2. Open the **File** menu and select **Save Copy As**.
3. Select the option to create an empty copy of the database. You might want to save the database to the drive/folder of the shared folder user.
4. When prompted, enter the My Record for the shared folder user.
5. Click **OK**.

Next, create an "inbox" folder for each shared folder user. The physical location of the folder is not important as long as the shared folder user has access to it. You might need to have the system administrator create these and set the access permissions.

In the master database, open the **File** menu and select **Synchronization Setup**. Enter the settings in the Synchronization Wizards as

➤ **With Other Users**
➤ **Send Updates**, **Receive Updates**, **Notes/History**, **Activities**, **Sales/Opportunities**
➤ The names of the shared folder users

You are now at the How? dialog box. Select **Use Shared Folders**. Click the **Browse** button to locate the folder to which master database synchronization files are to be sent for that user. Each shared folder user must have a unique inbox folder.

ACT! receives all synchronizations from all users to the same folder. The default folder is C:\Program Files\ACT\Sync.

Finish the Synchronization Wizards and add the settings as described under "Installing the Synchronization Settings for the Remote User," earlier in this chapter.

Modem-to-Modem Synchronization

The modem-to-modem method of synchronization requires both the master and remote ACT! databases to be open at the same time. That is, the synchronization file is transferred between the two computers in real time. The master database dials via the modem and tries to connect with the remote computer. The remote computer is on and the ACT! database open. The file is sent to the ACT\Briefcase folder. After receiving the file, the remote user can apply the update by manually running the synchronization.

In the master database, open the **File** menu and select **Synchronization Setup**. Enter the settings in the Synchronization Wizards as

➤ **With Other Users**

➤ **Send Updates**, **Receive Updates**, **Notes/History**, **Activities**, **Sales/Opportunities**

You are now at the How? dialog box. Select the names of the modem-to-modem users. You must enter a complete number, including any number to access an outside line.

The final setting in this dialog box is whether or not to wait for calls when synchronizing with this user. In most cases, as the master database, you will want to wait for the calls from the remote users. Otherwise, if you are synchronizing with multiple remote users, they will have to leave ACT! running and wait for the master ACT! database to dial them and send the synchronization file. If the situation exists where it is more efficient to send to them at a specified time, then do not check this box.

Finish the Synchronization Wizards and add the settings as described under "Installing the Synchronization Settings for the Remote User," earlier in this chapter.

When you are ready to synchronize, you will have to arrange the times with the remote users so that you can send or receive the synchronization files.

Deleting Records

The remote users cannot delete records. The contact records are marked for deletion and when they synchronize, ACT! alerts you by creating a lookup of those records. To see the records, open the **Lookup** menu and select **Synchronized Records** and **Deleted by Remote Users**. Once the record is marked for deletion, it is excluded from the transaction log and is not sent back to the remote user. If you want the record deleted, go to each via the lookup and use the **Contact** menu, **Delete Contact**. For any records that you want to keep, you must open the **Lookup** menu and select **Synchronized Records**. From the submenu, select **Deleted by Remote Users**.

The Records Deleted by Remote Users dialog box has the options to restore records or groups deleted by a remote user.

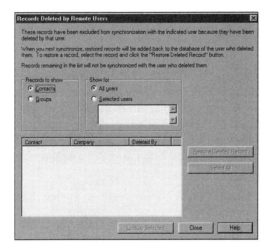

Database-to-Database Synchronization

This version of synchronization works between two databases only. In my experience, it is rarely used. I do recommend it to customers who have a severely corrupted database. By creating a new blank database (not using the File menu, Save Copy As method) and selecting the new database as the target of the synchronization, you can fix many problems.

Setting Group Rules

If you are adding new contact records to the master database and they need to be added to specific groups so that they are sent to the remote users, read the section in Chapter 15 on creating Group Rules. This new feature of ACT! relieves a problem that has bedeviled ACT! database administrators.

If All Else Fails, Ground Zero!

Ground zero is the term that Symantec employs when a synchronization process is not working properly. The idea is that you consider the next synchronization to be the same as the very first synchronization—you are starting from scratch. So, what happens then is what happens with every initial synchronization—ACT! goes record by record and matches unique IDs and, if found, merges the two records. If the unique IDs do not match, then ACT! does a secondary check using the fields set in the Duplicate Checking tab—the defaults are Company, Contact, and then Phone. If all three fields match in both records, they are merged into one record.

The Least You Need to Know

➤ Synchronization keeps records the same no matter where they are located.

➤ There are several methods for synchronizing databases, such as email, shared folder, and modem to modem.

➤ ACT! Certified Consultants can make the initial setup process much easier.

"Few people think more than two or three times a year. I have made an international reputation for myself by thinking once or twice a week."

George Bernard Shaw

ACT! Add-on Products

"It is one thing to show a man that he is in error, and another to put him in possession of the truth."

John Locke

In this chapter, we take a look at products that have been developed by other companies to work with ACT! or complement ACT!. There may be just the product you need to make ACT! the best tool for your business.

A Third-Party Endorsement

You might think that ACT! is perfecto right out of the box. But alas, because it is a general-purpose contact manager, some of the features and functionality that you might need or want are provided by other companies in cooperation with Symantec. These tools are called third-party applications. Why? Because, I guess, Symantec is the first party, and you are the second party. In any case, the party is just starting, and these are the candidates I endorse.

Area Code Updates

With the seemingly unending proliferation of new area codes, it is a big pain to go through your ACT! database and have to manually change each number every time a change is forced upon us. So, obviate the pain by ordering Split Wizard from CompanionLink Software. You can update all the phone fields in each contact record instantly. Plus, you can order a subscription service that sends you the new area code splits every 120 days. The Web site is www.companionlink.com and the phone number is (800) 386-1623.

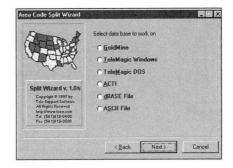

The Area Code Split Wizard from CompanionLink Software remedies the headache of area code changes.

Card Scan

Going to a convention and gonna get buried (sung to "Chapel of Love") by business cards from prospects. Sure, you can hire a typist to keyboard the pile into ACT!, but a better way is to scan the cards into your database. This product consists of a piece of hardware and the software. The card is scanned, and then you see it onscreen. CardScan tries to guess which information goes into which field. You can make adjustments, and then send the information directly into an ACT! database. Take a closer look at www.cardscan.com or call (800) 317-4811. About $300.

QwikQuote

Nearly every business needs to send quotations to its customers and prospects, and it is a pain! Especially if you are the unusual salesperson that tries to be accurate. Anyway, QwikQuote works with ACT! or as a standalone program. Working with ACT!, you can designate the fields from your ACT! database that are to be sent to QwikQuote.

You can import or create a database of your products, and then generate quotes that are accurate and—most importantly—easy for a salesperson to knock out. The software is not inexpensive—about $200 for a single user and $900 for a five-user license—but many ACT! certified consultants are equipped to demonstrate the software. To contact the company, visit its Web site at www.qwikquote.com or phone (800) 598-4465.

DAZzle, a.k.a. Envelope Manager Software

Direct mail, despite the Internet, continues to grow as a way to reach targeted prospects or customers with your sales message. ACT! does an admirable job of printing labels and such, but what if you need the barcodes and FIM codes for the post office? You know how friendly it can be to incorrectly generated bulk mail! DAZzle Plus takes care of this. Also, you can print Business Reply Envelopes from your desktop. Not only that, you can dial into the post office and connect with its computers to verify the integrity of the zip+4 codes that you have in your ACT! database for—get this—free! Well, free in that the cost is in every stamp you buy. Go to `www.envelopemanager.com` or call (800) 576-3279 to get this kick bulk software. $59.95.

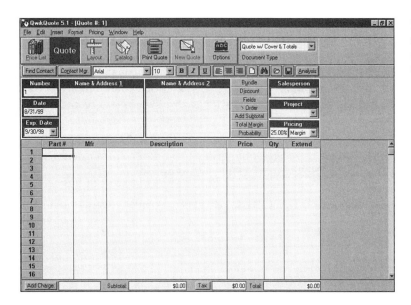

The QwikQuote screen makes it easy to develop complicated quotes in a matter of minutes.

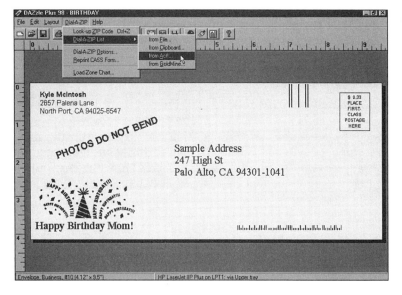

A DAZzle sample.

ACT! Utilities

One company that has been around almost as long as ACT! itself is OakHurst. I know, it is an unusual name—almost as unusual as its founder—an ACT! Certified Consultant. The following are two of the top products it sells:

➤ **ACT!PAK**   Has a series of programs. The first is the merge program, which makes it easy to send data to a spreadsheet from ACT! (and from a specific contact record) or to ACT! from a spreadsheet. You can create and save a data dictionary, which is a text file that has all of the field attributes and drop-down lists. Another program is auto-fill: Enter a zip code and the City and State fields are filled in for you. Another program allows you to calculate values based on the entries in two other fields. So, you can create two fields: one for sales price and a second for sales tax and this program generates the extended total. Finally, it has a program that generates a sequential number for each new contact record—you no longer have to worry about creating customer account numbers.

➤ **OAK!Script!**   If your firm is in the telemarketing business, OAK!Script! has a sophisticated scripting program that uses hyperlinks to branch from document to document and can update fields in an ACT! contact record.

To browse the Web site for the solution you need, visit www.oakhurst.com or call (704) 641-1265.

Easy ACT! *Newsletter*

I was the founding editor of *Easy ACT!*, published by Pinnacle Publishing. It is a monthly news/information letter that updates ACT! users on the best ways to use ACT! and has articles for beginning and intermediate users, many written by your never-to-be-humble author. Plus, there is a Q&A column written by a Symantec employee. Contact *Easy ACT!* at www.pinpub.com or (800) 788-1900.

Practical Sales Tools Inc.

Another ACT! Certified Consultant—like the folks at OakHurst—just had to have a special tool for ACT!, so he designed it himself. One of the products is called Proximity. You can enter a zip code and mileage range, and it looks at the entries in your ACT! database and returns the contact records that are within your designated range. Geo Lookup, another program, finds a zip code when you know the city and state, or locates a state when you enter an area code. Contact Practical Sales Tools Inc. at www.pstools.com or (888) 433-2891.

Commercial Real Estate Brokers

If you are in the commercial real estate business, the mountain of data that is requisite to be successful can be daunting. This program is called ARES and adds 150 customized fields and 3 relational databases to track contacts, properties, listings, and comparables. It also generates snazzy reports for prospective investors and tenants. See it at www.aresforact.com or call (310) 782-7700. (Tell Terry you read it in my book.)

Residential Real Estate

A great feature of the Residential Real Estate program is the capability to insert a photograph right into the ACT! layout. Imagine looking up a contact record and getting photos of both the owner and the property. This program can be had at www.recsnet.com or (800) 962-9651.

Address Grabber

Address Grabber from eGrabber is a program I use every day—literally. Because I also offer video training on ACT!, I frequently receive orders from my Web site. With this program, I grab the key information, and it is automatically transferred to ACT! and then on to QuickBooks. Address Grabber is remarkably accurate; it grabs address information from a variety of other programs and can then send the data to a bunch of other programs. Call (408) 872-3103 or browse to www.egrabber.com. $89.95 and well worth it.

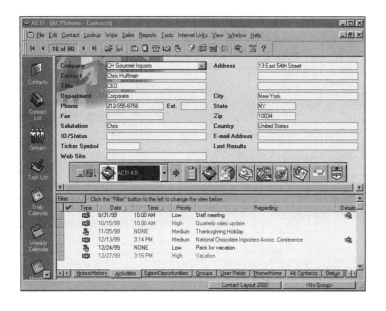

The highly useful Address Grabber, by eGrabber, can import information from other programs into ACT!.

WinFax PRO

Faxing software is fairly common, and fairly commonly is difficult to run. Fortunately, WinFax PRO is an exception. I think this program is a must-have for anyone using ACT!. It, too, is published by Symantec and makes it easy to send and receive faxes from your desktop, even on a network! No need for everyone to have a phone line and modem—just install WinFax on the network server, set up the users, and away they go. Go to www.symantec.com for more information on this vital product.

WinFax is an easy-to-run faxing program.

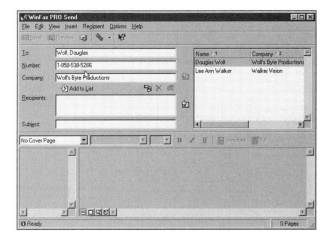

Dragon Naturally Speaking, Voice It Link

Drive ACT! by voice control! Yes, it is a reality. Dragon Naturally Speaking has a specific product just for ACT! users that allows you to run ACT! with a microphone. Plus, you get the hand-held gadget that allows you to record activities, notes, and so on and, when you return to the office, plug the recorder in and send the remarks directly to your ACT! database. This is too easy. The program takes about two hours to accommodate your voice and a high-powered machine is required. It is worth it. See the details at www.dragonsys.com or call (617) 965-5200.

Wolf's Byte Productions

As an ACT! Certified Consultant, I am frequently asked to train groups of salespeople and their staffs on ACT!. But, I cannot be everywhere. So, you can get me on video or

CDROM by visiting my Web site at www.howtosoftware.com or calling (800) 449-9653. Guaranteed results, and every *customer* (yes, you have to buy the stuff first) can call or email me for help.

Prototyping Management Corporation

ACT! has a very extensive set of sales opportunity tools built in, but one of the problems with all salespeople is that they dislike (okay, hate) paperwork of any kind, especially sales reports. Root canal sounds better than having to sit down and enter information on a day's worth of sales calls. Yet, it is necessary, and the better salespeople do it—reluctantly. A better way of getting salespeople to complete sales reports has been developed by the folks at PMC. The idea is that a company works with PMC to develop a sales script that the salesperson loosely follows while spending that all-important face time with a client. After leaving the meeting, the salesperson dials an 800 number and leaves a narrative report on a voice mail system. PMC then filters and refines the information and generates an email to both the salesperson and the sales manager. The next day the salesperson updates his ACT! record painlessly by reading the email. Contact PMC via an ACT! Certified Consultant, by browsing to www.pmcworldwide.com, or by calling (801) 253-0483.

Digitize Your Signature!

Skillnet produces digitized signatures directly from your handwritten signature. You send them several examples of your signature, and they not only scan the signatures but actually create a font file that you can insert into a document—such as fax sent directly from your desktop or a mail merge template—so that it looks as though you signed every letter! Holy forgery, Batman! What will they think of next. Contact Skillnet at www.sigfont.com. $29.95 per signature.

ACT! Certified Consultants

Sometimes they ride in on a white horse, sometimes in a BWM, but however he or she should arrive, a visit from an A.C.C. can bring calm to the storm. Symantec trains and certifies these folks to go out into the world and do those ACT! things that you refuse to, or cannot, do yourself. Of course, they charge for this service as they are not Symantec employees. But, what is your data worth? If the answer is not much, you do not need their services. On the other hand, if you are in the process of setting up a sales team with ACT! and want customized databases, layouts, synchronization that works, and training, make the call. To see the list of the certified and thereby sanctified, browse to www.symantec.com or my Web site, www.howtosoftware.com. I even list my favorites.

This Is Only the Beginning...

Many functions specific to your business cannot possibly be included in ACT!, so independent companies have developed them for you. When you purchase ACT!, you should have received a catalog with the companies that provide such. Really in over your head with ACT!? Call an ACT! Certified Consultant and sleep better.

The Least You Need to Know

➤ Many companies have developed add-on tools to work with ACT!, and the one you need may be listed in this chapter.

➤ Really have a problem or need guidance on the ACT! setup? Call an ACT! Certified Consultant. They are listed on the Symantec Web site.

➤ Enhance your use of ACT! with products such as Archer Enterprise, an SQL solution for ACT!, or PMC voice reports.

"This new development (automation) has unbounded possibilities for good and evil."

Norbert Wiener

Speak Like a Geek: The Complete Archive

ACT!   A software program designed to make it easier to do your job by automating the sales process.

activity   A type of action that can be scheduled in ACT!. Activities are available in three kinds: Calls, Meetings, and To-dos.

additional contacts   Persons added to a contact record who are associated with the contact, but do not require a separate record.

administrator   The person who has full access to ACT! and is usually in charge of maintaining ACT!, adding design changes, executing synchronization, and backing up the data. By default, the person who installs ACT! and creates the initial My Record is the administrator. Other users can be designated as the administrator.

alarms   An attribute that can be added to an activity to cause ACT! to pop up a dialog box alerting the user that an activity is scheduled.

Allow Editing   A field attribute that allows users to enter data into the field, or not.

applying updates   The process whereby synchronization files are applied to the open database.

attach file   Any type of file can be attached to a contact record. The attachment is shown on the Notes/History tab.

backing up   Making a copy of your working database. Something not done nearly often enough.

bitmap   A file format for graphics (with the extension BMP) that can be inserted into ACT! as a background or into a template.

browse level   On a network database, browse level access allows the user to look at records only.

By Example   Looking for contact records using entries in the fields that you suspect contain matching data.

calendar week   A user preference for calendars to start the week on Sunday or Monday.

check box   A small square preceding an option in a dialog box that can have a mark or not. When the box is checked, the option is active.

clearing   Disposing of a scheduled activity.

compressing   The process whereby the space in the database caused by deleting records from ACT! is eliminated.

conflict checking   The process whereby ACT! checks to see if the activity being scheduled conflicts with a previously scheduled activity.

contact record   A record in ACT!, consisting of a person's name, phone numbers, company, and so on. This term is used interchangeably with *record* throughout the book.

country code   The phone company number prefix for a country. The U.S., of course, is number 1.

database   A software program for storing information. ACT! is a semi-structured database in that it has many fields and other attributes already defined.

disk drive   A series of spinning metallic platters that are used to store computer software and data. Reminiscent of the guy on the Ed Sullivan show who used to spin dozens of plates on sticks. They crashed often, too.

DOS   Acronym for *Disk Operating System*. The original operating system licensed by IBM from Microsoft in 1982, sometimes called the deal of the century because Microsoft retained the rights to sell it to other computer makers. DOS was not written by Microsoft; Bill Gates and company bought it for $50,000 from another software company and then repackaged it for IBM. Windows 3x and 9x are based on DOS, while NT is not.

drop-down list   A list of items that can be quickly entered into an ACT! field.

duration   The length of time allocated to an activity.

email   Sending messages and files over an Internet connection.

exporting   Transferring data from ACT! to a file in several formats.

fax   A document sent from ACT! to WinFAX and from there to a fax recipient.

field   A space in the contact/group record in which specific data is entered, such as a phone number or a birthday.

field definition   The attributes of a field, such as the type of data that can be entered, length of the field, whether an entry is required, and so on.

field label   The descriptive text that precedes a field.

filters   A means by which you can decide what information is displayed on tabs, calendars, and the Tasklist. Similar to the process whereby management ignores bad news and hears only the good news.

groups   One or more contact records that you have designated as having something in common, such as your golfing group.

hardware   The computer and its concomitant components that seldom work the way they are supposed to and are often blamed for software problems.

history   Recorded actions and events that have occurred with the contact record.

ID/Status   An indexed field in ACT! that allows you to categorize the contact record by a single designation.

importing   Adding records to ACT! by bringing the data in from an ACT! database or a file format that ACT! can access.

Internet   The worldwide series of computers connected via phone lines, which a user can access to find data about everything. First created in the late 1960s by the Defense Department.

keyboard   A device for entering data into a computer. The alphabet is not arranged on the keys in a logical manner (A, B, C,...). A crazed individual with the strange last name of Qwerty is credited with the design.

layout   The mask on top of an ACT! database that determines the appearance of the ACT! interface.

lead time   The designated amount of time before an activity is to occur that an ACT! alarm appears.

List view   Looking at ACT! contact records in a columnar format rather than the Form view.

Live Update   Updating the ACT! program files direct from the Symantec computers via modem to your copy of ACT!.

menu   A drop-down list at the top of the ACT! window that holds a variety of items. ACT! allows for ala carte menu selections.

merge   While importing records into ACT! if two records are deemed nearly identical, (based on your criteria) the information is combined leaving a single record.

Mini-calendar   A one- or three-month calendar that you can pop up over the top of the ACT! contact record for date reference.

modem   Acronym for *modulator demodulator*, it is a piece of hardware that connects the computer to a phone line and, after doing so, sends or receives data. The data in your computer is digital; the modem translates it to analog format, and the phone line carries it to the receiving modem, which then translates the data back to a digital format.

mouse   A device for clicking and pointing at objects on the computer screen. Developed by Xerox in the late 1970s and "borrowed" by Steve Jobs and Apple for the Macintosh computer. Later, "borrowed" from Apple by the design team at Microsoft to run Windows.

My Record   The most important record in ACT!. It is your record and has your information. It is the first record you see in either a standalone or networked database. All users of a network database must have a My Record.

name prefix   Common prefixes, such as Dr., Mr., and Ms., are ignored by ACT! when they are included as an entry into the Contact field in ACT!.

name suffix   Common suffixes, such as MD., CPA, and Esq., are ignored by ACT! when they are included as an entry into the Contact field in ACT!.

network   Several computers physically connected via cabling, which allows all the computers to access the resources of all the other computers. Usually requires a minimum of a Ph.D. in computer science and a pocket protector to keep running.

NT   Microsoft's network software. NT stands for *New Technology*.

PDA   Acronym for *Personal Digital Assistant*. These devices can synchronize with ACT!.

Plug and Play   A Microsoft protocol intended to reduce hardware conflicts. More commonly known as *Plug and Pray*.

preferences   The settings that can be made to personalize ACT! for an individual user.

private record   An ACT! record in a network database that can only be seen by the creator of the record, as determined by the login name.

Purge   A maintenance tool in ACT! to remove unneeded data, such as old histories, notes, and so on.

record   Same as a contact record.

recurring activity   Any activity that occurs at regular intervals. ACT! allows you to enter the activity once, and will alert you to all subsequent occurrences.

Reindex   A maintenance tool in ACT! for maintaining the integrity of the database.

reports   Documents created by ACT! based on data in the database such as histories, cleared activities, sales opportunities, and so on.

rolling over   The process by which an activity that is not cleared is automatically moved to the next day. Also known as procrastination.

software   A computer program written by a 20 year old with no business experience for 40 year old who thinks a mouse is rodent. When it causes problems, the software company blames it on the hardware.

sorting   The default sort in ACT! is by Company, and then Last Name. You can change the sort order using any fields you choose.

standard level   A security level in a networked database that allows the user to add, modify, and delete records.

synchronization   The process where two records are updated so that they are mirror images—they both contain the exact same data, even though they are physically located on different computers.

Task List   The place where ACT! stores all scheduled activities in the database.

template   A "blueprint" for letters, memos, envelopes, reports, and other documents that automatically fill-in information from the database when opened.

timeless   A scheduled activity that has a date attached but not a specific time.

URL   Acronym for *Uniform Resource Locator*. The URL of a Web site might read www.howtosoftware.com or www.kellyrest.net or www.internic.org.

user fields   Existing generic fields in ACT! that can be modified for specific data.

Web site   HTML document(s) that can be located by a Web address.

Windows 95/98   Operating systems based on DOS that provide a graphical user interface (GUI).

Wolf's Byte Productions   Your humble author's company.

word processor   Software program for writing letters, memos, and so on. ACT! has a built-in word processor, or Word can be used in its place.

World Wide Web   A refinement of the Internet that allows pages to be displayed in graphical format.

Index

369

373